English Architecture

An Illustrated Glossary

By the same author

European Cities and Society (1970)
The Victorian Celebration of Death (1972)
City of London Pubs (1973)
Victorian Architecture: Its Practical Aspects (1973)
The Cemeteries and Burial Grounds of Glasgow (1975)
The Erosion of Oxford (1977)
Mausolea in Ulster (1978)
Moneymore and Draperstown. The Architecture and Planning of the
    Ulster Estates of the Drapers' Company (1979)
A Celebration of Death (1980)
Classical Churches in Ulster (1980)
The History, Architecture, and Planning of the Estates of the
    Fishmongers' Company in Ulster (1981)
The Egyptian Revival (1982)
The Life and Work of Henry Roberts (1803–76), Architect (1983)
The Londonderry Plantation, 1609–1914 (1986)

The first edition of this book was dedicated to my
daughters, Astrid and Ingrid, who embellished
most of the buildings illustrated with their lively
and agreeable presences. The second edition is
also inscribed to them both with a father's gratitude and love, in the hope that they will retrace
our steps in future years, and will discover anew
what we found so long ago.

English Architecture

An Illustrated Glossary

James Stevens Curl

With drawings by John J. Sambrook

David & Charles
Newton Abbot   London   North Pomfret (Vt)

'It is the deadness of our town life which produces the deadness of our architecture: the unutterable deadness which has come over English cities and villages in the last forty years, the stagnation and daily dying of the towns up and down the country.'

W. R. Lethaby (writing in 1917)

'The more closely, constantly, and carefully we study [the native architecture of our own country, and that of our forefathers], the more entirely shall we be convinced that our love and admiration cannot exceed what is due to its intrinsic excellencies.'

Sir George Gilbert Scott

'[The English Cathedrals] are more than buildings, more than art, something intangible was built into them with their stones and burnt into their glass. The work of a man, a man may understand; but these are the works of ages, of nations. They are serene, masterly, non-personal, like works of nature – indeed they are such, natural manifestations of the minds of men working under the impulse of a noble idea.'

W. R. Lethaby

'One of the most sad wastes of power to which men of good will are subject is vain strife about words, especially when pairs of words have been allowed to come into opposition – such as faith and works, or art and science. There is really no opposition between art and science. Show me your art, as St James might have said, and I will show you your science. The most of art is science in operation, and a large part of science is reflection on art.'

W. R. Lethaby

British Library Cataloguing in Publication Data

Curl, James Stevens
   English architecture: an illustrated
   glossary.—2nd ed.
   1. Architecture—England—Dictionaries
   I. Title
   720'.942   NA961

   ISBN 0–7153–8887–8

First published 1977
Second revised edition 1986

Printed in Great Britain
by Redwood Burn Limited   Trowbridge   Wiltshire
for David & Charles Publishers plc
Brunel House   Newton Abbot   Devon

Published in the United States of America
by David & Charles Inc
North Pomfret   Vermont 05053   USA

Contents

Preface

A new edition requires a revised Preface. Since I wrote *English Architecture* much has changed; many more historic buildings have been lost, although the orgies of destruction of the 1950s, '60s and '70s caused by 'Comprehensive Redevelopment' have somewhat abated. Value Added Tax (VAT) on repairs to existing buildings, appalling modern windows and doors, and hamfisted ignorant attempts to 'restore' or 'modernise' old buildings have done immense harm during recent years, however, and for this the Government and the Professions must take a great deal of blame. Architectural education, for example, still concentrates on new building rather than on careful rehabilitation, sensitive detailing, and an understanding of traditional and historic structures. The unfortunate result is that many buildings which could be saved are treated with something less than understanding: it is as though a surgeon was asked to operate on a patient without a sound knowledge of anatomy. Much more damage is caused by builders, odd-job men, and owners of property who do not appreciate what they have.

In his paper on 'The Education of the Architect', delivered at the Royal Institute of British Architects in 1917, W. R. Lethaby said that he could remember 'how beautiful were the towns throughout England' fifty years before. In the little town in which he lived 'no vulgarity had touched it at that time: it was a thing which had grown, a work of art and beauty, a work which Turner would have painted. But now it is . . . exploited and miserified. . .'

If Lethaby could be so aware of the damage done in 1917, it is perhaps worth speculating on how he would have reacted today. There is no doubt that the vocabulary, the language of architecture, has almost been lost.

This book is intended to provide an introduction to the language that describes the nation's built heritage so that the basic architectural elements can be identified. A glossary necessarily involves explanatory pictures where these are thought to be justified. Included in the book are Scots terms, many of which are encountered in the northern counties of England, and I make no apology for including them: many were collected during the three years when I was Architectural Adviser to the Scottish Committee for European Architectural Heritage Year, 1975, and many others are compiled from 'A Scottish Building Glossary: Survival of Craft Terms', by Ralph E. Bullock, published in *The Builder* of 20 June 1952. Glen L. Pride's *Glossary of Scottish Building*, published in 1975, is recommended to readers who wish to pursue a study of Scots terms.

The layman often feels at sea when confronted by even the simplest architectural descriptions, so I have tried to compile a list of historical terms, illustrated where possible, and accompanied with succinct explanations. I rejected the notion of including potted biographies of English architects: Howard M. Colvin has provided the definitive work in his *A Biographical Dictionary of British Architects 1600–1840*, published in 1978, which should be consulted by those interested in the personalities of that period. My Glossary is mostly my own compilation, but owes debts to *An Encyclopaedia of Architecture, Historical, Theoretical, and Practical*, by Joseph Gwilt, revised by Wyatt Papworth (1903), to *A Glossary of Terms used in Grecian, Roman, Italian, and Gothic Architecture*, published by John Parker (1850), and to many other sources listed in the Bibliography. For those who wish to know something of the sculptors who created so many monuments in churches, on buildings, in graveyards, and in public places, the *Dictionary of British Sculptors 1660–1851* by Rupert Gunnis is indispensable. Journals such as *The Builder, The Journal of the Royal Institute of British Architects,* and *The Architect and Building News* provide information concerning later architects and their works for those disposed to ferret out the details. A useful guide to terms in carpentry is found in *The Development of Carpentry, 1200–1700. An Essex Study*, by C. A. Hewett.

I have tried to provide as many unhackneyed pictures as possible, many from my own collection, but I am indebted to the staffs of the libraries and collections acknowledged with each illustration where it has not been possible to provide my own photographs. All photographs, in fact, are my own unless otherwise stated. I am very grateful to the late Mr Terence Davis and to Mr A. W. Pullan for providing several plates. I am indebted to Shropshire County Council Record Office, to the Hereford City Library, to the Library of the Royal Borough of Kensington and Chelsea, to the RIBA British Architectural Library, to the G.L.C. Department of Architecture and Civic Design, and to the Guildhall

Library, City of London, for the supply of the plates indicated. I am also grateful to all the vicars and other clergy, and to the various cathedral authorities for permission to photograph. My wife and daughters accompanied me in search of examples for this book, and I am very indebted to them for their patience, understanding, and enthusiasm: they often spent hours in cathedrals and churches while I made my notes and took photographs. My very old friend, Mr Rodney Roach, who has collaborated with me for many years, enlarged the pictures and processed my film in his usual expert fashion: I acknowledge a large debt to his kindness and efficiency.

Mr A. H. Buck, most helpful of dear friends, once more subjected his sensibilities to the tiresome task of reading my text. His help has always been invaluable, while his expertise as a proofreader was given to the First Edition, even when the delights of a Test Match offered their blandishments. The long sessions of going over scripts together were educational and hugely entertaining.

Many other friends accompanied me in search of the architecture of the past: Mr John Sambrook kindly contributed his clear and admirable drawings to help with the explanation of architectural plans and terms; Mr Victor Belcher, Mr Peter Bezodis, Mr John Greenacombe, and Mr Rodney Hubbuck all helped in one way or another; the late Mr Kit Norbury introduced me to some splendid places near his lovely home; Mr John Gerrard suggested one or two examples; and my late father also helped before his last illness made travel difficult for him. Miss Helen I. Logan typed the book from my unseemly notebooks, for which she gained my gratitude and sympathy. Dr Eileen Blackstock, my wife, helped me to check the first drafts of the texts during a holiday at Eílean Iarmaín, and Mrs Penelope Jessel aided my last labours on the book. Lord Muirshiel, my Chairman during my time in Scotland, kindly wrote the Foreword to the First Edition that was timed to come out during the aftermath of European Architectural Heritage Year: as that Foreword is now out of date I have omitted it from this new version of the book. I have included the late John Gloag's appreciation of the First Edition instead. Mrs Pamela Walker assisted to prepare material for the New Edition, and I record here my grateful thanks to her for her kindness.

It is my earnest hope that *English Architecture* will give pleasure to those who use it, and will stimulate a greater understanding of the unique riches to be found among the buildings of England.

JAMES STEVENS CURL
Oxford, Glasgow, Eílean Iarmaín and Leicester
1972–85

Foreword

James Stevens Curl's *English Architecture* exhibits the conscientious thoroughness of its compiler, and would enlarge and enrich the practical value of any reference library. It is the enlightened work of an architect, an antiquary and a perceptive historian.

Curl's *Glossary* is refreshingly free from tiresome wordiness, and the value of his succinct entries is enhanced by some 300 exceptionally clear illustrations, largely reproduced from his own extensive collection of architectural photographs and from drawings by John J. Sambrook. The format is large enough to allow ample space for the subjects shown, and the entries, set in two columns, are mostly short, pithy and always lucid. The exceptions, justified by the extent and character of the subject, are skilfully compressed essays, for Mr Curl has mastered the difficult art of conveying in a relatively small space all that it is absolutely necessary to say.

This work is far more than an illustrated assembly of technical terms; apart from its considerable value as a reliable reference book, it more than repays the attention of the casual browser, for so many pages reveal new aspects of familiar examples, drawn from our immense treasury of ancient buildings, and so many of the terms stimulate fresh thoughts about our architectural past and our often peculiar architectural present. For students, for teachers, and for all those who enjoy a vital interest in architectural history and development, this book should provide a stimulating experience.

JOHN GLOAG
The Journal of the Royal Society of Arts Vol. CXXV. No. 5254. September 1977
Reproduced by kind permission of The Editor, *The Journal of the Royal Society of Arts*

Abaciscus Synonymous with abacus, but more properly a square compartment enclosing part of a design of a mosaic pavement.

Abacus (pl **Abaci**) The slab at the top of a capital, crowning the column. In the Tuscan, Doric, and antique Ionic Orders it is flat and square, but in the richer Orders its four sides are concave, ornamented on the centres, and with the corners chamfered and moulded. The Greek Doric abacus is a simple square block, unmoulded and unchamfered; the Roman Doric abacus is ornamental with a cyma reversa mould capped by a fillet; the Tuscan abacus has a plain crowning fillet with a cavetto mould under it. The Greek Ionic abacus is very thin, with an ovolo edge, and is sometimes enriched with decoration. The Roman Ionic abacus has a fillet over the ovolo moulding. (See Figs **Orders**). The Egyptian abacus is thick, sometimes bell-shaped, sometimes a square block of considerable thickness, and sometimes elaborated in the form of a shrine. Saxon abaci are generally unmoulded and flat. Norman abaci are found square, circular, octagonal, and frequently moulded and decorated. During the Middle Ages, the abacus varied greatly, and is sometimes vestigial. In some instances, where the capitals consist of clusters of mouldings, the abacus is difficult to define.

Abbey The residence of the head of a convent or monastery; the term has come to mean the church and buildings of a monastic establishment. These were usually very grand and consisted of church, cloisters, chapterhouse, refectory, guest hall, locutory, dormitory, almonry, library, cells, and sometimes a prison for offenders. Often there were granges, schools with accommodation, common rooms, mints and treasuries, and sanatoria. All abbeys had graveyards, gardens and bakehouses. Kitchens, brewhouses, cornmills, stables, byres, piggeries, workshops, smithies and stores completed the complex. Abbeys were self-contained communities and played a positive part in economic, spiritual, and intellectual life. They often vied with each other as places of pilgrimage and were often richly endowed with relics and magnificent furnishings to attract the faithful. There were, of course, several religious orders with specialisations of their own. Many abbeys developed great traditions of musical performance, and the singing-schools of several were world-famous. Traditional plainchant and later polyphony were living parts of the great religious services.

a

b

Abbey
a) The nave of Fountains Abbey, looking west, showing the mid-twelfth-century style of architecture. The west window is fifteenth-century and replaces probably three Norman windows
b) Lay brothers' refectory and great cellar at Fountains Abbey. Note that the quadripartite vaulting runs from the piers without capitals, but springs from corbels on the walls. This beautiful vaulted room, completely intact, dates from the latter half of the twelfth century and the first decades of the thirteenth. The floor level has risen somewhat since the great cellar was built
c) The Chapel of the Nine Altars (1220–50) at Fountains Abbey. The huge Perpendicular window of the late fifteenth century has lost all its tracery

Abbey Plan of Fountains Abbey, Yorkshire

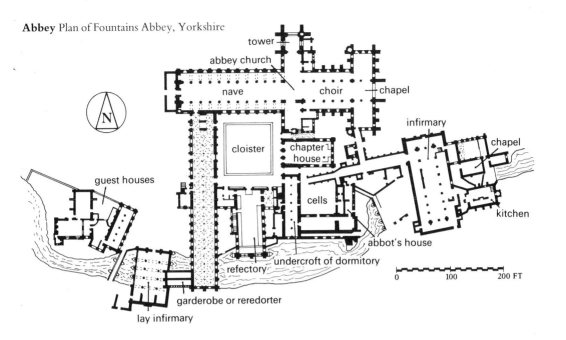

Abutment The solid part of a pier from which an arch springs. Abutments can be artificial, of stone, bricks, or concrete, to counteract the lateral thrust of an arch, but the term can also be applied to solid rock which receives the foot of an arch. (See Fig **Arcade**)

Acanthus A spiny plant with thick leaves said to be the model for the leaves of the Corinthian and Composite capital, and other similar classical mouldings. (See also Figs d, g **Orders**)

Acroteria Pedestals or plinths at the centre and sides of pediments for statues or ornaments. The

9

Abutment This magnificent arcade from Leominster shows a typical Norman arrangement of nave arcade, triforium over, and clerestory lights above. Note the massive abutments

Acanthus Leaf

singular, acroterium, is applied to the ridge of a building, and has been used to describe the statues or ornaments on the plinths. The term is also sometimes incorrectly applied to signify the pieces of wall between pedestals and balusters. Acroteria are also found at the apices of gables in Gothic architecture, especially in canopies. (See Fig A **Temple**)

Addorsed Timbers placed back to back.

Adit, Aditus The approach or entrance to a building.

Adytum The secret chamber or inner sanctuary of a Greek temple from which oracles were delivered. It was usually without natural lighting. In ancient Egypt it was known as the Secos.

Aedicule A shrine framed by two columns supporting an entablature and pediment, usually containing a statue. It is also used as a term signifying the framing of a door, window, or niche, with two columns, pilasters, or piers, carrying a gable, entablature and pediment, or a single lintel. An opening framed in such a manner could be said to be aediculated.

Aeolic A very early form of the Ionic capital, probably of Semitic origin. The Aeolic capital had a long abacus carried on two volutes with palmettes filling the gap between them.

Aesthetics That science in the fine arts which has its first principles in the effect which objects have on the mind and sensibilities. It is the science of the states and conditions of sensual perception. In the early nineteenth century, the term came to mean the philosophy of taste or the perception of the beautiful.

Aetoma, Aetos The tympanum of a pediment. (See Fig A **Temple**)

Agora The open space in a Greek city which doubled as market place and general rendezvous. It was usually surrounded by colonnades.

Aisle A lateral portion of a basilican building or a church parallel to the nave, choir, and chancel, and separated from the central portion of the building by arcades. The aisles are usually much lower in height than the central, main body of the edifice. (See also Fig **Basilica**)

Aedicule Aediculated opening at Kirby Hall, Northamptonshire

Aisle The south aisle of Wells Cathedral in the Early English style

Aedicule Aediculated and pedimented window opening

Ajutage A tube through which water in a fountain is played.

Alabaster A semi-translucent variety of gypsum, white and brown in colour, much used for decorative sculpture in churches. It is very common in Victorian work and is easily carved. It is frequently found in reredos, pulpits, ambones or monumental decoration. It is always inside a building.

Albarium Opus A variety of stucco used in Roman times, capable of being polished.

Alcove A portion of a room set aside for a bed, often raised above the level of a floor, and separated from the rest of the room by a balustrade with doors. The term is also used to denote small ornamental buildings with seats in gardens or to suggest large niches.

Alley An aisle. A narrow passage in an urban area. An enclosed walk in a garden.

a

Almeny (See **Aumbry**)

Almonry A closet for the reception of victuals for the poor. It also came to signify the building near a church in abbeys provided with offices for the distribution of alms, and with accommodation for the almoner.

Almshouse A house devoted to the shelter of poor persons and endowed for this use.

Aloring The parapet of a church, associated with the gutter path or alura.

b

Almshouse

a) The Beauchamp Almshouses at Newland, in Worcestershire. This interesting group, consisting of church and almshouses, was designed by P. C. Hardwick, and built 1862–4

b) The interior of the church at the Beauchamp Almshouses at Newland in Worcestershire. This interior is in the Gothic style, and is remarkable for the surviving Victorian decorations. This photograph shows the beautiful sedilia

Altar

The high altar and reredos of the church of St Francis of Assisi, Pottery Lane, Kensington, by John Francis Bentley, constructed in 1863 of alabaster richly inlaid with marble and mosaic. The altar frontal has short marble columns with ornate capitals and cushions

that support the table itself. The central panel is painted, while on either side are panels much enriched with inlays. The first super-altar is inlaid with triangular patterns of dark and light marbles, and the second super-altar has circular recessed panels separated from each other by inlays of black foliate patterns of Art Nouveau style. The reredos itself is surmounted by a leaf cornice and has four panels of eight-pointed star shapes, each containing a painted figure. A corbel carries a throne above with a Vesica Piscis panel inlaid with mosaics. The Pelican in Piety surmounts the gilded canopy over this throne. In the centre of the altar is a tabernacle set behind an aediculated front, with a brass door enriched with enamels and precious stones (*Greater London Council, Department of Architecture and Civic Design, serial No 70/11/80*)

Altar An elevated table or podium on which to place or sacrifice offerings to deities. In Christian churches they were of stone from the sixth century onwards, until the Reformation encouraged the use of wooden communion tables. The Christian altar was consecrated for the celebration of the Sacrament. Altars were usually built of solid masonry, and the slab forming the top was sometimes partially carried on columns or brackets. Five crosses were cut on the top to signify the five wounds of Christ. Altars were found at the east end of the church and in side chapels, each dedicated to a particular saint. The principal altar was termed the high altar, and stood at the east end of the chancel. From the period that stone altars were introduced, it was usual to enclose relics in the altar slab. Altars have sides or horns termed epistle (south) and gospel (north). In England there was much destruction of altars in and around 1550, although some restoration took place under Queen Mary I. Further desecration occurred under Queen Elizabeth I and more under the Puritans.

Altar Piece The decorations of an altar.

Altar Screen, Altar Wall The wall behind an altar, separating the choir from the east (usually Lady) chapel.

Altar Tomb A tomb or memorial resembling an altar. Such tombs often have recumbent effigies on top.

Alto-relievo (See **Relievo**)

Alura, Alure A passage or gangway, gallery, or garden walk. It may also be a covered pavement. The clerestory gallery in the nave of Ely is referred to in the sacristy rolls as an alura: *Pro sexdecim fenestris factis de novo in superioribus alluris ecclesiae.* The term may also be used to denote the passages on the roof of a building along the gutters, or for the galleries behind the battlements of a castle or city wall.

Ambitus A space round a tomb, or a niche for a body or an urn in a catacomb. The ambitus was often decorated and usually sealed in with slabs on which were inscribed the names of the dead.

Ambo An elevated lectern or pulpit in the nave, before the steps of the chancel, or sometimes associated with the balustrade dividing the chancel from the nave. Ambones usually had two ascents, and were sometimes isolated. Where they are associated with the choir, they are twinned, one on the south side being used for the reading of the Epistle, and the other, on the north, acting as a platform for the reading of the Gospel.

Ambry (See **Aumbry**)

Ambulatory A place in which to walk, such as a cloister. The term is also used to denote the semicircular, right-angled, or polygonal aisle enclosing a sanctuary, and joining the two chancel aisles behind the high altar. (See Fig **Cathedral**)

Altar Tomb A fine, late-Elizabethan altar tomb of Edmund Walter (d 1592) and his wife. Note the strapwork cartouche, and the ribbon-work in the spandrels. The Order is a coarse Corinthian (note the exaggerated entasis), and the entablature is surmounted by a central cartouche flanked by obelisks. Ludlow, St Laurence's Church

Amphi-prostyle A Classical building with a portico at each end, but with no columns along the sides. (See Fig D **Temple**)

Amphitheatre A circular or elliptical building with rising tiers of seats. The term is derived from the fact that the form of an amphitheatre is in reality two normal semicircular theatres joined together at the proscenium to form a theatre in the round. The amphitheatre was used by the Romans for large-scale spectacles and gladiatorial combat.

Anchor An ornament like an arrow head used with an egg design to enrich mouldings. It is also known as a dart. (See Fig **Egg and Dart**)

Ancones The trusses or consoles supporting the cornices above Classical openings. (See Figs **Console, Georgian**)

Andirons Firedogs.

Angle Bar Upright bar at the angle of a polygonal window.

Angle Bead A vertical bead of wood fixed to an angle and flush with the surface of the intended plaster on either side to secure the angle against accident and also to serve as a guide for floating the plaster. This was a common detail in houses of the Victorian period, and was supremely functional.

Angle Buttress A buttress at the corner of a building usually associated with another buttress at an angle of 90°. (See **Buttress**)

Angle Capital In the Ionic Order, the corner capitals often have the corner volutes placed at an angle of 135° with the planes of the front and returning friezes. (See Fig f **Orders**)

Angle Chimney A chimney placed in the corner of a room.

Angle Iron A plate of iron rolled into an L shape. Angle irons are now usually made of mild steel.

Angle Modillion A modillion at the mitring of a cornice, generally regarded as an abuse of Classical detail and decidedly decadent.

Angle Rafter Timber in a hipped roof in the line of the junction of the two inclined planes. More often called a hip rafter.

Angle Tie A small timber tying two timbers at an angle to each other.

Angle-tooled, Angle-droved Dressed stone with the tool marks running diagonally. (Scots)

Annulated Column Slender shafts clustered round a column, joined by bands of stone or metal, very commonly found in Early English architecture, and usually of Purbeck marble.

Annulet A small flat fillet encircling a column. It is used under the echinus of a Doric capital several times. It is also called a shaft ring. (See Fig d **Orders**)

Anta A species of pilaster used in Classical architecture to terminate the side walls or pteromata of temples. When the pronaos or porch in front of the cell is formed by the projection of the pteromata terminated by antae with columns between, it is described as being 'in antis'. (See Fig B **Temple**). The base and capitals of antae differ from those on adjacent columns. Antae may be said to correspond to the responds of medieval architecture.

Antechamber, Anteroom An apartment through which access is obtained to a room beyond.

Antechapel The part of a chapel between the western wall and the choir screen.

Antechurch Also called the forechurch, it is a narthex or porch to the west, several bays deep, and consists of a nave and aisles.

Antecourt The approach to the principal court of a house.

Antefixae Ornamental tiles placed above the cornice of a Classical building at the end of each ridge of tiling, concealing the ends of the harmi, or joint tiles. The term is also applied to ornamental heads, below the eaves, through the mouths of which water is cast away.

Antepagmenta Jambs or moulded architraves.

Antependium The frontal of an altar.

Anterides Buttresses for the support of a wall.

Anthemion Ornament based on the honeysuckle, associated with the palmette or fleuron design.

Anticum A porch to a front door. The space between the columns of a portico and the wall of the cella. It is sometimes ignorantly used to describe the anta.

Antefixae Ornamental antefixae above the Corinthian monument to William Huskisson, MP, who was killed by a steam engine at the opening of the Liverpool and Manchester Railway in 1830. The tomb is in St James's Cemetery, Liverpool, and was designed by John Foster

Apartment A part of a house, consisting of a set of one or more rooms which are self-contained. In Victorian times the term became misused and was corrupted to mean a single room, so that phrases such as a 'suite of apartments' became common. In Scots usage, an apartment still means one room.

Apiary A place for keeping beehives.

Apodyterium A place where a person took off clothes in preparation for a bath or for gymnastic exercise.

Apophyge The curve given to the top and bottom of the shaft of a column, where it expands to meet the edge of the fillet above the base, and beneath the astragal under the capital. It is also known as the apothesis and the apophysis. (See Fig e **Orders**)

Apotheca A store for wine, oil, and spices.

Applied Column An engaged column, that is, attached to a wall.

Approach A road leading to a building.

Apron Also known as a pitching piece, it is a horizontal timber, in double-flight stairs, for supporting the carriage pieces in the landings. It is also a panel below a sill.

Antefixae

Anthemion

Aqueduct
Aqueduct in Warwickshire, carrying a canal. Cast-iron sections are bolted together, and the whole trough and walk is carried on brick piers

Apse A semicircular or polygonal domed recess, usually found as a termination to a basilican building. Apses are found at the east ends of choirs or chancels, and sometimes in chancel aisles. Early churches sometimes had apses at the west ends. Chapels were frequently apsed. The term apsidal means shaped like an apse. An apsidiole is a subsidiary apse. (See Fig **Basilica**)

Apteral A classical building with no columns at the sides.

Aqueduct A channel for conveying water, often elevated on brick or stone piers.

Arabesque Geometrical and complicated decoration, involving intertwined tendrils and foliage, adorning walls, pavements and ceilings of buildings. The term does not necessarily derive from Arabian or Saracenic examples, for the Greeks and Romans used arabesque or capricious ornament, while the illuminations of the medieval period are often enriched with arabesque decoration. Also a term meaning grotesque.

Arabesque A design by John Francis Bentley used in the altar of the Dominican convent, Portobello Road, London

Arabian Architecture The Moresque, Saracenic, or Arabian architecture was occasionally the model for some late-eighteenth and nineteenth-century designs but was not common.

Araeostyle One of the five species of intercolumniation defined by Vitruvius. It includes cases where columns are set more than three diameters apart, usually approximately four diameters apart. (See **Intercolumniation**)

Arcade Arches carried on columns, piers, or pilasters, either freestanding or attached to a wall to form decoration. In the latter case it is referred to as a blind arcade. The term is applied to large arches and piers that divide a nave from an aisle. The Victorian 'shopping arcade' derives from another meaning of the term signifying a continued arch, a passage, a walk formed by a number of arches, or an avenue of trees. An arcade in the sense of a covered avenue with shops on one or both sides dates from 1731. Arcades are also the lines of vertical posts on either side of a timber-framed building. (See Fig **Gothic Architecture**)

a

b

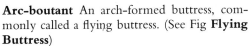

Arc-boutant An arch-formed buttress, commonly called a flying buttress. (See Fig **Flying Buttress**)

Arch A construction of blocks of material, disposed in a curve or curves, and supporting one another by mutual pressure. An arch so formed over an opening is capable of carrying a superimposed weight. Each block is called a *voussoir*, usually in the shape of a truncated wedge, and the block in the centre is called the *keystone*. The solid extremities on or against which the arch rests are called *abutments*. (See Fig **Arcade**). The lower or under curve of each stone is called the *intrados*, and the upper curve the *extrados*. The

Arcade
a) The Barton Arcade, Manchester, by Corby, Raby, and Sawyer, using parts cast in Macfarlane's 'Saracen' Foundry in Glasgow
b) The Central Arcade, Newcastle upon Tyne
c) Part of the chapel of Ludlow Castle, Shropshire. This blank or blind arcading is in the circular nave of *c* 1140, and has typical Norman work, with scallop capitals and zigzag mouldings

distance between the piers or abutments is the *span* of the arch, and the vertical distance between the level line of the springing to the intrados is the height of the arch. The *springing* or *impost* is the point at which an arch unites with its support. The simplest arches are the *semicircular*

c

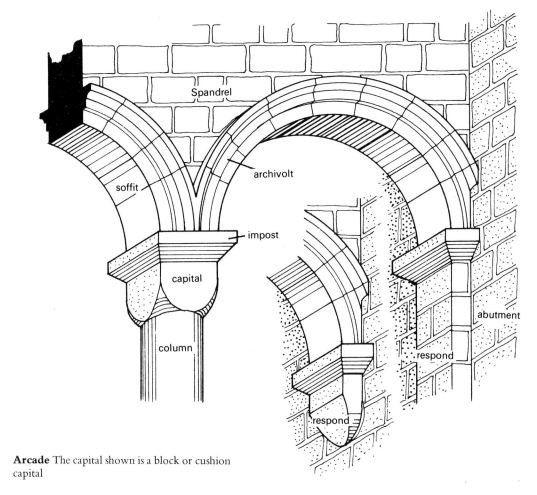

Arcade The capital shown is a block or cushion capital

Labels on figure: Spandrel, archivolt, soffit, impost, capital, column, abutment, respond, respond

and *segmental* arches, the former with its centre on the springing line and the latter with its centre below the springing line. In the Saxon and Norman periods, when semicircular arches were commonly used, the centre is often above the springing line, giving the arch an elongated or sometimes *horseshoe* shape. The elongated arch is called a *stilted* arch. Occasionally, elongated pointed arches are found, and when pointed arches have prolonged curves which narrow the arch at impost level, the effect is predominantly Moresque. The proportions of a pointed arch are governed by the position of the two centre points from which its curved sides are struck. An arch formed of two curves each with a radius equal to the span is called an *equilateral* arch. When the centres of the curves forming the sides of the arch lie far apart, the radius is longer than the span, and so the height is increased. This is called a *lancet* arch. In a case where the centres lie within this arch, the height is lessened, and the result is known as a *drop* arch. *Foil* arches are

found in Moresque architecture and in Romanesque buildings, as well as in medieval work. Simple *pointed* or *ogive* arches were used in all the periods of Gothic architecture. The lancet arch is a characteristic of the Early English period, while drop and equilateral arches are common in both Early English and Decorated buildings. Perpendicular Gothic often has both drop and equilateral arches, but the characteristic form of later Perpendicular Gothic is the *four-centred* arch, also known as the *Tudor*. The latter is a very depressed arch, and was sometimes found in a single stone lintel. During the Decorated period, the *ogee* arch was introduced, and is commonly found in tomb-canopies, small doorways and windows. The figures also show a *flat, relieving, shouldered, Venetian* and *Florentine* arch. (See also **Basket-handle, Compound, Diminished, Discharging, Gauged, Interlacing, Inverted, Jack, Mitre, Rampant, Rear, Scheme, Straight, Strainer, Surbased, Surmounted, Transverse,** and **Triumphal**.)

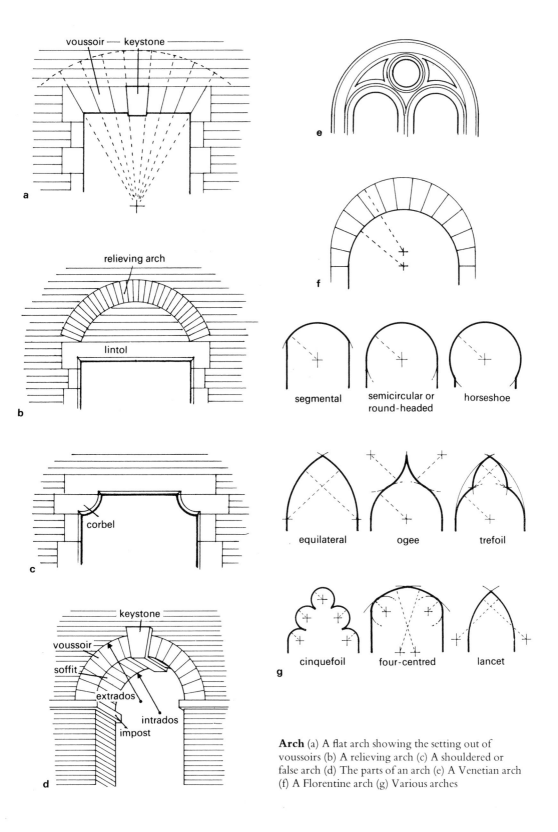

voussoir — keystone

a

relieving arch

lintol

b

corbel

c

keystone

voussoir

soffit

extrados

intrados

impost

d

e

f

segmental   semicircular or   horseshoe
             round-headed

equilateral   ogee   trefoil

cinquefoil   four-centred   lancet

g

Arch (a) A flat arch showing the setting out of
voussoirs (b) A relieving arch (c) A shouldered or
false arch (d) The parts of an arch (e) A Venetian arch
(f) A Florentine arch (g) Various arches

19

Arches
A fine example of brickwork in a warehouse, of Flemish bond. Note the segmental arches over the windows, and the inverted arch below the sill of the lowest window. The ends of the wall ties form a pattern, and there is a string course

Arch Brace A curved timber brace. (See Figs e, f **Roof**)

Arch Buttress A flying buttress, or arc-boutant. (See **Buttress**, Fig **Flying Buttress**)

Architect A person competent to design and superintend the execution of any building. A master builder. In the United Kingdom, the title of architect is protected by Act of Parliament which requires a person to pass professional examinations and receive practical training and experience before being admitted to the Register of Architects.

Architecture The art of designing and building according to rules and proportions regulated by nature and taste.

Architrave The lowest of the divisions of an entablature that rests directly on the abaci of columns. The term also refers to the lintels, jambs and mouldings surrounding a window, door, panel or niche. It is also the ornamental moulding round the exterior curve of an arch. (See Figs **Door, Orders**)

Architrave Cornice An entablature with no frieze.

Archivolt A group of concentric mouldings with which the face of a classical arch is decorated. The term was originally used to designate a vault, and is sometimes erroneously given to the soffit of an arch. (See Fig **Arcade**)

Arcuated A building dependent on the arch principle, as opposed to the trabeated form of construction.

Arcus Ecclesiae An arch dividing the nave of a church from the chancel.

Area A court or place, often sunk below the ground, allowing light into a basement storey. It is also used to denote a small courtyard, even when level with the ground. The term also means the superficial content of a figure.

Arena The central space of an amphitheatre where gladiators fought, or any building where public contests are held.

Argent Heraldic silver.

Ark A chest.

Armature Iron framework used in the construction of slender columns, or for supporting canopies, bosses and tracery.

Armoury A place where weapons are stored.

Aronade Embattled, with arches in the middle of each raised part.

Arris A sharp edge at the junction of two surfaces.

Arsenal A public store for arms and ammunition.

Artificial Stone A material resembling stone, but made by a mix of materials.

Artisan Mannerism The use of motifs in a different way, and outside their original usage, evolved by craftsmen as opposed to architects.

Art Nouveau A shop that opened in Paris in 1895 and gave its name to the style of decorative art characterised by undulating sinuous lines and a breakaway from Classical or Gothic ornament.

Ashlar Cut stone, worked to even faces and right-angled edges, laid in horizontal courses with vertical joints. When the work is smooth, the result is called plain ashlar, but when the surface is cut in a regular fashion, with parallel fluting, it is called tooled ashlar. Other finishes are random tooling, or irregular texturing using a broad tool; chiselling or boasting, created with a narrow tool; and pointed, if the surface is cut with a very narrow tool. Where the stones project beyond the joints, the finish is known as rustication. (See Figs **Masonry**)

Ashlaring, Ashlering The short quartering in timber roofs between the rafters and the ceiling joists to cut off the acute angle caused by the rafters. An ashlar piece is a short timber rising from the sole piece to meet the feet of rafters.

Aspect The direction in which a building faces.

Aspersorium The stoup, or holy water basin.

Asphalt A bituminous substance, impervious to damp.

Astragal A small semicircular moulding or bead, sometimes called a roundel. It is properly applied only to the ring that separates the capital from the column, and may be ornamented with a bead or reel. It may also denote the bead that separates the faces of architraves.

Astragals An illiterate use of the term in Scotland to denote glazing bars.

Astylar Without columns or pilasters.

Atkinson's Cement A quick-setting patent cement or stucco.

Atlantes, Atlantides Heroic male figures used instead of columns or brackets to support an entablature.

Atrium A court, usually colonnaded, found in Roman domestic architecture and in front of Early Christian churches. It was roofed to leave a large opening in the centre to admit light and rain. The latter was received in a cistern formed in the pavement.

Attached Column An engaged column.

Attic A low storey over the main entablature, not to be confused with a garret. An attic has ceilings square with the side walls, and is quite distinct from a roof space. An attic storey is found in Classical styles of architecture. (See Fig **Georgian**)

Attic Base The base of an Ionic column with two large convex rings between which is a concave moulding. These rings are described as upper and lower torus, with scotia and fillets between them. (See Fig c **Orders**)

Attributes Symbols associated with figures, and used decoratively. Hercules is indicated by a club, Neptune by a trident and Pallas by a spear.

Auger A tool for boring holes.

Aula A court or hall.

Aumbry Also known as an almeny, aumery, ambry, ambre, ambrie or aumbrye, it was a recess by the side of an altar to contain the sacred vessels. Ornate doors were provided, and the stonework surrounding aumbries was beautifully carved.

Aureole (See **Vesica Piscis, Mandala**)

Aviary A place for the keeping and breeding of birds.

Awning A covering to screen persons or parts of buildings from the sun or rain.

Axed Dressed. A finish to hard stone after the face has been reduced with a punch. (Scots)

Axonometric Projection A drawing showing a building in three dimensions, with verticals and horizontals to scale. (See Figs A and B **Projections**)

Azure Heraldic blue.

Back Boxing The back-lining of a sash frame, or that parallel to the pulley piece. (Scots)

Back of a Wall Its inner face.

Back of a Window The frame in the space between the sash frame and the floor.

Backs The principal rafters of a roof. The upper side of any piece of timber is the back, while the lower side is the breast.

Backset Stone cut back so that rendering over it is flush with the rest of the face.

Badigeon A mixture of plaster and freestone used to repair statues. It is also a mixture of sawdust and glue used to repair blemishes in timber. Sometimes whiting and glue, or putty and chalk are used.

Bagnio A bath, usually a Turkish bath. The term came to signify a brothel or 'stew' in the seventeenth century.

Baguette, Bagnette A small moulding similar to an astragal.

Bailey, Bail, Ballium The space between the circuits of the walls of a castle and the keep, also called a ward. The outer court of a castle or any court within the walls. The term originally meant the walls round a castle.

Bakehouse A place where bread is made.

Balanced Winders (See **Dancing Steps**)

Balcony A projection from a wall of a building carried on brackets, consoles, or columns, or cantilevered. It is usually placed before windows or openings and protected by a railing or balustrade. The term is also applied to a stage box in a theatre, or to the open part above the dress circle.

Baldachin, Baldaquin, Baldacchino A canopy placed over an altar, supported on columns, carried on brackets cantilevered from a wall, or suspended from the ceiling. The word originally signified a rich embroidered canopy over shrines borne in procession. Also known as a ciborium.

Balection (See **Bolection Moulding**)

Balistraria The narrow aperture in medieval fortress walls through which the bowmen discharged their balistae or arrows. It was often cruciform and came into general use in the thirteenth century. It is also known by the terms arbalestina or arbalisteria. A balistraria is also a room in which arbalests or crossbows were kept.

Balk, Baulk A piece of fir, rough-squared. In

Balistraria
Cruciform balistraria in the Micklegate Bar, or gate, at York. Note the Norman archway and shouldered arches to the doors that once led to the wall walks of the Barbican. Above are fourteenth-century bartisans with battlements

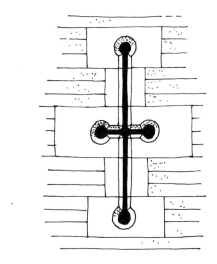

Balistraria From Tattershall Castle, Lincolnshire

Scots usage the upper tie between rafters.

Ball Flower An ornament like a ball enclosed within petals and usually placed in a hollow moulding. It is usually regarded as a characteristic of the Decorated style of Gothic architecture of the fourteenth century.

Ball Flower
Ball flower decoration on the Decorated windows of
Leominster Priory Church, Herefordshire

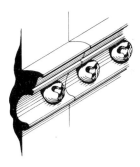

Ballflower

Ballium (See **Bailey**)

Balloon A globe on a column or pier, or the ball
on the top of a cathedral dome.

Balteus The wide step in theatres or amphitheatres which allowed people to walk without disturbing those seated. The term is also used
to describe the strap which appears to bind the
cushion or coussinet of the Ionic capital.

Baluster A small pillar or post forming part of a
balustrade and supporting the handrail or coping. (See Fig **Pedestal**). Balusters are also known
as columellae. A baluster shaft is a small pillar
with pear-shaped entasis dividing an opening in
Saxon churches.

Balustrade A parapet composed of balusters
and a coping or rail. (See Fig **Pedestal**)

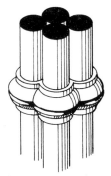

Band of a Shaft The drawing shows a clustered
column with a band

Band A flat face or square moulding encircling a
building or running across its façade. A continuous series of ornaments such as a band of
foliage, quatrefoils, or bricks. In Scots usage, a
band is a bond, where inband and outband will
occur.

Bandage A ring or chain of iron at the corner of
a stone wall or round the circumference of a
tower or drum which acts as a tie to keep the
walls together.

Banded Column A rusticated column consisting of a shaft broken by plain or rusticated
rectangular blocks.

Bandelet, Bandlet (See **Band of a Shaft**)

Band of a Shaft The moulding or series of

23

mouldings encircling pillars and shafts in Gothic architecture usually of the Early English period. They are also known as shaft rings, bandelets, or annulets.

Banister A vulgar term for a baluster. The plural, banisters, signifies a balustrade. (Scots)

Banquet A raised footway on a bridge.

Baptistery Part of a church or a separate building used for the rite of baptism and therefore containing the font.

Bar A piece of wood or iron used to fasten doors or windows. A place in courts where counsel have their places to plead. It is also the bar at which prisoners are placed to take their trials. It is any counter across which refreshments are served, but the term has come also to be applied to a building or room in which alcohol is served as well as to the actual counter.

Bar, Barred Door The term used in Scotland for a ledged door, as a bar is a ledge in Scots usage.

Barbican, Barbacan A watch tower. An outwork or defence before a gate, or a fortified gate.

Bares Parts of an image which represent bare flesh.

Bargeboards The inclined projecting boards placed at the gable of a building, covering the horizontal timbers of the roof, and set under the tiles or slates. They are frequently ornamented or carved. In Scots usage, a barge is a stone drip at the base of a chimney stack, a shaped timber drip

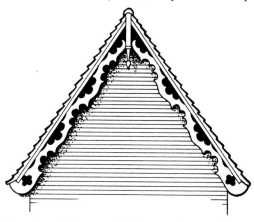

Bargeboards An example from London Road, Isleworth, Middlesex (c 1880)

at the bottom rail of a door, or an apron of lead or copper. It is also spelt 'berge', and can also be applied to bargeboards, as in England.

Barge Couples Beams mortised and tenoned together for the purpose of increasing the strength of a structure.

Barge Course Tiles projecting over the gable of a building and made good with mortar.

Barley-sugar Column A Classical column twisted like a stick of barley sugar also known as a Solomonic or twisted column. It is a Baroque motif.

Barmkin A defensive enclosure round a tower. (Scots)

Barn A covered building for storing grain, hay or straw. Many fine medieval barns exist throughout England.

Bar of a Sash, Glazing Bar Pieces of wood or metal dividing a window sash into compartments for glazing. (See Fig **Sash**). Angle bars are those standing at the intersection of two vertical planes.

Baroque A florid form of art prevalent during the seventeenth and eighteenth centuries. It is characterised by exuberance, movement, curvacious forms, theatrical and illusionist effects and by immensely contrived and complex spatial interrelationships.

Barrack, Barracks A building for the housing of troops.

Barrack Room A long room in country houses for the accommodation of a number of men in cases where individual rooms do not exist.

Barrel Vault A cylindrical vault, with a uniform concave ceiling with no groins or ribs. (See **Vault**)

Barrow A sepulchral mound or tumulus.

Bartisan, Bartizan A turret projecting from the angle of a top of a tower, castle, house or wall. In Scotland the term is also applied to the embattled parapet of a tower.

Bar Tracery Completely developed Gothic tracery.

a

b

Baroque

a) A composition by Rysbrack in the Church of St Michael, Great Witley, Worcestershire, completed *c* 1740. It is perhaps one of the largest funerary monuments of the eighteenth century. Note the sarcophagus, obelisk, and large urn

b) Late-Baroque interior of St Michael, Great Witley, with paintings from Canons, the house of the Duke of Chandos

Basilica

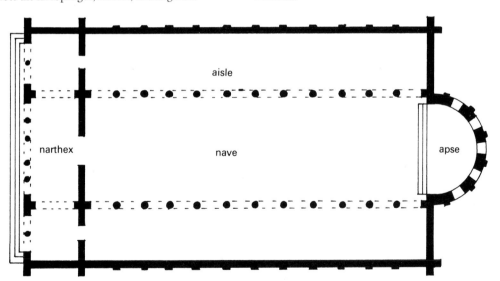

narthex   aisle   nave   apse

Base The base of a column is that part of it between the shaft and the pavement or pedestal. (See Fig c **Orders**). In Scots usage base blocks are plinth blocks, bases are built-up skirtings with plain bands and separate mouldings above, and a base course is a plinth.

Basement The lowest storey of a building, whether above or below ground. (See Fig **Georgian**)

Basilica A building divided into a nave and two aisles, the former being wider and taller than the

25

latter. The basilican form is that used in church plans. It originally had an apse at one end of the nave and was the basis of the Early Christian church designs. In Roman times, a basilica was a large hall, and the term referred to the type of building rather than to its form.

Basket-handle Arch An arch with a height less than half its span.

Basso-relievo, Bas-relief (See **Relievo**)

Bastille A fortification used as a prison, or a tower or bulwark in the fortifications of a town.

Bastion A projection at an angle of a fortress or wall, which enables the ground in front of the ramparts to be seen and defended.

Bat A piece of brick of less than half the length of a whole brick. In Scots usage, a bat is a metal cramp, or a lead wedge; also part of a hinge built into a wall; to caulk.

Bat Bolt Rag bolts. (Scots)

Bath An apartment or series of apartments for bathing.

Batten A scantling or small rectangular piece of timber used to provide fixing for slates, or in order to receive laths for plasterwork. In Scots usage, a batten door is a ledged door.

Battening The fixing of battens or the battens in the state of being fixed.

Batter An inclined face. It is applied to walls that are sloping, thick at the bottom but thinner at the top.

Battlement A parapet that is notched or indented. It consists of rising parts called merlons or cops, separated by spaces which are called crenelles, embrasures, or loops. It is a very ancient form of parapet. To say that a wall is crenellated means that it has battlements.

Baulk (See **Balk**)

Bay A principal compartment or division in the architectural arrangement of a building, marked by buttresses or pilasters, or by the main vaults or principal rafters of the roof. (See **Gothic Architecture**)

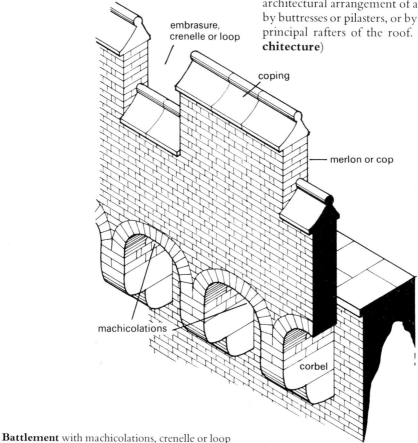

embrasure, crenelle or loop

coping

merlon or cop

machicolations

corbel

Battlement with machicolations, crenelle or loop

Battlement
Battlemented wall at York

Bay
Segmental bays, or bows, on houses in St Andrew's Place, London. *(Photograph by E. R. Jarrett, kindly lent by Mr Terence Davis)*

Bay Window
A tall semicircular bay window with mullions and transoms at Fountains Hall, Yorkshire. Note the battlements, the balustrade with statues on the pedestals, the niches with statues, and the entrance door with engaged Ionic columns on either side

Bay-leaf Garland Torus enrichment in Classical architecture.

Bay Stall The seat in a bay of a window.

Bay Window A window forming a bay or recess in a room, projecting out from the wall either in a rectangular, polygonal, or semi-circular form. On an upper floor only, cantilevered out, it is called an oriel. A segmental bay is sometimes called a bow, and is particularly

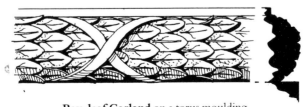

Bay-leaf Garland on a torus moulding

associated with architecture of the Regency period.

Bead A small cylindrical or partly cylindrical moulding often enriched with beads and reels. It is similarly any small moulding with a curved section.

Bead and Butt Frames in which the panels are flush, with beads struck or run upon the two edges. *Bead, butt and square work* is framing with beads and butts on one side, and square on the other. *Bead and flush work* is a piece of framed work with beads run on each edge of the panel enclosed. *Bead, flush and square work* is framing with bead and flush on one side, and square on the other, used chiefly in doors. *Bead and quirk* refers to a bead stuck on the edge of a piece of wood, flush with its surface, with only one quirk, or without being returned on the other surface.

Bead and Reel Enrichment of an astragal resembling a string of beads and reels.

Bead and Reel

Beak A hanging fillet left on the edge of a larmier, sometimes formed by a groove recessed on the soffit of the larmier. (See Fig **Mouldings**)

Beak Head An ornamental moulding resembling a beak or beak head, found in Norman work.

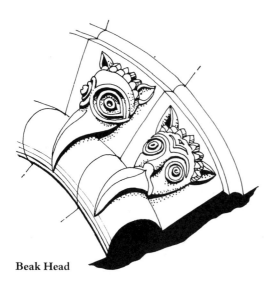

Beak Head

Beak Moulding A moulding which forms an ovolo or ogee with or without a fillet under it, followed by a hollow. It is found in the cap of an anta of the Doric Order.

Beam A principal horizontal member of a building, spanning from wall to wall and carrying a weight.

Beam Filling Brickwork or masonry brought up from the level of the under to the upper sides of beams. It can also be the filling of the space from the top of the wall plate to the underside of the slate.

Bearer A support carrying something, such as a gutter.

Bearing The length of a beam or joist carried on a wall or other support.

Bed The horizontal surface on which stones, bricks, etc, lie.

Bed Moulding The moulding under a corona, between it and the frieze, or any moulding under any projection.

Beehive Structure A circular stone building with courses decreasing in diameter as the height is increased, thus forming a pseudo-domed structure.

Belection (See **Bolection Moulding**)

Belfast or Bowstring Roof A roof of curved timber trusses and horizontal ties, with timber lattice work.

Belfry The upper part of a tower where bells are

Belfry
The cemetery chapels and belfry in Paddington cemetery, by Thomas Little (1853)

Bellcote, From Little Coxwell, Berkshire

hung, or the timber framing by which bells are supported.

Bell The 'bell' of a capital in Classical or Egyptian architecture.

Bellcast Pieces Sprockets or fillets at the bases of roughcast or harled walls. (Scots)

Bellcote A small turret or gable in which bells are hung. Sometimes a bellcote may be found on the gable of the eastern end of the nave, known as a sanctecote, for the sanctus bell.

Bell Gable, Bell Turret (See **Bellcote**)

Belt A term in masonry to denote a course of projecting stones. In Scots usage, a belt course refers to any string course or hand course.

Belting Plugged bearers, or hat and coat rails. (Scots)

Belvedere A turret or lantern or room built above a roof or on high land for the enjoyment of a view. The term is also applied to a summer house or gazebo.

Bema The sanctuary or chancel of a church.

Benatura The holy water vessel at the entrance to a church, generally on the right of the porch.

Bench-end The end of a pew.

Bench Table, Bench A low stone seat on the inside of walls and sometimes round the bases of pillars, porches, cloisters, etc.

Bend An oblique band across a shield.

Bend

Béton Brut Concrete left in its natural state from the formwork.

Bevel A sloped or canted surface.

Bevel-checked Joint Bevel halving. (Scots)

Bezant A gold roundel in heraldry.

Bier A portable carriage for the dead.

Bilection (See **Bolection Moulding**).

Bilgate A wood fixing slip, for joinery, built into a wall. (Scots)

Billet Moulding An ornament used in Norman work, formed by cutting a moulding in notches so that the parts left resemble short wooden billets or cylindrical dowels, two or three inches long, placed sometimes in hollow mouldings. The billets are arranged in several bands, and are placed at regular intervals. Sometimes the billets are square or rectangular instead of cylindrical.

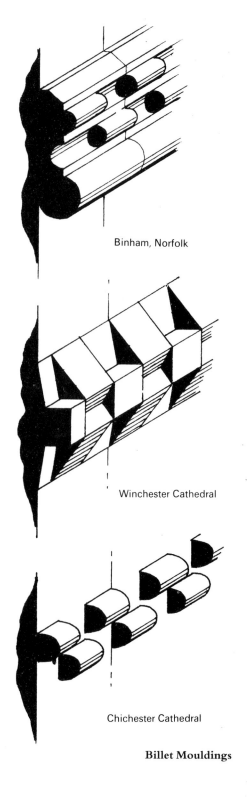

Binham, Norfolk

Winchester Cathedral

Chichester Cathedral

Billet Mouldings

Bin, Binn A subdivision in a cellar for wine bottles.

Binding Beam A joist which supports bridging joists above and ceiling joists below. A binding rafter is a purlin.

Bird's Beak Moulding A moulding which in section forms an ogee or ovolo with a fillet under it.

Bird's Mouth An interior angle cut on the end

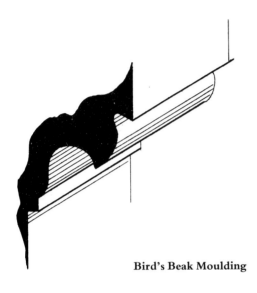

Bird's Beak Moulding

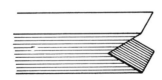

Bird's Mouth

of a timber to obtain a firm fixing upon the exterior angle of another piece.

Biss A stall division in a byre. (Scots)

Blades The principal rafters or backs of a roof.

Blaes, Blaze Poor bituminous sandstone. (Scots)

Blank Door A fake door. The same term

'blank' is used for windows that are false.

Blind A draw-down covering for windows. The term also means forms of wood or metal, covered with opaque material, to cover the whole or part of a window to protect it from the sun. Blind also means blank.

Blind Storey A triforium. The term can also be applied to a fake storey, or heightened parapet wall which is there for visual effect and usually conceals a roof behind it.

Blind Tracery Tracery which is purely decorative and is applied to walls without glazing or openings (See Fig c **Gothic Architecture**)

Blocking Course The plain course of stone which surmounts a cornice at the top of a Classical building. It is also a projecting course without mouldings at the base of a building.

Blocking-out A masonry term referring to boasting, and a joinery term referring to rough grounds or fir battens. (Scots)

Blockings Pieces of wood glued to the backs of timbers for additional strength.

Board A piece of timber more than four inches wide and not more than two and a half inches thick. Trapezoidal sections are called feather-edged boards; wider boards are called planks. Boards for valleys, or valley boards, are boards fixed to the valley rafters for the lead guttering.

Boarding Joist A joist to which boards are to be fixed.

Boarding for Pugging, Soundboarding This means short boards between joists of floors fixed to fillets with a substance, usually plaster, placed between them to prevent sound transmission. The plaster is known as pugging.

Boast To boast a piece of stone or wood is to shape it into the simple form approaching its ultimate appearance when carved. Often stone carvings or capitals are boasted and built into position, to be carved at leisure. Boasted work may frequently be seen, the carving never having been completed. In Scots terminology, droved is also used to signify boasted.

Body of a Church The nave. The body of a compound pillar is the central shaft.

Boss A mid-thirteenth-century example from Westminster Abbey

Boiserie Wainscoting. The term is commonly applied to seventeenth- or eighteenth-century panelling elaborately decorated with shallow-relief carvings.

Bolection Moulding Mouldings which project beyond the surface of a panel or frame, usually found in panelling or in doors. It is used to cover the joint between the members with different surface levels. Also spelt balection, belection or bilection. (See Fig c **Panel Mouldings**)

Bolster, Pillow The return side of an Ionic capital resembling a baluster. (See Fig f **Orders**)

Bond Bond timbers were formerly built into walls to tie them and allow fixings for furnishings. Bondstones are those placed to cover the full thickness of a wall. (See **Brickwork**).

Boneing Judging or making a surface level.

Booth Any temporary structure for shade and shelter.

Border A piece of wood or other stuff round the edges or along the upper edge of any thing.

Bordure A border round an heraldic shield.

Boss An enriched ornamental block at the intersection of the ribs of a vault. (See also Fig A **Vaults**)

Bossage Projecting stones laid in a wall to be carved later. The term is also applied to rusticated work.

Boss Head A box staple for a bolt of a lock. (Scots)

Bossing A recess in a wall on the inside under a window. (Scots)

Bottled Rounded. (Scots)

Bottle-nosing Rounded nosing. (Scots)

Bottoming Hardcore or filling. (Scots)

Boudoir A room for the use of the lady of the house as a sitting-room.

Boulder Wall A wall constructed of round stones.

Boultine, Boltel A convex moulding, or an ovolo. (See **Bowtell**, Fig **Roll Mouldings**)

Bound Framed. (Scots)

Bound Masonry Bonded stonework.

Bow A projecting part of a building, semi-circular or segmental on plan. Bows on polygonal plans are called canted bows.

Bower (See **Boudoir**).

Bowlers, Bolders Pebbles six to nine inches deep used for paving.

Bow Room A room having a bow on one or more sides.

Bowstring A truss formed of a segmental arch and a horizontal tie.

Bowtell A round moulding or bead, or the small shafts of clustered pillars, window jambs, or mullions. It is an old English term for an astragal. Also called bowtel, boltel, boutell and boultine. (See Fig **Roll mouldings**)

Bow Window (See **Bay Window**)

Box A small dwelling.

Boxed Shutters The cases on either side of a window where the shutters are folded inside the room.

Box Frame A structure where loads are carried on the cross walls, usually only suitable for flats or hotel apartments.

Box of a Theatre A partitioned-off compartment, usually on either side of the proscenium, in tiers, where parties can attend the play.

Box Pew A Georgian pew with high wooden partitions around it, usually large enough for one family.

Brace An inclined piece of timber used to stiffen roofs, partitions, and the like. When a brace supports a rafter, it is called a strut.

Bracket A projection from the face of a wall, frequently ornamented, to support a statue, colonnette or other weight. Brackets may also be termed corbels. Simple brackets of wood or metal can support shelves, seats or other objects. A bracket moulding is a Gothic moulding of two ogees with joined faces.

Bracketing to a Cornice The wooden frame

to support large cornices. A bracketed cornice is one where the modillions have become transmogrified into large brackets, usually found in coarser Victorian work.

Braggers Brackets.

Branches The ribs of a Gothic vault rising up from the tops of pillars to the apex.

Brandering Battening to give better fixing to laths for plaster ceilings. Branders are thus the battens. The term is also known in Scotland.

Brandrith A fence round a well.

Brass, Brasses Monumental plates of brass laid on or in stone slabs in the pavements of churches, incised with figures and lettering to celebrate the dead. The incised work was filled with black resin, mastic and enamel. English sepulchral brasses offer a rich field of study and beautiful medieval examples may be found in abundance.

Brattishing Also known as brandishing, bretizment, bretaysing, bretise, bretisement. An ornamental cresting above a parapet, screen or cornice, usually composed of foliate decoration, battlements or floral enrichment. The term is also applied to carved open work over shrines.

Breast The portion of a chimney projecting into a room. The breast of a window is the solid under the sill. In Scots usage, a breast is a riser. A breast lining is panelling between a window-board and the skirting.

Breastsummer, Bressumer, Breastsommer The beam supporting the front of a building, rather like a massive lintel. It carries the whole of a superstructure as opposed to only a small portion over a window, and has the first-floor joists tenoned into it. It is not to be confused with a fascia-board planted onto normal jetty construction as described falsely in some other architectural reference books.

Bretasche A defensive wooden gallery. (Scots)

Bretexed Embattled.

Brewhouse A building for the manufacture of malt liquors.

Brick A block made of clay, sand and lime, or concrete. Clay bricks may be sun-dried or burnt

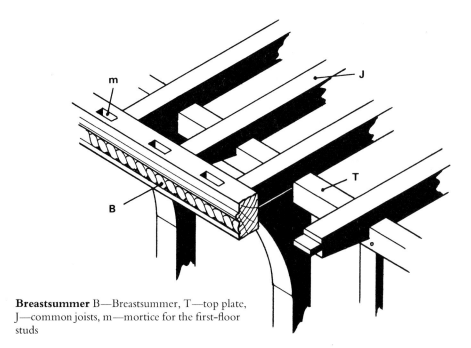

Breastsummer B—Breastsummer, T—top plate, J—common joists, m—mortice for the first-floor studs

in a kiln after moulding or cutting. Fine clay bricks have widely differing colours and textures depending upon the types of constituents and the manufacturing process.

Brickwork and Brick Bond A selection of the commonest types of bond is shown here. A *header* is a brick laid so that only its end appears on the face of the wall; a *snapped header* is a brick laid so that only its end appears on the face of the wall, but, when used on $4\frac{1}{2}$-in thick work it must be cut in two, or snapped; a *stretcher* is a brick laid so that its longest side appears on the face of the wall; *brick bats* are cut bricks less than half the length of a whole brick. A *closer* is a brick at the end of a horizontal length of wall, which is of less size than other full-size bricks and is used to close the row and keep the bond. Traditional *English bond* consists of alternate courses of stretchers and headers, and was in use before the reign of King William III, when Flemish bond was introduced from the Netherlands. *Flemish bond* consists of alternate headers and stretchers in each row. Brickwork may be carved and moulded for decorative effect. Bonds are frequently confused in early work, and Georgian Flemish bond often turns out to be $4\frac{1}{2}$-in thick brickwork with snapped headers.

Bridge A construction with one or more open intervals under it to span a river or other space. It is constructed of rope, wood, iron, stone, brick or concrete, or a combination of these.

Bridgeboard A board into which the ends of the steps of wooden stairs are fixed.

Bridge-over A piece of timber fixed over parallel timbers. Rafters bridge over purlins.

Bridgestone Stone laid from the pavement to the entrance door of a house over a sunken area, usually supported by an arch.

Bridging Joist A principal joist spanning between walls and into which common joists are tenoned.

Bridging Pieces Pieces placed between beams or joints to prevent bending towards each other.

Bridging to Floors Herringbone strutting between floor joists.

Bridle A trimmer. (Scots)

Bridling Joist A trimming joist. (Scots)

Brig, Briggs Divisions between flues. (Scots)

Brise-soleil A sunshade outside a building, usually composed of fins.

Broach An old English word for a spire. The term now means an octagonal spire that springs from the tower without a parapet. (See **Spire**)

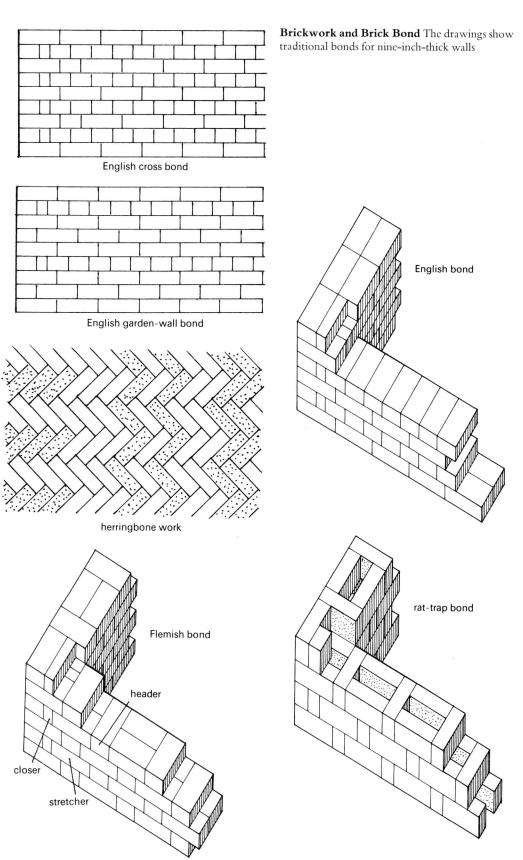

Brickwork and Brick Bond The drawings show traditional bonds for nine-inch-thick walls

English cross bond

English garden-wall bond

herringbone work

English bond

Flemish bond

header

closer

stretcher

rat-trap bond

Broached Stone worked to show diagonal or horizontal furrows. (Scots)

Broadstone Freestone.

Brutalism A term used in the 1950s to describe an architectural expression using raw exposed concrete on which the impression of the shuttering is left. The word derives from the French 'béton brut'.

Bucrane, Bucranium An ox skull, garlanded, found in Classical architecture.

Buhl Work Also known as boule, or boulle work, this consists of one or more metals inlaid on a ground of tortoiseshell.

Built Docks Fixing pads or hardwood plugs. (Scots)

Built Steps Built into, or on, support walls. (Scots)

Bulker A beam or rafter.

Bullen or Boleyn Nails Nails with round heads and short shanks, turned and lacquered, used in the hangings of rooms.

Bull's Eye A small circular aperture for the admission of light and air. The term is also applied to the thickening of a pane of glass produced by the Crown glass method.

Bundle Pillar In Gothic architecture, a column consisting of a central column with a number of shafts around it.

Bungalow Derived from the Hindu term for a thatched house, it has come to mean a single-storey dwelling.

Bush Hammering A technique to obtain an even textured surface on concrete. The work is carried out by operatives using a hammer with a grooved head. The smooth surface of the concrete is chipped away to expose the aggregate. The method is time-consuming and expensive.

Butment Synonymous with abutment.

Butment Checks The two solid pieces on either side of a mortise.

Butt A square or fitted end or heading joint,

but it is not a term used to describe hinges. (Scots)

Butt End That part of a timber which was nearest the root of the tree.

Buttery A store for provisions, usually on the north side of a building. The term has come to be applied to places in pubs where food is served.

Butt Hinges, Butts Hinges on which doors and windows are hung; the two halves of the hinge close against each other as opposed to strap hinges. Rising butt hinges cause a door to rise as it opens in order to clear a carpet.

Butting Joint One formed by two pieces of wood, the grain of one being at right angles to the other, or at an oblique angle.

Button A small piece of wood or metal, fixed with a screw to turn, for fastening a door or drawer.

Buttress A projection from a wall to create additional strength and support. Saxon and Norman buttresses are often wide but of small projection, and are commonly not subdivided into stages. Early English buttresses are normally of considerable depth, but are much less wide than Norman work, and are often staged, with reduction in their width and projection. Each stage is marked by set-offs, and the buttresses are capped either with a plain slope or with a triangular head or pediment. Buttresses at the angle of a building usually consist of a pair meeting at an angle of 90° at the corner (*angle buttress*) or of a large square buttress encasing the corner (*clasping buttress*) in the Early English style. Sometimes buttresses will be surmounted by a pinnacle. In the Decorated style, buttresses are almost invariably worked in stages and are usually ornamented with niches, crocketed canopies and other carved decorations, and they frequently terminate in pinnacles rather than in the familiar triangular pediment. With the introduction of the Decorated style, buttresses were often set diagonally at corners, forming 135° angles. During the Perpendicular period, buttresses were often panelled, the heads taking on the forms of the architectural character. Another type of buttress is the *setback buttress*, which is like an angle buttress but set back from the corner on the face of the wall so that it does not join its counterpart but leaves the corner or angle of the building freely expressed. A *flying buttress*, as the name

Buttress

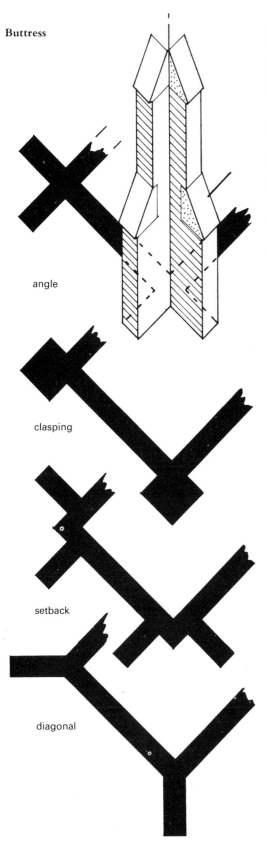

angle

clasping

setback

diagonal

implies, transmits the thrust of a vault or roof from the top of a wall to an outer support via an arch or part of an arch. It is then known as an *arch buttress* or arc-boutant. (See Fig **Flying Buttress**).

Byewood Flushing Planing down joints of boarded floors. (Scots)

Byzantine A style of architecture which was developed in the eastern Roman Empire from the foundation of Constantinople to AD 1453. It was the highest achievement of late Roman and Greek work, and differs greatly from Classical architecture as the Orders were abandoned, although Classical forms could still be discerned, transmogrified and often simplified. Christian symbols replaced pagan sculptural motifs, and Roman structural techniques were evolved even further using brick, concrete, and the arch. Decorations were usually rich and glowingly coloured. During the nineteenth century several buildings of a Byzantine style were built including Westminster Cathedral by John Francis Bentley.

Cabin A hut or cottage.

Cabinet A chamber set aside for study, private converse or the display of treasures.

Cable Moulding A Romanesque moulding resembling a strand of twisted cord or rope. It was much used during the late-Norman period.

Cabling A convex moulding in the flutes of columns or pilasters in Classical architecture, nearly filling up the hollow flute to less than one third the total height of the shaft. (See Fig **Pilaster**).

Caen Stone Stone from Caen in France, frequently found in the south of England.

Cage An outer work of timber surrounding another.

Cairn A monument or pile of stones for marking or memorial purposes.

Caisson A structure driven down to a firm foundation used to facilitate building below water level. The term also refers to the sunken panels in ceilings, vaults, and cupolas.

Caldarium A room in Roman architecture

where perspiration was induced by steam, hot water or heated air.

Caliducts Channels in walls for the passage of hot air.

Calvary Cross A cross on a mound or on steps.

Camber A curve in the form of a very shallow, almost flat arch. A camber beam has a slight curve so that its centre is higher than its ends, thus avoiding a sagging effect.

Came Slender rods of lead used in stained-glass windows and other leaded lights.

Camerated Arched.

Campanile A bell tower, generally attached to a church but sometimes unconnected with it. There are detached bell towers at Evesham and Ledbury, among other places.

Camp Ceiling A ceiling with a sagging inward curve. In Scots usage, the term camp is also used, but more often the words coom or comb are used to mean the same thing.

Camp Sheeting, Camp Shot The sill or cap of a wharf wall.

Canal A duct for carrying a liquid. The term is also used to suggest the flutings of a column or pilaster.

Cancelli Latticed windows. The balusters or rails surrounding an altar are also thus named.

Cancello A latticed screen separating the chancel from the nave.

Candelabrum A stand for the support of lamps.

Canephorae Figures of young persons bearing baskets on their heads. They are not to be confused with caryatides.

Canopy The tester and curtains of a bed, or any covering or hood over an altar, statue, pulpit or other object. Canopied tombs are common in English churches.

Cant An external angle of a building. The term is also used by carpenters to express the cutting off of an angle of a square. Any part of a building on a polygonal plan is said to be canted. A canted

a

b

Canopied Tomb
a) Tomb of Bishop Stafford (d 1419) in Exeter Cathedral. The effigy is delicate and beautiful. The canopy is fifteenth-century work, and was the model for Bishop Bronescombe's monument
b) Effigy of Bishop Bronescombe in Exeter Cathedral (d 1280)

column is a column that is polygonal on plan. In Scots usage it means a tilt, and can also signify stone laid with its natural bed vertical and showing on the face.

Cantharus A fountain or pool in the atrium of ancient churches where worshippers washed before entering the building. The holy water stoup is a vestigial survival of the cantharus.

Canthers, Canterii In ancient carpentry, the common rafters of a roof the ends of which may be represented by the mutules of the Doric Order.

Cantilever A bracket built into a wall to support eaves, cornices, balconies or canopies. It is essentially any projecting member supported by a downward force the far side of a fulcrum. Canopies and balconies are nearly always cantilevered.

Cant Moulding A moulding with bevelled rather than curved surfaces.

Cantoned A building enriched by columns, pilasters, rusticated quoins or anything projecting beyond the façade.

Cap A capital, a cornice, or an uppermost finishing member.

Cap House The upper covering of a stair leading to a parapet or a gallery. (Scots)

Capital The upper part or head of a column or pilaster. The *Aeolic capital* is an early form of the Ionic capital (see **Aeolic**). The *bell capital* has a bell-like form, reversed, which is found in Egyptian architecture and as the basis of the Corinthian capital. The *crocket capital* is a Gothic capital with rolled leaves resembling Classical volutes. The *cushion capital* is a Norman capital, basically cubic in form, but with the lower parts rounded to fit the circular column. The flat faces remaining are referred to as lunettes from their half-moon forms. The *scalloped capital* is similar to the cushion capital, but with the curved portion carved with part-cones as enrichment. (See also Figs **Moulded Capital**, **Orders**)

Capital Different types of capital

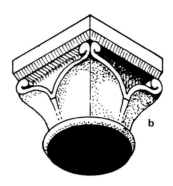

water-leaf capital

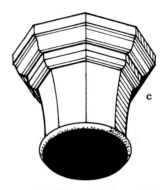

moulded Perpendicular capital

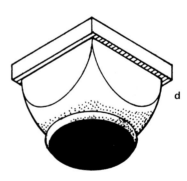

cushion capital

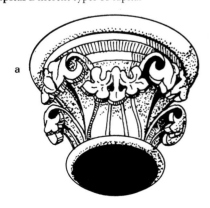

stiff-leaf capital

scallop capital

39

Caput Ecclesiae The caput, or head, of a church is usually the east end, but the term was also sometimes applied to the west.

Caracol A spiral staircase.

Carcass The shell of a building. Similarly, carcass flooring or roofing refers to the frame of timber that carries boards.

Carol, Carrol, Carrel A small closet or enclosure in which to study. The term is sometimes used to describe a small bay window or a niche in a cloister.

Carolitic Column A column with a foliated shaft.

Carpentry A structure of timber, distinguished from joinery in that it is constructed using the simple tools of axe, adze, saw and chisel, whereas joinery implies the use of a plane and more sophistication. The term is also applied to the trade of carpentry.

Carrara Marble A white Tuscan marble commonly found in Victorian monuments and decorative architecture.

Carriage The timber frame on which steps of a stair are supported.

Cartouch, Cartouche A modillion, usually internal. The term is more commonly applied to a decorative tablet or frame for inscriptions in the form of a scroll or curling piece of parchment.

Caryatides Figures of females used instead of columns for the support of an entablature. The term is also given to any support carved in the form of a human figure, but is not strictly speaking correct. Male figures, usually heroic in scale and proportion, are called *atlantes* or *telamones*. Figures of young persons bearing baskets on their heads are called *canephorae*. *Herms* are portions of figures on pedestals, while *terms* are pedestals merging at the top into human or other figures.

Case Bays Joists framed between girders. When the ends of flooring joists are let into a wall and the other ends into a girder, they are called tail bays.

Cased Facing to a building. The term signifies that the outside of a building is covered with

Cartouche
a) A beautiful mural monument in the Curl chapel at Soberton, Hampshire, in the Baroque manner, in memory of Sir Walter Curl
b) Cartouche of 1691 on the Mico Almshouses, Stepney

materials of superior quality to those used in its construction.

Cased Sash Frames Those which have their interior verticals hollow for the weights to balance the sashes.

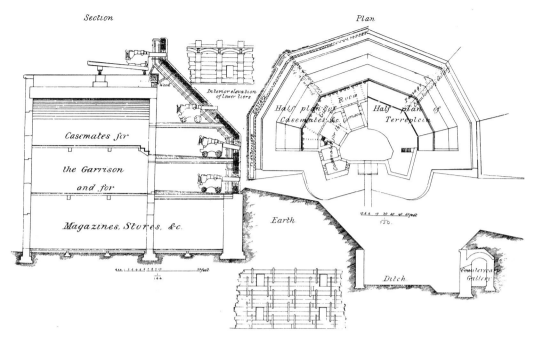

Section   Plan

Wood

Interior elevation
of lower tiers

Casemates for

the Garrison

and for

Magazines, Stores, &c.

Half plan of Guard Room in Garrison

Half plan of Terreplein

Earth

Ditch

Counterscarp Gallery

Exterior elevation showing position of vertical ties.

Casemate

Plan and section of an iron fort showing the casemates. From *Papers on Fortification in Iron* by Sir Edmund Du Cane, 1862. (*Kindly lent by Mr A. W. Pullan*)

Casemate A vaulted chamber in the thickness of fortified ramparts, with embrasures. The term is also used to signify a barrack or a battery. In archaic usage the term also meant a hollow moulding, such as the cavetto. Casemated means provided with casemates, ie fortified strongly.

Casement A frame enclosing part of the glazing of a window, with hinges to open and shut. A casement window is a metal or timber window with the opening frame hinged vertically. The term was also used to describe the deep concave moulding, similar to the cavetto or scotia, prevalent in Gothic architecture in cornices, door and window jambs. It was often enriched.

Case of a Door The wooden frame in which a door is hung. The term door-case is also applied to the whole of an elaborate timber Classical frame to a doorway.

Case of a Stair The wall around a staircase.

Casing Lining.

Casino A small country house, or a lodge in a park. The term was formerly applied to a de-

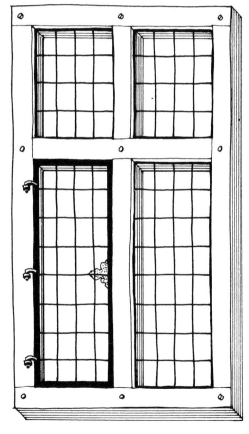

Casement A seventeenth-century cross-casement of oak, from the brewhouse at Crostwight Hall, Norfolk

Castle

a) Stokesay Castle, Shropshire. One of the earliest fortified houses in England, built in the latter part of the thirteenth century. On the left is a timber-framed structure of the late-sixteenth century
b) Ludlow. The castle on the left is of the twelfth and thirteenth centuries. The keep is twelfth century. To the right is the tower of St Laurence's Church, dating from the fifteenth century

fence post, but later came to be applied to a summerhouse or decorative lodge. The word also means any public room for social meetings, especially a public music – or dancing – saloon, but now is used to describe a room or building used for gambling.

Castellated With battlements and turrets.

Castelle, Castellum, Castella A receptacle for the collection of water for distribution. In ancient times the castelle was often a large chamber with vaulted rooms or cisterns.

Casting In joinery, the term means warping or bending. In metalwork, it means the pouring of molten metal into a mould, or the result of such a pouring when set, eg a gulley – grating or a bell.

Castle A building fortified for defence. It is also a habitation with towers and surrounding walls and moats. The chief parts of a castle are the valla or embankments, fossae or ditches, walls with battlements, bastions at angles or intervals along the wall, and the central tower or keep. The *fosse* or moat had a bridge that could be raised leading to the gates which were guarded by descending metal-reinforced grilles called *portcullises*. The *barbican* was in advance of the castle and defended the entrance, being constructed on a mound or tower principle with terraces facing the castle. The *gatehouse* was flanked by towers and crowned with projecting *machicolations*. Inside the castle was the *outer bailey* or ballium, separated from the *inner bailey* by a wall and gatehouse, and usually containing stables and offices. The inner bailey was the innermost defence, in the corner of which was a *keep* or donjon. The latter was the stronghold and contained the state apartments, a well, a chapel, and other important rooms.

Catabasion A place under an altar where relics are placed.

Catacomb An underground place for the de-

Catacomb
Catacombs at the General Cemetery of All Souls, Kensal Green, dating from 1836–7, designed by J. W. Griffith. The catafalque to bring coffins down from the chapel above is visible. (*G.L.C. Department of Architecture and Civic Design, serial No 70/12203*)

positing of the dead. In early times catacombs were hollowed out of the solid rock and were used as prisons, burial places, stores and places of worship. In England, several catacombs were built rather than hollowed out and used for the depositing of coffins. The great Victorian cemeteries, for example, often had catacombs.

Catafalque, Catafalco A temporary structure, decorated and usually draped, representing a tomb or cenotaph and used in funeral cere-

monies. It is often used to support the coffin and some permanent catafalques may be found in funerary chapels in cemeteries and in later crematoria. Both in Victorian mortuary chapels and crematoria, catafalques often have mechanical lifts to carry the coffin downwards to vaults or furnaces.

Catch Drain A drain on the side of a large open canal to take the surplus water.

Catenary Curve The curve formed when a heavy cord or chain hangs freely from two supports.

Cathedra A bishop's chair or throne, originally placed in the apse behind the High Altar but in Gothic architecture usually found in cathedrals associated with the choir stalls.

Cathedra
The Bishop's throne (1313–17) and east end of Exeter Cathedral are largely Decorated work

Cathedral The principal church of a diocese in which the cathedra or bishop's throne is placed.

Catherine Wheel Window Also called a marigold window, it is a geometrically patterned window with radiating divisions or spokes. (See **Rose Window**)

Cathedral
The Decorated nave of Exeter Cathedral

Caulicoli, Caulicolae, Caulcoles In the Corinthian capital, the eight stalks that spring from the four greater stalks. The eight volutes of the capital are carried by four stalks from which the caulicolae arise. (See **Orders**)

Caulking, Cocking The mode of fixing the tie beam of a roof or the binding joists of a floor to the wall plates. The term is also used to mean the stopping-up of crevices.

Causeway In English usage, the term means a raised dam or bank across a marsh for a road. It also means any paved road. In Scotland it means a paving of setts or squared stones.

Cavaedium An open court within a house.

Cavalier A raised platform of earth for the placing of guns, or as a lookout post.

Cathedral The drawing shows a plan of Norwich Cathedral. The curved east end, with ambulatory and chapels, is the 'chevet' plan of French Gothic cathedrals

chapels

ambulatory

altar

chapter house (site)

chapel

crossing with a tower and spire over

choir

screen

cloister

nave

locutory

0   100 FT

Caveae Subterranean cells in an amphitheatre. Cavea is also applied to an amphitheatre.

Cavetto A hollow moulding with its profile a quadrant of a circle, principally used in cornices.

Ceele, Seele A canopy.

Ceiling Joists Small beams fixed to the binding joists for the attachment of lathing which will take plaster on a ceiling.

Cell A small closet in which to sit or read, especially the bedsitting room of a monastic establishment. Part of a temple enclosed within the walls, otherwise the naos, or cella. (See Fig H **Temple**). A chamber in which a prisoner is confined. The term is also applied to a compartment of a groined vault.

Cellar The lowest storey of a building, wholly or partly underground, used for storage. The word is also applied to an underground store-room.

Cellarium Monastic buildings with stores and cellars on the west side of the cloisters.

Cellular Beam Beams of iron plates with cells at the top of the web.

Celure The panelled and painted roof or ceiling over an altar or rood. A canopy.

Cement An adhesive composed of a powdered substance made into a paste with water which hardens on drying to bind bricks or stones together. It is also any substance, when applied to the surfaces of solid bodies, that makes them cohere firmly.

Cemetery Any place where the dead are interred or deposited.

Cenotaph A monument that celebrates the memory of a person or persons buried elsewhere. An empty tomb.

Centering Wooden framework used in arch or vault construction, and struck or removed when the arch or vault is completed or the mortar has set. In some early vaults which were constructed of rough-hewn stone, the centering was covered with a thick layer of mortar, so that when it was struck the impression of the wooden structure was left.

a

b

Cemetery
a) The strange, Italianate landscaping of Highgate Cemetery (late 1830s) designed by Stephen Geary, J. B. Bunning, and David Ramsay.
b) The South Metropolitan Cemetery, Norwood, designed by Sir William Tite, laid out in the late 1830s. (*Author's collection from J. C. Loudon's* Gardener's Magazine)

Centrie Garth A cemetery.

Ceroma An apartment in baths where anointing took place.

Cesspool A pit for the collection of soil and human wastes. It is also any well sunk below the mouth of a drain to receive sediment which might block the drain.

Chain Moulding An ornamental moulding resembling a chain.

Chair Rail A dado rail or moulding around a room to prevent the backs of chairs from damaging the plasterwork.

Chalcidicum A building for the administration of justice.

Chamber A room. The great chamber was contiguous to the hall and was the equivalent of a drawing-room. The term camera is used to signify a suite of rooms or an apartment. The camera of an abbot was a suite of lodgings. In Scots usage this is a chalmer.

Chamber Storey A storey for bedrooms.

Chambranle An ornamental border on the sides and tops of doors or windows.

Chamfer An arris or angle which is pared off is said to be chamfered. A chamfer resembles a splay, but is much smaller. A hollow chamfer is concave.

Champ, Champe The field or ground on which carving is raised.

Chancel The choir and sanctuary in the eastern part of a church appropriated for the use of those who officiate during services. The term was originally applied only to that part of the church where the altar was placed. (See also Fig **Isometric Projection**)

Chancel
The Church of St John, Plymtree, Devon, with beautiful decorated screen

Chandry An apartment for storing candles.

Channel A gutter sunk below the surface of, say, a street to collect and run off rainwater.

Chanelling Rebates on ashlar to form rustications. (Scots)

Chantlate A piece of timber fixed to the ends of rafters and projecting beyond the wall to support slates.

Chantry An endowment to provide for the chanting of masses. A chantry chapel was a small chapel devoted to the saying of masses for the dead. Most chantry chapels were in abbeys, cathedrals, and the grander churches in which it was considered a privilege to be buried, and thus were often over or attached to the grave of the person who provided the endowment. In the reign of Edward VI all the chantries in England were dissolved, but many fine examples of chapels survive.

Chapel A small building or part of a building set aside for worship, and dedicated separately. Before the Reformation all great houses, castles and granges had chapels attached to them. The parish churches and cathedrals had numbers of chapels, usually to the east of the High Altar and often in the aisles. The largest of all these chapels attached to a church was always dedicated to Our Lady. The term chapel generally signifies a building endowed with fewer privileges than churches, and in which the sacrament of baptism could not be administered. Chapels generally had no burying ground annexed. Chapel also signifies a building used for forms of worship

Chantry Chapel
Perpendicular stone screens set round the chapel (c 1508) in Exeter Cathedral. Note the cadaver, warning passers-by: *Sum quod eris, fueram quod es, pro me, precor, ora*

practised by dissenting or nonconformist sects. In Ireland, chapel signifies a Roman Catholic church, probably because Mass was said in chapels attached to other buildings before freedom of worship was granted. (See Fig **Cathedral**)

Chapiter, Chaptrel A capital.

Chaplet A moulding carved with beads, olives, etc.

Chapterhouse The building attached to a cathedral or collegiate church where the dean and prebendaries or monks and canons met for the transaction of business. Chapterhouses are often very ornate and magnificent, and are frequently polygonal on plan, eg Wells, Southwell, York, Salisbury, Lincoln and Worcester.

Chaptrel An impost, or a capital.

Char, Chare To hew or work.

Charged A frieze is charged with the ornament on it, so the term means the dependence of one

Chapterhouse
The magnificent central column that branches into the vault of the chapterhouse at Wells Cathedral

part of a work of architecture upon another.

Charnel House A building where the bones of the dead were stored. Charnel houses were usually vaulted and often had chantry chapels attached. Charnel houses ensured that churchyards never filled and ground could be used over and over again. The Reformation, with concepts of ownership of graves and the destruction of chantry chapels, heralded the end of charnel houses.

Chartophylacium An apartment for the storing of records.

Chase An indent in a wall for a pipe or for the joint with another wall.

Chase Mortise A long mortise in one of a pair of parallel timbers for the insertion of one end of a transverse member.

Chatri A parasol-shaped dome over a flat, carried on columns, found in Indian architecture.

Check A rebate. (Scots)

Checky Divided into heraldic squares or chequers.

Cheeks Two upright and equal similar parts of any piece of timberwork, eg the sides of a dormer window. The cheeks of a mortise are the solid pieces of timber on either side of the mortise.

Chequerwork Decorative treatments of pavings or walls involving squares of contrasting materials in a chessboard pattern.

Chests Receptacles for all kinds of goods. In churches, chests are usually for the storage of copes or linens, or even for vessels. The term is also used to denote coffins.

Chevet The east end of a church built in the French style, that is, with an apsidal form and ambulatory, usually with radiating chapels. (See Fig **Cathedral**)

Chevron A zigzag ornament found in Norman work, usually on the archivolt. An heraldic pointed gable charge.

Chief The upper third part of an heraldic shield.

Chimney A fireplace. The term now includes

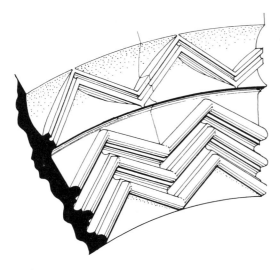

Chevron An example from Chichester Cathedral

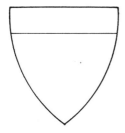

Chief

Chinoiserie
The pagoda in the Chinese style at Kew Gardens by Sir William Chambers (1763)

the flue and the structure above a roof. In early medieval times chimney shafts appear to have been rare and they did not become common until as late as the early sixteenth century. In domestic buildings chimneys are often found as massive stacks in the core of the house, and sometimes at the gable ends. Where walls were very thick chimneys were formed within them, but chimneys are more usually found expressed as projections and definite structures. The opening into a room is called a *fireplace*, and the floor of the fireplace is the *hearth*. The part of the flue that contracts as it ascends is called the *gathering*. The stone or brick structure that contains the chimney is called the *chimneybreast* while the bar above the fireplace opening which supports the chimneybreast is called the *chimneybar*. The *chimneypiece* is also called the *mantelpiece*, and is essentially the decorative surround to a fireplace with a shelf over it. The *chimneystack* is the structure containing several flues that projects above a roof. On top of the chimneystacks are often placed *chimneypots*, which cap the flues. A *chimney-shaft* is a chimney with one flue only. The chimneys for furnaces and boilers are called *stalks*. In Scots usage, a pot is known as a can, while the head is the portion above a roof.

Chinoiserie A style of art and decoration that evoked Cathay. It first appeared in the seventeenth century, but reached its finest flowering in the eighteenth century. Chinese porcelain and imitations of it became popular, while furniture and decoration in the Chinese taste rivalled the Rococo for delicacy and ingenuity. Pagodas, teahouses and pavilions became all the rage, while the interior of the Royal Pavilion at Brighton might be regarded as containing some of the most important examples of chinoiserie.

Chiselled Work The finish given to the surface of stones by a chisel.

a

Choir Stalls

a) Exeter Cathedral. Originally dating from 1309–10, these are now largely by George Gilbert Scott of the 1870s

Choir, Quire Strictly speaking, it is that part of a church with stalls for singers, but has come to mean the entire space that is used for the performance of services, including the choir and presbytery. In cruciform churches, it is therefore the eastern limb. A choir screen is a screen which divides the choir and presbytery from the side aisles, although the term also means the screen between the chancel and nave.

Choir Stalls Elevated seats in the chancel of a church. They are fixed seats enclosed wholly or partially at the backs and sides. In cathedrals or large churches they were enclosed at the back with panelling, surmounted by overhanging canopies of openwork, and formed part of serried rows of stalls. The open canopies were enriched with pinnacles, crockets, tracery, and other ornament. The choir stall seats, if hinged, frequently had carved grotesques on the underside. (See **Misericord**)

b

b) Choir stalls in Wells Cathedral dating from the late 1840s

Chrismatory A recess like a piscina near the site of a font which contained chrism, or holy oil.

Church A building for public Christian worship. In its simplest form, it consists of an area for the congregation known as the nave, and a smaller part (usually divided from the nave by an arch) known as the chancel. (See **Abbey**, **Aisle**, **Cathedral**, **Chancel**, **Chapel**, **Nave**, **Sanctuary**, **Tabernacle**, **Temple** etc.) (See Fig **Isometric Projection**)

Chymol A hinge.

Ciborium A domed canopy on columns and arches over an altar.

Church

All Saints Church, Fittleton, Wiltshire. This is a typical medieval parish church, built of flint and stone dressings, with a fourteenth-century tower. The different parts of the church may be clearly seen—the west tower, the chancel on the right, the clerestory, south aisle, and porch

Cilery Drapes or foliage on a capital.

Cill (See **Sill**)

Cimbia A fillet, a string course or a cornice.

Cimborio A raised lantern over a roof through which light is admitted.

Cimeliarch The place where vestments and plate were kept in churches.

Cincture A ring at the top or bottom of a column that divides the shaft from the capital and base.

Cinquefoil An ornamental foliation in tracery or panels of the Gothic style, formed by projecting points or cusps arranged so that the intervals between them resemble five leaves.

Cippus A small low column, often with no base or cap and often bearing an inscription. The cippus was used as a milestone and as a funerary monument.

Circle A name given to a megalithic site such as Avebury or Stonehenge.

Circus A long narrow building with a central barrier, curved ends and tiered seating, used by the Romans for chariot races.

Cistern A reservoir for water.

Citadel A fortress situated in a fortified town or city.

Civic Crown A garland of acorns and oak leaves used in architectural ornament.

Cladding An external face or skin of a building. In Scots usage the term means rough boarding or cleading.

Clapboard Weatherboarding.

Clapper Bridge A bridge of stone formed of piers with slabs bridging across them.

Clasping Buttress A large buttress, square on plan, encasing the corner of a building. (See **Buttress**)

Classical Architecture Architecture based on the Classical principles of Greece and Rome. During the Renaissance, theories of architecture were evolved based on the treatises of Vitruvius which had been rediscovered in the fifteenth century. In the eighteenth century, a scholarly return to Classical principles was led by William Kent, Lord Burlington and Colen Campbell who revered the works of Palladio and Inigo Jones: this movement was known as Palladianism, and dominated significant architecture for most of the century. Palladianism was, in a sense, a purifying of style after what was regarded as the excesses of Baroque. Studies of the buildings of antiquity, notably those of Greece by Stuart and Revett, led to the Neo-Classical movement of which the Greek Revival was the most important element in the 1840s.

Neo-Classicism tended to become severe and ultra-simple, and architects such as Dance and Soane reduced decoration to a few motifs, preferring the possibilities of basic geometrical forms, blank walls, and the simplest of elements. From the 1830s an Italianate style based on the *palazzi* of the Quattrocento and Cinquecento led to a general Renaissance revival that coexisted with the Gothic Revival throughout the Victorian period. (See **Orders**)

Clavicula A quarter-circle rampart preventing direct entry to a Roman town or camp.

Cleam To glue.

Clean Wrought timber, or timber free from knots. (Scots)

Clepsydra A water clock.

Clerestory, Clear-story Any window, row of windows, or openings, in the upper part of a building. Also known as an overstorey. It is usually applied to the upper part of the nave, choir or transepts of a church in which windows are formed above the roofs of the aisles. (See Figs **Gothic Architecture**, **Isometric Projection**)

Cling To shrink. (Scots)

Clink A jail. In Scots usage, a welt.

Cloister A covered ambulatory forming part of a monastic or collegiate establishment, arranged round three or four sides of a quadrangular area known as a cloister garth. The ambulatory was roofed, sometimes with timber as at New College, Oxford, and sometimes with stone as at Gloucester. The arches which admitted light from the garth often had fine tracery, and sometimes were glazed or partially glazed. Cloisters

Cloister
Norwich

Cloister Garth
Salisbury Cathedral

gave access to several buildings or apartments. They often contained carrels or places for study, and frequently had lavatories or places to wash. There were benches and niches, and often memorials, for cloisters were sometimes used for sepulture. The sides of a cloister were its panes. (See also Fig **Cathedral**)

Cloister Garth (See **Cloister**).

Close End The stopped end of an eaves gutter. (Scots)

Closer A brick or stone at the end of a horizontal length of wall which is of less size than other full-size bricks or stones, to close the row and keep the bond.

Close String or Closed String (See **Stair**)

Closet A small room to communicate with a bedchamber.

Clour Hack or hammer-dressed stonework. (Scots)

Club Skew A springer or spur stone. (Scots)

Clustered Pier or Column Several columns or shafts clustered together, also known as a compound pier. (See Fig **Band of a Shaft**)

Coade Stone Artificial cast stone manufactured in London from the 1770s onwards and used for decorative keystones, quoins, statuary etc.

Cob Wall Walls of mud and straw.

Cocking Caulking.

Cockle Stair A winding stair.

Coddings The base or footings for chimneys. Padstones, or templates. (Scots)

Coenaculum A supper room. The term also means an upper storey, or lodgings for hire.

Coenatio An apartment in a Roman villa in which to eat, sometimes used to describe a summerhouse.

Coffer A sunken panel in a ceiling, or a caisson. It is also used to describe a chest.

Coffer Dam A watertight piled dam in a river to enable piers or walls to be built.

Coffin A chest to enclose a dead body. In the medieval period coffins of ecclesiastics and wealthy persons were often of stone, with shaped and carved lids, that frequently formed part of the paving of a church. The body of the coffin had a circular cavity to receive the head and there were generally holes in the bottom to allow moisture to drain off. Medieval burial was never deep even when no coffins were used, so churchyards could be used over and over again. Lead coffins were fairly common among the more wealthy members of society, especially when burial took place within churches or in vaults. Royal corpses were inevitably embalmed and placed in leaden coffins. (See **Charnel House**)

Cogging Caulking.

Coin, Coillon, Coyning The same as quoin.

Coliseum, Colosseum A huge amphitheatre built by Vespasian in Rome. The word became popular in Victorian times to describe large theatres and music-halls, of which the great theatre in St Martin's Lane in London is perhaps the best-known example.

Collar A horizontal tie connecting a pair of rafters at any point below the ridge and above the wall plate. (See Fig **Roof**)

Collar Purlin A horizontal timber above a crown post that ties the collars of trusses. (See Fig **Roof**)

Collarino The cylindrical part of the capital of the Roman Doric and Tuscan Orders, lying between the annulets under the ovolo and the astragal. It is termed the neck and is the hypotrachelium of Vitruvius. (See Figs a, d **Orders**)

College An establishment for education in the higher branches of study. The traditional college in England consists of one or more quadrangles around which the rooms are disposed – a library and chapel, a refectory, commonrooms, kitchens, etc.

Colonnade A row of columns. If there are four,

Colonnade
Range of Ionic columns at Park Crescent, London, by John Nash. *(Photograph by E. R. Jarrett, kindly provided by Mr Terence Davis)*

the range is called tetrastyle; if six, hexastyle; if eight, octastyle; if ten, decastyle, etc. When a colonnade stands before a building it is called a portico; if it surrounds a building it is called a peristyle. Colonnades are further described in terms of the spaces between columns (see **Intercolumniation**). In Classical architecture, two columns between antae would be described as distyle in antis. A front portico of four columns is described as prostyle tetrastyle, and a building with porticos of four columns at both the front and rear is described as amphi-prostyle tetrastyle. A circular building with columns all round it would be a peripteral circular building, while the term peripteral octastyle means a rectangular building surrounded by columns, with eight at each end forming porticos. The term pseudo-peripteral means that half columns are engaged with the walls and are not free-standing. To say that a colonnade is dipteral means that there are double rows of columns, so dipteral octastyle means a building surrounded by two rows of columns, with two porticos of sixteen columns at each end, eight columns wide. (See Figs **Temple**)

Colonnette A small column.

Colossal Order An Order where the columns rise several storeys, also known as a Giant Order. (See Fig **Giant Order**)

Columbarium A dovecote, formed of a building with holes or niches in the walls. A building for the reception of urns containing cremated remains is also known as a columbarium from the resemblance to the niches for pigeons or doves.

Columellae Balusters.

Columen The ridge piece.

Column A pillar, circular on plane, consisting of a base, a shaft and a capital. A canted column is polygonal on plane. (See also **Annulated, Barley-sugar, Bundle, Carolitic, Cippus, Clustered Pier, Colonnade, Engaged, Grouped, Intercolumniation, Orders**)

Columniation A building with columns, or an arrangement of columns.

Comitium An assembly building.

Commissure The joint between stones.

Common House A room in a monastery where there was always a fire. It was the prototype of the university commonroom.

Common Joist A joist in a floor to which boards are fixed.

Common Rafter A rafter to which boards or laths for a roof are fixed. (See Fig **Roof**)

Common Roof A roof consisting of common rafters only, bridging over purlins.

Common Round A roll moulding.

Communion Table A wooden table for the bread and wine in post-Reformation churches.

Compartment Ceiling A panelled ceiling.

Compass Roof A roof with a ridge in the centre, as opposed to a lean-to or flat roof.

Compass Window A projecting bay window or oriel.

Compluvium An open part in the middle of a roof of an atrium that admits water to an impluvium or cistern in the pavement.

Composite Order A Roman Order consisting of a mixture of Ionic and Corinthian. It is generally similar to the Corinthian except that the capitals have Ionic volutes and echini instead of the Corinthian caulicoli and scrolls. It was very grand and festive, and somewhat coarse. (See Fig g **Orders**)

Compound Arch A number of concentric arches successively placed within and behind each other, also called a recessed arch.

Compound Pier A pier with several shafts attached to it, or clustered about it, also called a clustered pier.

Concamerata Sudatoria An apartment where sweat could be wiped off the bodies of athletes or bathers.

Concamerate To arch over.

Conch, Concha The semi-dome of an apse, sometimes also applied to a pendentive or even to a whole niche with a semi-dome over it. A shell is sometimes carved in the semi-dome.

Concrete Cement mixed with fine and coarse aggregates. It was used by the Romans very extensively, especially in vaults and in dome construction. The discovery of Portland cement enabled concrete development to proceed in the nineteenth century and the use of concrete, which is strong in compression, reinforced with steel rods, strong in tension, revolutionised building construction in the twentieth century.

Conductors Rainwater pipes. (Scots)

Conduit A reservoir for water, a canal or pipe.

Confessio A recess for holding relics.

Confessional A recess, box or seat, where a priest sits to hear confession. Pre-Reformation examples are extremely rare.

Conisterium A room in a gymnasium where wrestlers were sprinkled with oil and dust.

Conservation The conserving of a building is its retention and possibly adaptation to new uses, properly avoiding any drastic changes to its character or architectural detail.

Conservatory
The Palm House at Kew, erected by Richard Turner of Dublin to designs by him and Decimus Burton in 1844–8

Conservatory A building for conserving plants, a grander version of a greenhouse. The finest conservatories date from the nineteenth century when glass-and-iron construction reached its zenith. Conservatories are heated and kept humid by large tanks of water. The word is also given to establishments where the arts of music are practised and perfected.

Console A bracket or corbel, ornamented, with

Console

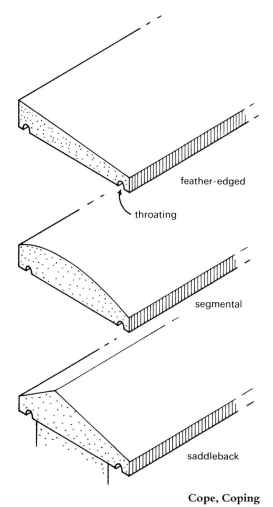

feather-edged

throating

segmental

saddleback

Cope, Coping

a greater height than projection. Consoles are sometimes known as ancones.

Convent A building used by a society of religious persons or by an order, usually of nuns.

Conventual Church The church attached to a convent.

Coom, Comb A sloping soffit or ceiling. (Scots)

Cope, Coping The covering course of a wall, designed to throw water off it, also called capping. Coping thinner on one side is called feather-edged coping, while that with a ridge is called saddleback coping. In Scots usage, a cope is the top of a pipe box or stair stringer, or a timber edge to the top of a sink.

Copper Tacking Copper nailing. (Scots)

Cops The rising parts of battlements, or merlons. (See Fig **Battlement**)

Corbeil A carved basket with sculptured flowers and fruit. The term is sometimes given to the bell of a Corinthian capital or to the baskets on the heads of caryatids.

Corbel A projecting block that supports a parapet or a beam. It is essentially a cantilever. (See Fig **Battlement**)

Corbel Table A range of corbels carrying a parapet or battlement, running just below the eaves. (See Fig **Battlement**)

Corbelling Courses built out over the corbels below to support a projection.

Corbiesteps Crowsteps on a gable. (Scots) (See Fig **Crowsteps**)

Cordon The stone moulding below a parapet of a rampart in a fort.

Corinthian Order A Greek and Roman Order of architecture. The Corinthian Order was less used by the Greeks than by the Romans. It is the most festive of the Greek Orders. The distinctive feature is the capital, which is about $1\frac{1}{6}$ diameters high, and very ornate with acanthus leaves and caulicoli, each of which is surmounted by a calyx from which emerge volutes. These volutes, or helices, support the angles of the abacus and the central ornaments on each face of the abacus. There are simpler forms of the Corinthian capital, with a row of acanthus leaves above which is a row of palm leaves. The abacus has moulded concave faces, meeting at points, or with chamfered points. Corinthian columns are slender, and, in the Greek Order, were fluted. In the Roman Order, they were sometimes unfluted. The entablature is very ornate. (See **Orders**)

Corner Bead A timber bead forming the arris of plastered walls. (Scots)

Corners Quoins. (Scots)

Cornice A moulded projection which crowns an entablature, moulding, wall or opening. (See Figs **Orders**)

Cornicione The large elaborate crowning cornice of the Italian palazzo, imported by Barry in the nineteenth century and used on many of the London clubs.

Corona The lower member, with a drip, of a Classical cornice, with a vertical face.

Corona Lucis A crown or circlet, suspended from the roof of a dome or vault, containing lights.

Corps de Logis The main part of a building.

Corridor A gallery or passage round a quadrangle. Any passage in a building giving access to rooms.

Corsa A fascia whose height is greater than its projection.

Cortile A small domestic court surrounded by the house, usually with arcades.

Cosmati Work Inlaid decorative panels of marble, mosaic and coloured stones.

Cottage A small house for artisans.

Cottage Orné A small villa in a rural setting, much favoured at the end of the eighteenth and beginning of the nineteenth centuries. It was used not only to ornament parks and to house labourers, but also as retreats for the gentry. Arch and picturesque effects were achieved by the use of thatch, fretwork bargeboards and rough wooden colonnades.

Counter Check A rebated meeting–rail of a folding door. (Scots)

Counterfort A buttress.

Coup A rubbish tip. (Scots)

Couple A rafter. In the North, couples signify rafters framed together in pairs with ties above their feet. (Scots)

Course A continuous level range of stones or bricks of the same height. Coursed rubble is rough stone walling laid in courses, as opposed to random rubble.

Court An uncovered area before or behind a building, or in the centre of it; sometimes an open area in densely built parts of cities. It is also a building where law is administered.

Coussinet, Cushion A stone placed upon the impost of a pier for receiving the first voussoir of an arch.

Coving The concave moulding between ceilings and walls. Rood screens often have covings under the rood loft. Cove bracketing is the framing for a cove.

Cowl A covering, of metal or pottery, over a chimney.

Coyn (See **Quoin**).

Cradling Framing for ceilings or for a shop front.

Cramp Metal bent to fasten stones together. Iron rusts and so has often caused splitting; copper or bronze cramps are best.

Crampets Cramps, wall hooks, holdfasts and gutter brackets. (Scots)

Crapaudine Doors Doors on pivots not hinges.

Creasing, Tile Creasing Two or three rows of tiles corbelled out under copings to throw off rainwater. They are often found at eaves.

Credence A small shelf or table, to the side of an altar, where the sacraments are placed before consecration. The term prothesis is also used. The word also signifies a buffet table where food was tasted as a safeguard against poison.

Crematorium A place or building where bodies are burnt. Modern crematoria contain a hall, transfer room and furnace room where bodies are consumed in gas-fired furnaces. There are ancillary rooms for the grinding of bones, storage of ashes and various offices.

Crenelle, Crenellation A battlement, but

Crematorium
The crematorium at the General Cemetery of All Souls, Kensal Green (1938)

more properly the term refers to the embrasures or loopholes. Crenellated mouldings are those which resemble battlements. A crenelle is also known as a kernel. (See Fig **Battlement**)

Crepido A projecting ornament or cornice.

Crescent A series of buildings planned on the arc of a circle, developed during the eighteenth century at Bath and Buxton.

Crest, Creste An ornamental finish to a wall, ridge, canopy or other part of a building. Crest tiles cover the ridge of a roof and may be of stone, clay or lead. In Victorian times, cast-iron cresting was popular and decorative.

Crinkle-Crankle Wall A wall that is serpentine on plan.

Crocket Projecting knobs of leaves, flowers or bunches of foliage used in Gothic ornamentation. (See Fig **Pinnacle**)

Crocket Capital (See **Capital**)

Croft (See **Crypt**)

Cromlech Three or more upright stones capped by a large flat stone, usually associated with burial. Sometimes known as a dolmen.

Crescent
The Quadrant, Regent Street, designed by John Nash. *(Kindly lent by Mr Terence Davis)*

Crope The bunch of leaves by which spires are often terminated, also known as a pommel but now usually called the finial. (See **Finial**, **Pinnacle**)

Cross The symbol of Christianity, used often as an architectural ornament to crown gables and to enrich altars. Consecration crosses are found in several churches, notably the Church of St Mary of Ottery in Devon. Crosses were also erected in cemeteries to mark graves and were also used as boundary stones. Several celebrated crosses were

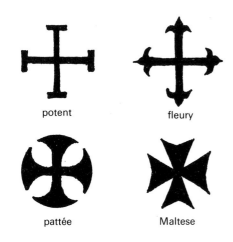

potent   fleury

pattée   Maltese

Cross Types of cross

erected to commemorate the funeral of Queen Eleanor. Crosses were also set up in market-places.

Cross Aisle A transept.

Cross Banded A term used when veneers are placed on handrails across the length.

Cross Beam A large beam going from wall to wall, or a beam that holds a building together.

Crossettes Projections in architraves at the junction of jambs and head, like ancones or consoles, but usually smaller. The term also signifies a ledged projection in the voussoirs of an arch.

Cross Garnet A T-shaped hinge, the tail being fastened to the door.

Crossing The junction of nave, chancel and transepts of a church, usually crowned by a tower.

Crossquarters A row of quatrefoil openings with each quatrefoil arranged so that the lobes are set diagonally. The effect is like a row of saltires.

Cross Springers Ribs that spring diagonally.

Cross-tailed Hinge Cross Garnet or T-hinge. (Scots)

Cross Vaulting That formed by an intersection of two or more vaults.

Cross Window A window with a mullion and transom forming a cross. (See Fig **Casement**)

Crowde, Croft A crypt.

Crown The upper part of any building or part of a building.

Crown Glass Window glass cut from a sheet blown into a disc when molten, and having therefore a thickened bull's eye in the middle.

Crown of an Arch The highest point, also called the extrados.

Crown Post The king or joggle post of a roof sustaining the tie beams and rafters. (See Fig **Roof**)

Crowsteps Stepped gables. In Scots usage, corbiesteps.

Crowstone The top stone of a gable.

Crucks Pairs of large timbers resting together at one end to join the apex of a structure.

Crypt A vault beneath a building, wholly or partly underground; also known as a crowde, croft, undercroft or shroud. Crypts are usually found only under chancels and chancel aisles. They were usually fitted with altars and were often used for burial. Large crypts exist in Canterbury, Gloucester, Winchester and other cathedrals.

Crypto-porticus An enclosed gallery or portico, with walls instead of columns.

Cubiculum A small chamber or tent.

Cullis A groove or channel.

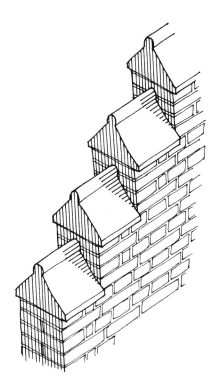

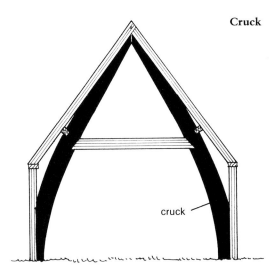

Cruck

Culvert An arched channel for conveying water.

Culvertail A dovetail.

Cuneus A wedge-shaped block of seats in an ancient theatre.

Cupboard Originally it was a sideboard, but now the term means a recess or piece of furniture with shelves.

Cupola
Robert Adam's square towers at the church of St Mary, Mistley, Essex, built in 1776. These towers are decorated with medallions and Tuscan columns, and are surmounted by cupolas with Ionic decorations.

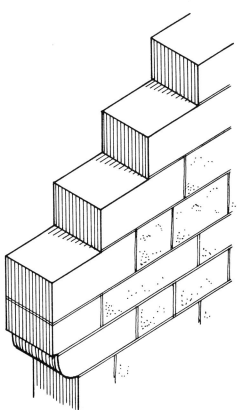

Crowsteps Capped and uncapped crowsteps

Cupola A concave ceiling covering a circular or polygonal area. The term is usually applied today to a small dome on a circular or polygonal base.

Curb A nosing to protect the edge of steps.

Curb Plate The wall plate of a dome or circular skylight.

Curb Roof A mansard roof. (See **Roof**)

Curbstone The stone in the foot paving of a street at the point where the footpath drops to the gutter. It is also spelt kerbstone.

Curia A council house.

Curstable A course of stones forming a string course.

Curtail Step The first step of a stair, with a curved scroll at the point furthest from the wall.

Curtain Wall A wall between two towers or pavilions. The term is sometimes applied to the side wall between buttresses in churches. In modern usage it is any non-loadbearing wall placed as a weatherproof membrane round a structure, and usually made of glass and metal. The proliferation of industrialised curtain walling accounts for much that is boring in modern architecture, while also causing grave problems of solar heat gain and internal heat loss.

Curvilinear Tracery Tracery composed of flowing ogee curves used in the Decorated period. (See Fig d **Tracery**)

Cushion Capital A Norman capital resembling a pressed cushion. A cube with the lower angles rounded off. The cushion of a capital is the same as a coussinet. (See Figs **Arcade**, **Capital**)

Cusp A point formed by the meeting of two curves, thus the term is applied to the points formed by the meeting of small arches or foils in Gothic tracery. Cusps are often ornamented. (See **Tracery**)

Cut Brackets Those moulded on the edges.

Cut Roof A truncated roof, with the part above the collar beams flattened.

Cut Splay Oblique cutting of bricks at door reveals, etc.

a

b

Cutwater
a) The cutwater masonry of the piers is clearly visible in this fine bridge at Bradford-on-Avon, Wiltshire
b) Cutwater at the fifteenth-century bridge at Ludlow

Cut-String Stairs Strings cut to the profiles of the steps. (See **Stair, Staircase**)

Cutwater The bow-shaped point of the pier of a bridge, also called a starling.

Cyclopean Masonry Masonry constructed of huge stones with no mortar, sometimes polygonal in form.

Cylindrical Vaulting A wagon-head, barrel, or cradle vault without groins resting on parallel walls. (See Fig **Vault**)

Cyma A moulding of a cornice, the section through which consists of a convex and concave line, like an elongated 'S'. An ogee.

Cyma Recta An S-shaped moulding at the top of a cornice, with the concave part uppermost.

Cyma Reversa As cyma recta, but reversed.

Cyma Recta (above), with Cyma Reversa (below)

Cymatium The top member of a group of Classical mouldings, usually the cornice.

Cymbia A fillet.

Dabbed, Daubed, Pitched Stone tooled with a sharp point to form a series of minute indentations. In Scots usage, also dabbed, or dabbled.

Dado The solid block or cube forming the body of a pedestal or plinth in Classical architecture, between the base and the cornice. It is also called a die. (See Fig **Pedestal**). Rooms are often found decorated with a base, dado course and cornice, resembling a continuous pedestal. In internal use, a pedestal corresponds to a chair rail, dado and skirting, as well as to a plinth.

Dagger A form found in Decorated tracery resembling a dagger contained within a fish shape. The dagger shape consists of two small ogee arches separated by cusping. (See Fig d **Tracery**)

Dairy A building or a room for the preservation of milk and the manufacture of butter, cheese or other dairy produce.

Dais A raised table in a hall where distinguished guests sat during feasts. The term is also applied to the platform on which the high table was placed, or to any raised platform. A raised platform or dais is also known as a footpace, halpace, or estrade. Another meaning is that of a canopy over a seat or throne.

Dam A barrier to confine water.

Damp-proof Course A course of impermeable material to prevent damp rising from the earth and penetrating a wall.

Dancette The chevron, or zigzag moulding. (See Fig **Chevron**)

Dancing Steps Steps in a curved stair, the narrow ends of which are widened. They are also called danced stairs or balanced winders.

Days The lights of a window, ie the spaces framed by mullions and transoms.

Deafening Pugging or sound-boarding.

Deal Small thicknesses of timber. The term now means softwood.

Deambulatory An ambulatory.

Dearn, Dern A doorpost or a threshold.

Decastyle A colonnade or portico of ten columns.

Decorated Style A term that is given to English Medieval architecture as it developed from the late-thirteenth century until the second half of the fourteenth century. As the term implies, its chief characteristics were the use of decoration covering surfaces, especially diaper work and crocketing. The ball flower and four-leafed flower largely replaced the Early English dogtooth enrichment. In tracery, the style developed the ogee or S-shaped curve in tracery of remarkable richness and flowing lines. Foliage is stylised rather than naturalistic. Clerestoreys are often very large while the triforium went into decline. Vaulting became complex, and intermediate and lierne ribs formed star-shaped patterns. The use of intermediate and ridge ribs in the nave vault at Exeter Cathedral is a tour-de-force of Decorated design. Decorated work is also referred to as Second or Middle Pointed. (See Fig **Gothic** – Decorated Bay, **Tracery**)

Degrees Steps or stairs.

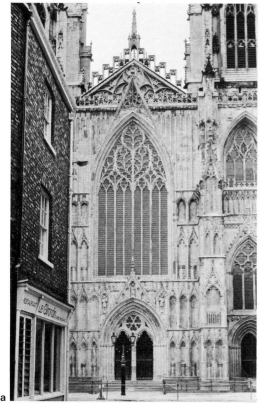

a

b

Decorated Style
a) West front of York Minster (1338), a fine example of curvilinear tracery and detailing
b) Cathedral of St Peter in Exeter looking west. Largely Decorated work of the fourteenth century.

Demi-column Half a column applied to a wall, as an engaged column, quite distinct from a pilaster.

Demilune A triangular or crescent-shaped outwork to a fortress.

Dentils Ornaments resembling teeth used in Classical mouldings. They are small rectangular or cubic projections. Dentilated means cornices with dentils in the bed mouldings. (See Fig e **Orders**)

Dexter The right-hand side of an heraldic device (left-hand when viewed from the front).

Diaconicum The place in, contiguous to, or near ancient churches where sacred vessels, vestments and ornaments were kept. It was also used as a treasury and library. It is the equivalent of the modern sacristy.

Diagonal Rib A rib crossing a bay or compartment of a vault diagonally. (See Fig b **Vault**)

Diamicton A Roman method of wall building consisting of ashlar faces with rubble between, similar to emplecton, but without binding stones.

Diamond Panes Lozenge-shaped panes of glass in wooden glazing bars or lead cames.

Diamond Pavement A pavement with the slabs or tiles laid in lozenge patterns.

Diaper Work Surface decoration consisting of repetitive patterns of diamonds or squares, often enriched with stylised flowers or other ornaments, and either carved or painted. It is found extensively in buildings of the Gothic style on walls and in the spandrels of arcades.

Diaphragm Vault An arch across a space carrying masonry walls dividing timber roofs into sections. The idea is similar to that of a party wall, and helps to minimise the spread of fire.

Diastyle One of the five species of inter-

61

Diaper Work Diaper pattern in flared headers from Ranworth Old Hall, Norfolk

columniation defined by Vitruvius. In this case, the distance between columns is equal to three diameters of a shaft. (See **Intercolumniation**)

Diatoni Binding stones.

Diazomata Passages or spaces encircling the seats of an ancient theatre.

Dicasterium A tribunal or hall of justice.

Dictyotheton Masonry worked to resemble the meshes of a net. The term is also applied to open latticework which resembles a net.

Die The cube or dado of a pedestal, ie that part between the base and the cornice. It often has half balusters attached if it is part of a balustrade. (See Fig **Pedestal**)

Diglyph A projecting face with two vertical channels or glyphs cut into it.

Diminished Arch One lower or less than a semicircle.

Diminished Bar or Sash One thinner on the edge facing the interior of a building.

Diminution of a Column The continuing contraction of the diameter of a column with its height in order to give it the appearance of strength and elegance.

Diocletian Window
This window is in the tomb of Julius Beer, Highgate Cemetery, by John Oldrid Scott and H. Hugh Armstead of 1877–78. Note the stepped pyramidal roof based on the mausoleum at Halicarnassus

Diocletian Window A semicircular window divided into three by two vertical mullions, common in Palladian architecture. Also known as a thermal window.

Dipteral A Classical building with two rows of columns on its flanks. (See **Colonnade**, Fig F **Temple**)

Discharging Arch A relieving arch built over a lintel to relieve it from the weight above. It is usually a segmental arch. (See Fig b **Arch**)

Dishing Out Cradling.

Displuviatum A place from which rain was conveyed in channels after collection, often the open court in a building.

Distemper Whiting mixed with size and water.

Distyle With a portico or colonnade of two columns. (See **Colonnade**, Fig B **Temple**)

Ditriglyph An interval between two columns admitting two triglyphs in the entablature above.

Dodecastyle A portico or colonnade with twelve columns.

Dog-leg Stair A stair with no well, the face of one string being set above the other. (See Fig C **Stairs**)

Dogtooth

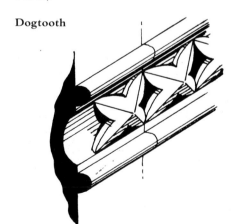

Dogtooth An Early English ornament of stylised star-shaped leaves raised and set in cavetto strings. The dogtooth is sometimes a V-shape in elevation.

Dolmen A cromlech.

Dome A vault over a circular or polygonal base, semicircular, segmental, pointed or bulb-shaped in section. Domes are often found on square bases and if so the corners must be built up so that the dome can sit comfortably. Squinch arches and pendentives are used to accomplish this purpose.

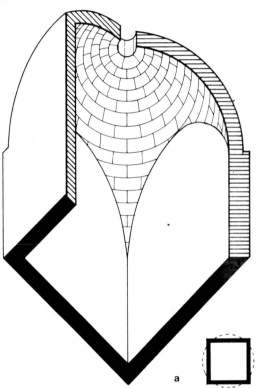

a

Dome
a) sail dome
over page
b) dome on pendentives and a square base
c) dome on squinches
d) domical vault

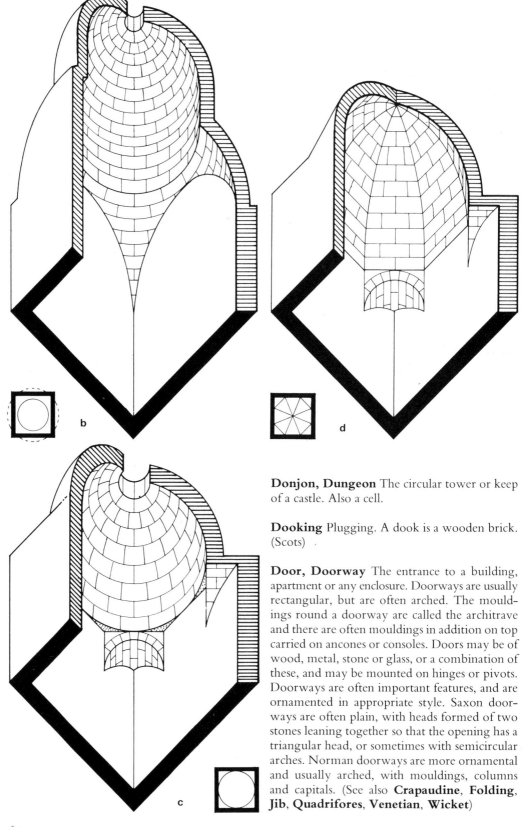

Donjon, Dungeon The circular tower or keep of a castle. Also a cell.

Dooking Plugging. A dook is a wooden brick. (Scots)

Door, Doorway The entrance to a building, apartment or any enclosure. Doorways are usually rectangular, but are often arched. The mouldings round a doorway are called the architrave and there are often mouldings in addition on top carried on ancones or consoles. Doors may be of wood, metal, stone or glass, or a combination of these, and may be mounted on hinges or pivots. Doorways are often important features, and are ornamented in appropriate style. Saxon doorways are often plain, with heads formed of two stones leaning together so that the opening has a triangular head, or sometimes with semicircular arches. Norman doorways are more ornamental and usually arched, with mouldings, columns and capitals. (See also **Crapaudine**, **Folding**, **Jib**, **Quadrifores**, **Venetian**, **Wicket**)

a

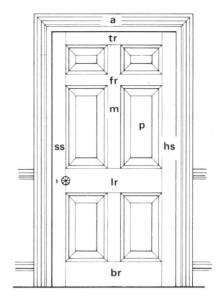

Door, Doorway m—muntin, a—architrave, hs—hanging stile, ss—shutting stile, br—bottom rail, lr—lock rail, fr—frieze rail, tr—top rail, p—panel

b

Door, Doorway
a) The west door of the church of St Mary the Blessed Virgin, at Stottesdon, Shropshire, with Saxon carvings in the tympanum *(Salop County Council SRO 770/ Large Box 1—No 1)*
b) Norman doorway from Selby Abbey. Note the chevron or zigzag moulding

Doorcase
Doorcase from Stepney Green. Note the fluted Corinthian pilasters, dentils, modillions, and exaggerated projections of the architrave fasciae

Early-eighteenth-century doorcase from 37, Stepney Green. Note the scallop-shell canopy and large ancones or consoles

Doorcase, Doorframe The wooden frame enclosing a door.

Doorstop The slip of wood against which a door shuts in its frame.

Doric Order The earliest of the Orders of Greek architecture. There is also a Roman Doric Order. The Doric Order is the sturdiest of the Orders, and is considered by many to be the most pure, most essentially Greek of all the Orders. It consists of a stylobate supporting a fluted base-less column with a distinctive capital consisting of annulets, echinus and abacus. The annulets or horizontal fillets, from three to five in number, stop the vertical lines of the arrises and flutes of the shaft. The entablature, usually one quarter the height of the Order, is carried on the capitals, and consists of an architrave or principal beam with its face in one plane. The Ionic and Corinthian Orders have their architraves stepped in three

planes. Separating the architrave from the frieze is a moulding called the tenia, and under this, at intervals immediately under each triglyph, is a narrow band called the regula, with six guttae. The frieze is composed of alternate metopes and triglyphs. Often the metopes were ornamented with groups of exquisite sculpture, whilst the triglyphs were incised with three vertical channels. The cornice consists of cymatium and bird's beak moulding. (See **Orders**)

Dormer A window placed on the inclined plane of a roof, the frame being placed vertically on the rafters. Also known as a luthern. A dormer will be roofed separately. (See Fig c **Roof**)

Dormitory A sleeping apartment, usually for large numbers of people.

Dossel Hangings round the walls of a hall or at the east end of a chancel. They are also found in sedilia and are usually of tapestry, silk or carpet-work.

Dosseret A block set above an abacus and placed between it and the springing of an arch above.

Double-cone Moulding A moulding like double cones, placed base to base, found in some Norman work.

Double Floor A floor with binding and bridging joists.

Double-framed Roof A roof with purlins and a ridge piece, usually with principal rafters and smaller common rafters.

Double-hung Sashes A window with two sashes, one to go up and the other to come down, both set in the same frame.

Doubling Eaves boards, or tilting fillets. (Scots)

Dovecot A building for keeping pigeons or doves, usually with small niches around the walls. In Scotland it is called a doocot.

Dovetail A joint formed in the shape of a spreading pigeon's tail.

Dovetail Moulding An ornament of running bands or a triangular fret.

Dowel A pin of wood or metal.

Drafts Margins of stone tooled separately. (Scots)

Dragging Tooling soft stone with a steel comb.

Dragon Beam A beam laid diagonally, supporting the corner post where a building jetties on two adjacent sides. (See Fig **Timber Framing**)

Dragon Piece A short piece of timber lying diagonally at the corner of a building at wall-plate level for receiving the foot of the hip rafter.

Drawbridge A bridge which can be raised or lowered.

Drawing Room A room to which company withdraws after dinner.

Dressings Dressings of a door or window or other opening are the mouldings and ornaments that surround them. The term is also used to describe stone used in such positions, usually in conjunction with brick walls.

Drip The projecting edge of a moulding, channelled or throated beneath so that rain will be thrown off. A dripbox in Scotland is a cesspool in a lead flat or a gutter.

Dripstone A label, weather moulding, or hood mould over a doorway or window which enriches and defines the opening. (See Fig A **Mouldings**)

Drop A drop arch is a pointed arch of less height than span. The term is also applied to the lower projecting end of a newel post. Drops are the conical shapes of the Doric Order under the triglyphs, known also as guttae, although the term is also applied to any carved pendent ornament. Similarly drop tracery is pendent tracery on the soffit of a Gothic arch. In Scotland, a drop is an outlet to an eaves gutter.

Droving Chiselled ashlar. Droving and boasting is finishing the stone with a fine texture of parallel lines. (Scots)

Drum A circular or polygonal structure supporting a dome or cupola. The term is also given to the shaft blocks of a column.

Dubbing Out The filling of an uneven surface with pieces of tile or daubs of mortar before plastering to an even surface.

Dungeon A donjon.

Dwang Bridging or herringbone strutting. Nogging of partitions or floors. (Scots)

Dwarf Wainscoting A dado.

Dwarf Walls Low walls used as fences or enclosures of any space. They are also used to carry the joists of a ground floor.

Dyke A drystone wall. (Scots)

Early English The first of the Pointed or Gothic styles of architecture in general use in England

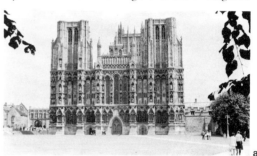

Early English
a) The west front of Wells Cathedral, a mass of niches, statuary, and fine shafts. (First half of the thirteenth century)
b) The nave of Wells Cathedral, with fourteenth-century supporting arches, and inverted arches. Note the rood above

from the end of the twelfth to the end of the thirteenth centuries. It succeeded the Norman style, although there was a brief period when early Gothic work was distinctively French in manner, due to the Burgundian sources of Cistercian architecture. The rib vaulting of Durham Cathedral is the earliest in England and possibly in the whole of Europe, but the first really Gothic building is the east end of Canterbury Cathedral. This was begun by William of Sens in 1175 and is almost completely French in style. The first example of Early English Gothic is probably Wells Cathedral, closely followed by Lincoln, both dating from the end of the twelfth century. Early English mouldings consist largely of contrasted concave and convex rolls, sometimes with fillets, producing a strong effect of light and shade. Arches are usually of the lancet type, or are equilateral. Trefoil and cinquefoil arches are found in smaller openings, while larger doorways are often divided into two by a single shaft with a quatrefoil or a Vesica Piscis set above. Numerous hood mouldings add emphasis, while clusters of shafts, usually detached and of black Purbeck marble, further ornament, emphasise and enrich the architecture. Circular windows are found in plenty, and simple geometrical cusped openings form the commencement of tracery. Groined vaulting came into common use, with bosses at the intersections. Columns are often composed of large piers with clusters of contrasting marble shafts around. In country churches, columns are usually simpler, either circular or polygonal on plan, with plain moulded capitals or foliage enrichment. Buttresses are prominent and are terminated in pointed pediments. Pinnacles only came into use towards the end of the style. Roofs were steeply pitched. Ornament consisted largely of the dogtooth, while foliage was deeply carved and stylised, often with trefoil leaves. (See Figs a **Gothic Architecture**, a **Tracery**)

Ears Crossettes.

Earth Table The plinth of a wall, or the lowest course of projecting stones above the ground.

Easter Sepulchre A recess under an arch or canopy associated with a tomb chest, situated on the north side of a chancel, used for the sacred elements, including an effigy of Christ, placed there from Maundy Thursday to Easter Day.

Eaves The lower edge of a sloping roof which overhangs the face of a wall.

Echea Sonorous vessels used in the construction of theatres to magnify voices.

Echelon Parallel lines of varying length.

Echinus An ovolo moulding below the abacus of a Doric capital. In the Ionic capital, the echinus is carved with egg-and-dart enrichment. (See Figs a, b, e, f **Orders**)

Edge Hinge A butt hinge. (Scots)

Edge Roll A rounded or convex moulding.

Egg and Dart Also called the egg-and-anchor, or egg-and-tongue enrichment, it is an ovolo moulding decorated with alternate egg shapes and arrowheads.

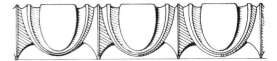

Egg and Dart

Egyptian Revival Features peculiar to Ancient Egyptian architecture include pyramids, obelisks, sphinxes, steeply battered walls, huge cavetto cornices, massive blank walls, and large lotus- or papyrus-headed columns. Elements from such architecture became part of the language of Neo-Classicism, first in furniture design, but scholarly use of Egyptian motifs began with the Napoleonic surveys of Egyptian antiquities published by Denon and the French Government. Egyptian motifs became an important part of *Empire* design and were adapted in Regency work in this country. In England, the style became popular for tomb design and for cemetery buildings, while certain factories and utility buildings are Neo-Egyptian in manner. The commonest elements are pylon-shaped chimney-pots, lotuses, and obelisks. Pylon forms were ideal for suspension bridges and dams. Many cinemas and factories were built in the Egyptian Revival style in the 1920s, and there are significant elements of Egyptian design in the movement known as Art-Déco. An Egyptian hall has an internal peristyle with a superimposed peristyle, but is Palladian and has no connection with Egyptian architecture.

Eke Piece A length of timber used to make up to a required size. (Scots)

Elaeothesium An apartment in baths where, after leaving the bath, bathers were anointed.

Egyptian Revival
a) The entrance to the catacombs at Highgate Cemetery (c 1839) by J. B. Bunning and Stephen Geary
b) Solar disc with outspread wings, a symbol of protection. From the Marshall Mills, Leeds, by Ignatius Bonomi (1838–40)

Elbow The upright side flanking panelling, or the vertical linings of windows at the sides, under shutters.

Elevation A geometrical projection on a vertical plane perpendicular to the horizon to show any one face of a building. The term also means the external face of a building. (See Figs **Projections**)

Elizabethan Style That which prevailed during the reign of Queen Elizabeth I of England. The style was a mixture of Renaissance motifs, Flemish decorative work, such as strapwork, and late-Gothic mullioned and transomed windows with large areas of glass. Symmetry, large win-

a

b

a

b

Elizabethan Architecture
a) Kirby Hall, Northamptonshire, commenced in 1570. Note the immense bay windows and the importance of chimneys
b) Condover Hall, Shropshire. An Elizabethan house, probably by Walter Hancock. The E-plan is clearly discernable in the entrance front. Note the typical windows with transoms and mullions

dows, Flemish gables and exuberant decoration characterise the grander houses. The vernacular buildings of the Elizabethan period were often timber-framed and continued in the traditional medieval manner.

Embattled Notched with embrasures, or provided with battlements. The term is synonymous with battlemented or crenellated. (See Fig **Battlement**)

Embossed Work The raising or forming in relievo of any sort of design, chiselled or carved.

Embrasure The crenelles or intervals between the merlons of a battlement. The term also means the splay of a window. (See Fig **Battlement**)

Emplecton A method of constructing walls in which the outside skins were formed of dressed stone and the interior was filled with rubble. Binding-stones joined the two skins.

Encarpus A festoon of fruit, flowers and leaves, used to decorate a frieze.

Encaustic A method of decoration where painted surfaces were waxed over after completion, or where the decorations were painted on using tints mixed with hot wax. Encaustic tiles, however, are earthenware tiles that are coloured and glazed. Decorative encaustic tiles were much used in medieval and in Victorian times.

Enceinte The main centre of a fortress, protected by walls, earthworks and ditches.

Enfilade In Baroque planning, the system of aligning internal doors connecting rooms in palaces so that long vistas through rooms are achieved.

Engaged Columns Columns attached to walls, by which a part of them will be concealed. Also known as applied, attached or inserted columns.

English Bond Brickwork laid with one course of headers and the next course of stretchers. (See Fig **Brickwork**)

Engrailed Edged with a series of concave curves in heraldic devices.

Entablature In Classical architecture, the superstructure of an Order, consisting of architrave, frieze and cornice. (See Figs **Orders**)

Entail Elaborate portions of carving, or a term meaning sculptured ornaments.

Entasis The swelling curve on the shaft of a column of Classical architecture. It was used to prevent the columns appearing concave or coarse. In the Elizabethan and Jacobean periods, and in the Domestic Revival of the 1880s entasis was often grossly exaggerated, giving columns a squat appearance.

Enterclose A passage between two rooms in a house, or leading from the door to the hall.

Entresol Where a floor can be introduced adjacent to a building with sufficient ceiling height, the intermediate floor is the entresol or mezzanine.

Envelope The outside of a building that contains the interior space, including the roof.

Eopyla A church with an apse at the east.

Eothola A church with an apse at the west.

Ephebeium A building for wrestling.

Epicranitis Tiles forming the cymatium or upper part of the cornice.

Epinaos The open vestibule within the portico of a Classical temple at the rear of the naos.

Episcenium The upper Order of the scene in a theatre.

Epistle Side The south side of a church.

Epistylium The architrave of an entablature.

Epitithedes Upper mouldings of an entablature, or the cymatium.

Equilateral Arch (See **Arch**).

Erased An heraldic term meaning torn off, leaving a ragged edge.

Escallop A scallop shell.

Escape That part of the shaft of a column where it springs out of the base moulding, also called the apophyge.

Escarp The bank in front of and below the ramparts of a fort.

Escoinson The interior edge of a window jamb, often ornamented with a pilaster or a shaft.

Escutcheon, Scutcheon A shield for armorial bearings. Also a plate for protecting the keyhole of a door, or a plate to which a handle is attached.

Escutcheon
a) From the spandrel of an arch of a gatehouse at Waxham Hall, Norfolk
b) An escutcheon or finger plate at Hornton Street, Kensington

a

b

Estipite A pilaster wider at the top.

Estrade A level place or space, or a public road. The term also means a raised platform or dais for a bed or a throne.

Etruscan The architecture of Etruria in northern Italy, now called Tuscany. The main structural materials were wood and clay, and sometimes rubble. The Etruscans favoured unfluted short columns and much terracotta decoration. Their most celebrated surviving works are tomb architecture and some city walls.

Eurithmy Regular, just and symmetrical measures resulting from harmony in the proportions of a building or Order.

Eustyle One of the five species of inter-columniation defined by Vitruvius. In this case the distance between columns is equal to two and a quarter diameters of a shaft. (See **Inter-columniation**)

Ewery A place where ewers were kept. A scullery.

Exchange A building for the meeting and resort of merchants.

Exedra An apartment for conversation or repose, usually open to the sun and air. The term also means an apse, a recess or a large niche.

Exposed Face A fair face. (Scots)

Extrados The exterior curve of an arch measured on top of the voussoirs as opposed to the soffit or intrados. (See Fig d **Arch**)

Eye The centre of any part. The eye of a pediment is a circular window in its centre and the eye of a volute is the circle at the centre.

Eyebrow A fillet.

Eyecatcher A decorative feature in a landscape as the terminating focus of a vista. Eyecatchers were often described as follies and were frequently built as sham ruins or as Classical temples in eighteenth-century parks.

Façade The exterior face or front of a building.

Face Mould A pattern for marking the timber out of which handrails are cut.

Facettes The flat projections between the flutes of columns.

Facings Any finishings applied to the exterior of a building, such as ashlar stonework. In Scots usage, a facing is a moulding or an architrave.

Factabling Coping.

Faldstool A portable seat made so as to fold up. Medieval examples were richly covered and were used as bishops' portable thrones. Also known as a folding stool or a faldstory, the faldstool was synonymous with the cathedra.

Fall of Land Thirty-six square yards. (Scots)

False Attic An attic storey without pilasters, casements or balustrades.

False Roof The roof between the ceiling of the upper floor and the covering of the roof.

Fanlight A window, often semicircular and over a door, found in buildings of the eighteenth and nineteenth centuries, and so called because the radiating glazing bars suggested the shape of an opened fan. The term has come to be applied to all glazed openings over doors, whether the glazing bars are in the shape of a fan or not. The term is also applied to any upper window or part of a window that is hinged to open.

Fan Tracery or Vaulting A system of vaulting used in the Perpendicular period, in which all the ribs that rise from the springing of the vault have the same curve and diverge equally in every direction, producing an effect like an opened fan.

Fan Vaulting
St Andrew's Church, Cullompton, Devon. The Lane aisle, of the early sixteenth century

Fanlight
Duncan Terrace, Islington, 1791. Note the typical fanlight over the door

Fan vaulting was frequently used over tombs, chantry chapels and small structures. Fine large-scale examples survive at King's College Chapel, Cambridge, and in Henry the Seventh's Chapel at Westminster. (See Fig E **Vault**)

Fascia A broad fillet, band or face, used in Classical architecture, usually in conjunction with other mouldings. Architraves are divided into two or three fasciae, or faciae, each of which projects beyond the face of that below it. (See Fig a **Orders**). The term is also applied to the name-board above shop-fronts, as it is derived from Classical prototypes which included fasciae. Similarly, it is applied to any board mounted in an elevated position to appear as a band or stripe.

Fastigium The point of a gable or pediment.

Fathom Six feet.

Faucet End A socketed end. (Scots)

Feather-edged Any section which is trapezoidal or thicker on one side than on the other.

Feathering Sometimes referred to as foliation, feathering is an arrangement of small arcs or foils separated by projecting points or cusps.

Feeder A channel by which water is conveyed.

Felt Grain Timber grain achieved by the cutting of pieces across the annular rings, as opposed to quarter grain, which is achieved by cutting the piece in the direction of the annular rings. Felting is the act of splitting timber by the felt grain.

Femerell, **Fomerell**, **Fumerell** A lantern, louvre or cover placed over a hall for ventilation or to allow smoke to escape without admitting rain.

Fence Any construction to enclose land, including banks, ditches, hedges, walls, palings, etc.

Fender A dwarf wall in the basement, built up to carry the front of the hearth of a fireplace. The term is also given to the structures of wood, brick, stone, marble or eta that rest on the outer extremity of a hearth to prevent coals from falling out onto the carpeting. Fine decorative metal fenders were produced in Victorian times.

Fender Piles Piles driven into the ground to protect buildings, corners, etc, from damage.

Fenestella The niche at the side of an altar containing the piscina, or water drain into which the water in which the priest washed his hands, and that with which the chalice was rinsed, was poured. There is often a shelf above the piscina which served as a credence for the sacred vessels. The fenestella is almost always on the south side of the altar.

Fenestral A window – blind or a casement closed with paper or cloth rather than glass. The term was also applied to the shutters or leaves which closed lights rather than glass, which was expensive. These shutters were generally simple, hung on hinges and fastened by a bolt, but sometimes they were fretted or panelled and became highly decorative features. Occasionally, windows closed with such shutters are themselves termed fenestrals.

Fenestration The arrangement of windows in a façade.

Fereter A bier, a catafalque, a coffin, a tomb or a shrine. The term seems properly to refer to portable shrines in which the relics of saints were carried, but was also given to the fixed shrines or tombs in which relics were deposited.

Feretory The enclosure or chapel within which a fereter was placed.

Fesse A horizontal band across the centre of a shield in heraldry.

Fesse Point The centre point of an heraldic device.

Festoon A sculptured design composed of flowers, drapes, fruit and foliage, suspended in swags on walls, friezes, altars, tablets and other situations and commonly found in Classical architecture. The carved garlands are represented as tied and hung with ribbons and are also known as swags.

Fielded A term applied to panels with a raised central part. (See Fig A **Panel**)

Fillet A small face or band used principally between mouldings to separate them. It is not always flat, but is often found cut into two or more narrow faces with sharp edges between them. If it is a narrow flat band it is also known as a listel or annulet, and can best be used to give firmness or emphasis to a moulding such as a crowning cornice. The small bands between the flutes of columns are also called fillets. In carpentry, a fillet is any small timber scantling equal to or less than a batten. In Scots usage, a fillet is a batten used for tiling. A *fillet gutter* is a sloping gutter. A *tilting fillet* is a wedge-shaped fillet used to cause a slope.

Fine Stuff This is plaster used for walls and ceilings, composed of slaked lime sifted with a fine sieve and mixed with fine sand and hair.

Finial The ornament which terminates pinnacles, canopies, pediments, gables or the tops of bench ends. The term used to be applied to the whole pinnacle. The medieval term for a finial was a crope or a pommel. (See Fig **Pinnacle**)

Finishing The completion of a building, but more often applied to the last coat of plasterers' work or to joinery such as architraves, etc.

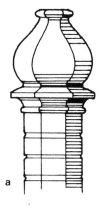

Finial
a) Jacobean finial
b) Perpendicular finial

Fireplace Early fireplaces were often in the centre of a room. From the twelfth century, the grander castles had large fireplaces, recessed, with arched openings and occasionally hoods. Perpendicular fireplaces are common and from this period enrichment of fireplaces became usual. Renaissance and Classical fireplaces became highly decorative foci for rooms, a trend that was continued until recent times. (See **Chimney**)

Fir in Bond A technical expression to denote lintels and other timbers built into walls.

Fir Framed Rough-framed timber.

Fir Wrought Planed softwood.

Firring, Furring The fixing of thin scantlings of timber on edges of other pieces in order to bring a surface level. The timbers themselves are called firrings, furrings or sometimes shreddings.

First Coat Plaster on laths, or first rendering on brickwork. When it is the first coat on laths it is called pricking up, and when on bricks it is called roughing in.

First Floor The floor over the ground floor.

Fish To secure a piece of timber by fastening another piece above or below it, and sometimes both, to strengthen it. The fish as a representation of the aquatic animal is a sacred symbol of Christianity and of Christ. When two circles overlap, a figure consisting of two pointed arches is formed, known as the Vesica Piscis.

Fished Beam A beam formed of two timbers placed end to end and covered by a long piece of wood placed over and under the joint.

Fistuca A pile-driving instrument consisting of a weight raised on ropes via a system of pulleys, sometimes called a monkey.

Flags, Flaggs Stones used for paving.

Flamboyant The style of Gothic architecture prevalent in France at the time of the Perpendicular in England. It was so-called from the flamelike shapes found in its tracery. Occasionally Flamboyant Revival may be found in England, as in the Victorian Carmelite Priory by Goldie, Child & Goldie in Kensington. Flamboyant crockets and ornaments are often surprisingly like Art Nouveau designs and may have been the inspiration for some aspects of the decorative effects of that style.

Flange A projection round a pipe or other article of metal to allow its fixing. L-shaped pieces of metal are termed flanges when used for fixing.

Flank The side of a bastion. That part of a body which forms a side of it. The party walls of a terrace are called flanks. In Scots usage a flank is a valley.

Flanning The internal splay of a window jamb.

Flashing Pieces of metal, usually lead, copper or zinc, let into the joints of brickwork to lap over gutters, or along the slating of a roof, to prevent water penetrating junctions.

Flat A horizontal covering of a building.

Flèche A slender spire on the ridge of a roof, often replacing the tower over the crossing. It is usually constructed of wood or metal.

Flemish Bond The laying of each course of bricks as headers and stretchers. (See Fig **Brickwork**)

Flemish Bricks A species of hard Dutch or Belgian brick used for paving.

Fleur-de-lis Also known as the fleur-de-lys or flower-de-luce, it is a lily-like ornament often used as a finial.

Fleuron A decorative carved flower resembling the fleur-de-lis, but the term can be applied to any floral or foliate carved decoration.

Flight A series of steps from one landing place to another.

Flint A material used in building where chalk abounds. Flints occur in chalk as irregular nodules and are usually built in walls with brick or freestone quoins and copings, or used in decorated panels or flushwork, especially in East Anglia.

Float A straight-edge by which plastering is reduced to a plane surface.

Floated Lath and Plaster Three-coat plaster on laths, the first is called pricking up, the second is

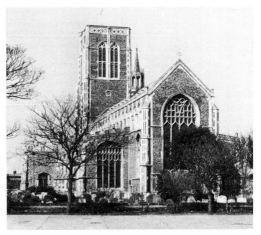

Flint
The Parish Church of St Edmund, King and Martyr, Southwold, Suffolk, built of flint facings with freestone dressings

floating, and the last, the setting coat, is done with fine stuff.

Floor The pavement or boarded lower horizontal surface of any apartment. It may be of earth, brick, stone, tile, wood or other materials. The term is also applied to the storey of a building. A sunken floor is the basement, the next the principal or ground, the next the first, and so on. The expression 'one pair' implies a storey above the first flight of stairs from the ground.

Floor Cloth Stout canvas covered with oil paint and then printed with a pattern. It was found in Victorian times, but only rare examples survived as it was replaced by linoleum and other coverings.

Floor Joists The joists supporting the floor surface. (See **Bridging Joist**)

Florentine Arch An arch with intrados and extrados of different form. (See Fig **Arch)**

Floriated Carved in imitation of flowers or leaves.

Flory-counter-flory An heraldic tressure with fleurs-de-lis pointing alternately out and in.

Flue The tube of a chimney through which smoke passes. It was formerly parged, or lined with plaster, but today's practice is to provide a flue liner of asbestos, concrete or steel, to ensure that the smoke is contained.

Fluing Splayed.

Flush On the same plane. In masonry and brick-laying, flushing signifies the splintering of stones at the joints from pressure, also termed 'spaulter-ing'. A *flush bead moulding* is a bead set in a channel so that its outer surface is flush with the wall. Flush is also a term used to denote the bedding of stones or bricks in mortar leaving no vacant space. *Flush pointing* is where the mortar is brought out to the face of the brickwork. A *flush bolt* is a metal bolt let into the woodwork so that it does not project.

Flushwork The use of knapped flint in panels to form patterns.

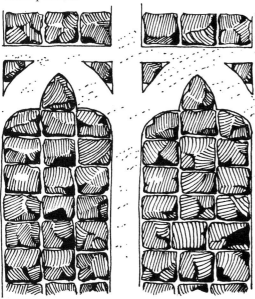

Flushwork An example of squared flint and ashlar from the gatehouse to St Osyth's Priory

Flutings, Flutes The hollow channels in the shafts of Classical columns, cut perpendicularly. They are used in all orders save the Tuscan. There are twenty in the Doric Order separated by sharp arrises, and there are twenty-four in the Ionic, Corinthian and Composite Orders separated by small fillets. Except in the Doric Order, flutes are sometimes partly filled with a convex moulding or bead one third of the height of the shaft, called cabling. (See Figs **Orders**)

Flyers Steps that are parallel to each other.

Flying Buttress A buttress in the form of an arch, springing from a solid mass of masonry and abutting against the springing of another arch which rises from the upper points of abut-

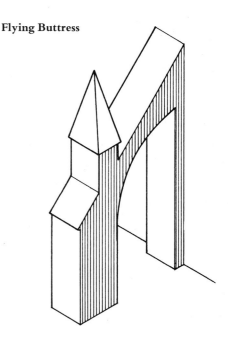

ment of the first. It acted as a counterthrust to the weight of nave vaulting. It is also known as an arc-boutant or arch buttress. (See **Buttress**)

Foil A small arc in the tracery of Gothic windows or panels. Foils are separated by cusps and the number of foils is indicated by a prefix, eg trefoil, quatrefoil. Similarly, an arch with foils and cusps is called a foil arch. (See Figs **Arch**, **Tracey**)

Folding Doors Doors made to meet each other from the opposite jambs. They are hinged and often are tracked. When closed they appear to be a panelled wall or one door.

Folding or Folded Floor A floor in which the boards are laid so that their joints are not continuous but in bays or folds of three, four, five or more boards each, as opposed to straight-joint floors.

Foliage Sculptured leaves forming ornaments. The term foliated signifies leaf ornament, or the use of arcs and cusps in the formation of tracery.

Folly A building erected as an eyecatcher, as a vista stopper or for some other effect. Follies were usually expensive and relatively useless buildings erected during the eighteenth and nineteenth centuries. They varied in style but were often built as 'ruins', or as imitation Gothic

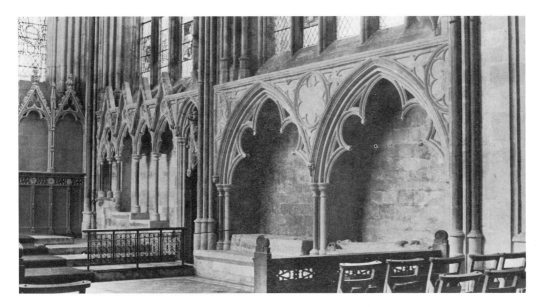

Foil
A series of foils in Exeter Cathedral

a

remains. Some follies were merely built as extravagant structures to satisfy vanity or whim and may have been landmarks, monuments, mausolea or merely objects in space.

Font The vessel which contains the consecrated water for baptism. The body of the font was usually a large block of stone hollowed out and carried on a short column or pier or a clustered shaft, and usually elevated on a base. Many Norman and Early English fonts survive, often lead-lined. Fonts were covered, and many fine late-Gothic canopies carried on pulleys survive. Lavish ornament is often applied to both font basins and to the canopied covers.

b

Font
a) Norman font with scrollwork in the Church of St Mary the Blessed Virgin, Stottesdon, Shropshire
(By courtesy of Salop County Council Record Office SRO 770/ Large Box 1—No 9)
b) The interior of the Church of St Edmund, King and Martyr, Southwold, looking through the fifteenth-century painted chancel screen to the font with its elaborate canopy

Beam The tie beam.

of a Wall Courses at the base of a wall which project beyond its face, or the lowest parts of a foundation.

Footpace A dais. A landing or broad step. A hearth stone.

Foot Stall A plinth or a base.

Footstone Upright stone at the foot of a grave.

Foreyn A cesspool.

Formeret An arch rib which in Gothic work lies next to the wall and is less than the other ribs dividing the vaulting. It is also known as a wall rib. (See Fig C **Vault**)

Form Pieces The stones forming the tracery of a window.

Formwork A structure of wood or metal which forms the mould for wet concrete.

Fortress A castle or a military structure constructed for defence and comprising walls, earthworks, ramparts, bunkers, etc.

Forum An open urban space surrounded by public buildings. It was like the Greek agora, but was more formal.

Fosse A ditch, either wet or dry, for defence.

Foundation The ground prepared for the footings of a wall. The concrete and footings are now called foundations, together with piling. In Scotland, founds means foundations.

Foundry An establishment where metals are cast in moulds.

Fountain A natural or artificial aperture from which water springs. In natural fountains the effect is produced by the pressure of the water head, while in artificial fountains a head must either be provided by placing the source above the aperture or by the installation of machinery.

Four-centred Arch (See **Arch**)

Foyer The entrance hall of a theatre or opera house.

Fractable Wrought stonework running up gable ends. Coping on a gable end is called fractabling. (See Fig **Isometric Projection**)

Frame The timber structure of a building. Generally, any wooden structure that encloses. A framed building is any structure carried on a frame, whether timber, concrete or steel, rather than a load-bearing wall.

Franche-botrass A buttress of stone.

Fraterhouse, Fratery A refectory in a monastic establishment.

Freemason A stonecutter who worked with a chisel. A member of the medieval guild of Freemasons. In recent times, the term has no connection with stonecutting, but denotes a member of a secret society of that name.

Freestone Any stone that can be worked.

French Window A window or glazed door opening in two leaves to give access to a balcony or a garden.

Fresco Painting Wall or ceiling decoration where the colours are added before the plaster is dry.

Fret, Frette, Fretwork Ornaments of fillets meeting at right angles, arranged in bands of angular key patterns.

Frieze The middle division of the entablature lying between the cornice and the architrave. It is always plain in the Tuscan Order, but is ornamented with triglyphs and sculpture in the Doric. It may be convex or cushioned in the Renaissance or Italianate Ionic, and in the Corinthian and Composite Orders it is decorated with figures and foliage. (See Figs **Orders**). The frieze of a capital is called the hypotrachelium. (See **Hypotrachelium**). A *frieze panel* is the upper panel of a six-panelled door. Similarly, the *frieze rail* is the upper rail but one of a six-panelled door.

Frigidarium The room for the cold bath in ancient architecture.

Frithstool, Fridstool, Freedstool A seat or chair near the altar which was literally the seat of peace where those who claimed sanctuary sat. Violation of a frithstool brought the severest punishment.

Front Any façade of a building, but usually the main elevation. The garden front would be the elevation facing the gardens.

Frontal The hanging or antependium in front of an altar.

Frontispiece The face of a house or its decorated entrance.

Fronton A pediment.

Frosted A type of rustic work. Frosted glass is roughened glass, made opaque by acid etching or sand blasting.

Functionalism A dogma that holds it is the duty of a designer to ensure a building functions, without any decoration, softening or humanising. This brutal dogma completely ignores the fact that it is a duty of architecture to function as architecture, ie work well, be sound in structure and give delight or aesthetic pleasure.

Furniture Metal fittings to doors and windows, etc, including knobs, levers, hinges, bolts, locks.

Furring (See **Firring**).

Fusarole A member with a semicircular section carved into beads. It is generally found under the echinus of the Doric, Ionic and Corinthian Orders.

Fust The shaft of a column or the trunk of a pilaster. It is also the ridge of a roof.

Gabbart Scaffold A scaffold of squared timbers put together with bolts. (Scots)

Gable, Gavel The end wall of a building, the top of which conforms to the slope of the roof which abuts against it. In contemporary usage, however, the term is applied only to the upper part of such a wall above eaves level, and the entire wall is called a gable end. In some instances, the large end window of a building was sometimes referred to as a gable window. Norman gables reflecting the pitch of the roof were steep, while Early English roofs were usually very nearly equilateral triangles in section. During the Decorated and Perpendicular periods, gables were often much lower. Gables were often coped or battlemented or, if the roof was carried over the gable, surmounted by ornamental bargeboards. During the sixteenth and seventeenth centuries, gables were often varied, stepped, curved or angled, reflecting a Flemish influence. A Dutch gable is one with curved sides crowned by an arch or a pediment. (See **Bargeboards**, **Crowsteps**)

Gable

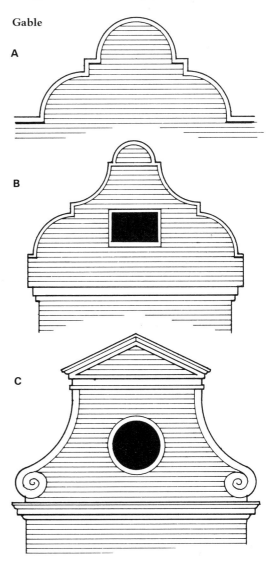

A shaped gable, Blickling, Norfolk
B shaped gable, Knodishall, Suffolk
C Dutch gable, Raynham, Norfolk

Gablet A small ornamental gable over a niche, a buttress or some other feature. (See Fig c **Roof**)

Gadroon, Godroon Enriched moulding of beads and cablings.

Gadrooned, Godrooned Enriched with convex rods, the exact opposite of fluted.

Galilee A porch or chapel at the west end of a church. The term is sometimes applied to the western portion of a nave. A Galilee is also called a narthex or a paradise. One of the finest of Galilees is that at Durham Cathedral. Galilees were often reserved for women.

Gallery An apartment of great length in proportion to width used as a passage or a place for the display of pictures and sculpture, commonly found in Elizabethan and Jacobean houses. The term is also used to denote an upper floor or loft with an apartment to accommodate musicians and spectators. Screens in churches and cathedrals often have galleries for the rood loft or for the placing of the organ. The triforium or tribune above the aisles opening to the nave is sometimes called a gallery. In post-Reformation times, galleries or scaffolds were erected above aisles and at the west end of the nave to accommodate more people, often to the detriment of the architecture. The whole or a portion of the upper storey of theatre seats is called a gallery.

Galleting, Garreting Small pieces of stone, brick, flint, etc, placed in the mortar joints of a building for decorative reasons or to reduce the amounts of mortar used.

Gambrel Roof A hipped roof with a small gable near the apex. (See Fig d **Roof**)

Gaol A prison.

Garden City, Garden Suburb A garden city is a town built in the countryside consisting of houses with gardens and all amenities, with shops and industries, etc. It was based on the ideas of Ebenezer Howard and the first examples, Letchworth and Welwyn, were the prototypes for the New Towns of the post-war period, although these were again based upon model towns such as Saltaire, Bourneville and Port Sunlight. A garden suburb was an early-nineteenth-century invention with its roots in the Romantic English landscape tradition. Its earliest prototypes were the designs for the Eyre Estate, the Ladbroke Estate in Kensington and Nash's work in the Regent's Park Area. Hampstead Garden Suburb and Bedford Park were later developments.

Garderobe A wardrobe. It is also a closet for defaecation, etc, usually situated over a river or even the street.

Gargoyle, Gurgoyle A projecting spout to throw the water from a gutter away from a wall. Sometimes they are plain but often are carved into representations of figures or animals, often grotesque in treatment. Gargoyles are also found unassociated with waterspouts. (See Fig **Pinnacle**)

Garland A band of ornamental work round a building. Also ornaments of flowers and fruits.

Garnet A T-shaped hinge, also called a cross garnet.

Garret The upper part of a house, wholly or partially within the roof, usually for servant accommodation or for storage.

Garreting (See **Galleting**).

Gate A large door, wood or metal.

Gateway An opening in an enclosure or fence. Gateways to large establishments are imposing and in the Middle Ages usually had apartments for gatekeepers. Gateways to towns, castles, etc, were fortified.

Gauge The length of a slate or tile below the lap.

Gauged Arch One with voussoirs radiating to a centre, with cut bricks finely rubbed, or stones precisely cut.

Gavel A gable.

Gazebo A small apartment on a roof with a view, also called a belvedere. A summerhouse.

Gemmel A hinge.

Genlese, Gentese Cusps or featherings.

Geometrical Decorated A period in Medieval architecture where the tracery and other ornament consisted almost entirely of geometrical forms. (See **Gothic**, **Tracery**)

Geometrical Staircase One in which the flight of stone stairs is supported by the wall at only one end of the steps, each step resting on the next. There are no newels.

Georgian Architecture of the reigns of the first four Georges. Georgian architecture is usually Classical and often very simple. Interiors are of-

a

b

c

Georgian

a) Houses of 1819–23 by J. and W. J. Booth in Clerkenwell, London, showing Greek Revival influence in the pediments.

b) St Chad's Church, Shrewsbury, by George Steuart, completed 1793. This very original Georgian church has an elegant tower, and a circular nave. Note the portico of Tuscan columns carrying the pediment, and the elegant Ionic pilasters around its rotunda. The tower is in three stages: a square base, an octagonal stage above enriched with Ionic pilasters; and a crowning circular domed stage with detached Corinthian columns

c) Double-fronted shop of two bow windows flanking a door with fanlight over it. Note the consoles and the enrichment. This is a fine example of a type of shopfront that was common in Georgian times

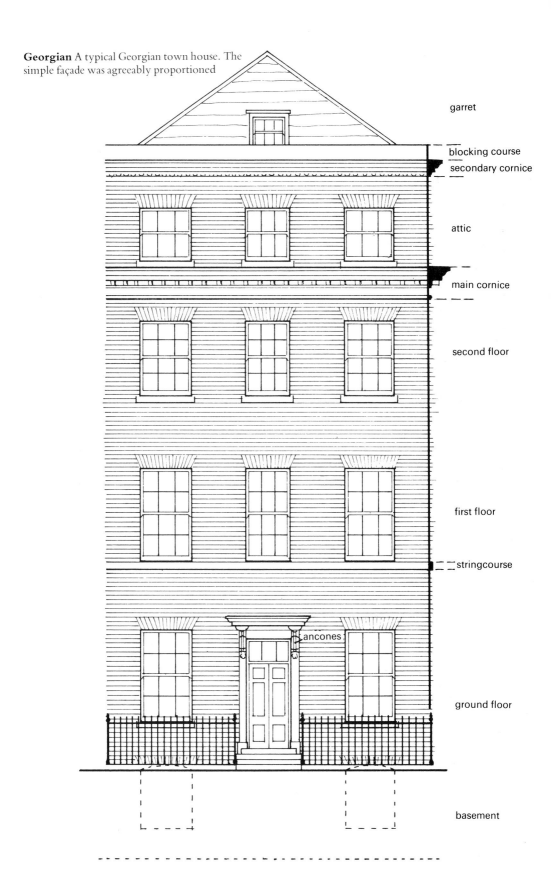

Georgian A typical Georgian town house. The simple façade was agreeably proportioned

garret

blocking course

secondary cornice

attic

main cornice

second floor

first floor

stringcourse

ancones

ground floor

basement

ten fairly elaborate, sometimes with Chinese or Rococo influences. Gothick made its appearance in the Georgian Period. The architecture of Adam, with its Pompeian motifs, became fashionable in the latter half of the eighteenth century, then the grander glories of the Regency period took over.

Giant Order
Pilasters at Kirby Hall, Nothamptonshire. Note the sculpture instead of capitals, and the very free adaptation of Renaissance motifs

Gesso A prepared surface of plaster to give relief to a painting.

Giant Order An Order where the columns rise several storeys, also known as a Colossal Order.

Gibbs Surround The architrave or surround of a door or window consisting of large blocks of stone interrupting the architrave. It is named after James Gibbs (1682–1754).

Giblet Check, Check A rebate in stone for a door or shutter, where there is no wooden door-case or frame. (Scots)

Gilding Laying of gold leaf on a surface.

Gesso (*left*)
Gesso work in the chancel screen of the Church of St Edmund, King and Martyr, Southwold, Suffolk, *c*1500

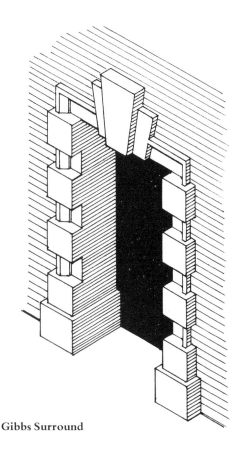

Gibbs Surround

Gin Palace

a) Etching by Cruikshank in the series *The Drunkard's Children* showing an early gin palace interior. *(Guildhall Library)*

b) The Angel Tavern, Crutched Friars, at the corner of Vine Street, City of London. The front is based upon a gin-palace type. The brass gas-light rails behind the large plate glass windows should be noted, as should the enormous lamp suspended over an exuberantly decorated bracket of iron. *(Guildhall Library)*

Gin Palace An ornate public house that developed in the 1830s after the passing of a law to encourage the drinking of beer in alehouses licensed for the sale of beer only. The large breweries and owners of public taverns saw independent beer shops as a threat and began buying up licensed houses where spirits including gin and other liquors could be sold. Plate glass, newly available in large sizes, engraved and acid-etched, gaslight, coloured tiles and advertisement mirrors were all part of the gin-palace decor, designed to attract custom from the drab streets. The architects Stephen Geary (died 1854) and J. B. Papworth (died 1847) are both credited with the design of the first original gin palace, but the first such building appears to have been Thompson & Fearon's establishment of 1829–31, attributed to Papworth. The gin palace was the result and not the cause of the gin-drinking habit.

Girder The main beam which carries the joists of a floor. Any main structural beam in a building.

Girdle A circular band or fillet surrounding part of a column.

Glacis Sloping ground falling from the parapet of a fortress so that it could be raked by fire.

Glass, Glazing During the Middle Ages the use of coloured glass set in lead was almost universal and surviving examples are among the greatest glories of medieval art. Stained and painted medieval glass is a major subject in itself. Windows contained brilliant colouring and told vivid stories in symbol and in stylised form. Although glass was used by the Romans, the material was not widely used for windows until late-Saxon times. The art of glazing developed from the Norman period and reached its zenith in the Gothic. Much glass was destroyed at the time of the Reformation and the art of stained-glass manufacture fell into a sad decline. Where coloured glass was used, colours became muddy, yellow, or dull. Glass was used in small panes because of the difficulties of manufacturing it, and was either placed in lead cames or in small panels secured by glazing bars. It was not until the 1830s when techniques of manufacturing large sheets of glass were perfected that large panes were available for domestic, commercial and other uses. The Victorians developed techniques of acid etching, sand blasting, etc, which created a whole rich field of decorative possibilities, especially in pubs. The revival of Gothic also brought about a revival of the art of stained-glass manufacture, and many thousands of fine Victorian windows still exist, although vandalism, church redundancies and neo-Puritanism are fast reducing the wealth left to us.

Glyph A sunken channel, usually vertical. The term is used to denote the perpendicular fluting in the Doric frieze. (See Fig e **Orders**)

Glyptotheca A building for the display of sculpture.

Gobbets Blocks of stone.

Godroon (See **Gadroon**).

Gola, Gula The cymatium.

Golgotha A place of interment, a graveyard, or a charnel-house. The Golgotha of a rood is the base-beam into which the three figures are set. This beam was carved to represent skulls and bones, set among rocks and grasses. (See Fig **Rood**)

Gorge Throating. (Scots)

Gorged Encirclement of a throat in heraldry.

Gorgoneia Keystones carved with the heads of gorgons.

Gospel Side The side of the altar at which the Gospel is read, that is, the north side.

Gothic Architecture The style of architecture prevalent in Europe from the latter part of the twelfth century until the sixteenth century. It is characterised by the pointed arch, pillars which owe nothing to Classical architecture, clustered shafts, ribbed vaults, elaborately traceried windows, and by an essentially vertical emphasis. Classical architecture is earthbound, based on columns and beams, while Gothic seems to spring upwards, striving for the heavens. Openings are large and walls are supported by buttresses. Some features of Gothic were developed in Norman times but it was not until the pointed arch came into general use that the style really developed. Early English Gothic windows were long, usually lancets and devoid of tracery, placed singly or in groups in walls. Mouldings were deeply cut and bold, while enrichments were frequently employed. During the Decorated period, windows were made larger and filled with ornate flowing tracery, while increased richness and more daring effects were achieved. In the Perpendicular period flowing lines were replaced by vertical emphases and rectangular motifs occurred. Arches became flatter and mouldings became mechanical and dull. Fan vaulting was perhaps the finest achievement of the Perpendicular period. Early English, Decorated and Perpendicular styles are also known respectively as First, Middle or Second, and Third Pointed. The Gothic style did not die with the Tudors, but continued, often in a vernacular form, until well into the seventeenth century. The Gothic Revival began in the eighteenth century, largely as a result of a growing interest in romantic ruins, antiquities, and irrationalism, as opposed to the Enlightenment. Many 'Gothic' buildings were erected by Wren and Hawksmoor, but fashionable 'Gothick' really began with Horace Walpole's Strawberry Hill (1750–70) although it owed little to period pre-

Gothic Architecture

a) Typical bay of the Early English period, from Salisbury Cathedral. Note the arch from the nave arcade, and the triforium over, with cusped openings and quatrefoils. Above this is a clerestory light of three lancets.

b) Typical bay of the Decorated period, from Exeter Cathedral. Note that the piers have now become very clustered, and the arches of the nave arcade are heavily moulded. The triforium has declined in importance, but the clerestory window has fully developed tracery.

c) Typical bay of the Perpendicular period from Winchester Cathedral. Note the heavily panelled effect, the obsessional use of verticals, the typical low arch of the nave arcade, vestigial triforium, blind panels of tracery, and vaulting

cedent and was perhaps more Rococo in spirit than really Gothic. In the early nineteenth century, many 'Gothic' churches were built which were in reality Georgian preaching boxes with simplified Perpendicular or Early English windows. True Gothic Revival, based upon a scholarly study of the medieval buildings, began with Rickman and Pugin. From the 1840s onwards many fine Victorian churches were built in a correct Gothic manner with fittings and glass to match, and these were largely made possible by the revival of the medieval liturgies as a result of the activities of the Ecclesiologists.

Gothick (See **Gothic Architecture**)

Goufing Underpinning with wedges. (Scots)

Gradetti Annulets.

a

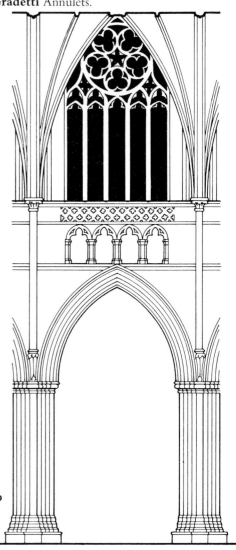

b

Graining, Combing Imitation grains or textures achieved by paint worked over with a comb and subsequently varnished.

Granary A building for the storing of corn.

Grange A farm, usually attached to a monastery.

Greek Architecture All examples of Grecian architecture may be ranged under three Orders, Doric, Ionic and Corinthian, each of which has its own characteristics. (See **Orders**). Although

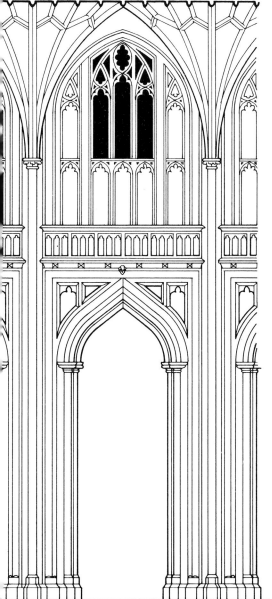

Gothic Revival

a) Fan-vaulted ceiling in Strawberry Hill

b) Alfred Waterhouse's Manchester Town Hall (1868–77)

87

a

b

Greek Revival
a) Prostyle tetrastyle Ionic Dissenter's Chapel by
John Griffith at the General Cemetery of All
Souls, Kensal Green (1834)
b) Prostyle tetrastyle Doric chapel designed for
Stephen Ralli at the South Metropolitan Cemetery,
Norwood by John Oldrid Scott (1872–4). Note the
elaborately carved metopes and tympanum

the Greeks favoured an architecture of columns
and beams, they refined the system to its ultimate
beauty. The eternal verities of proportion and
scale are nowhere demonstrated so aptly as in
Greek architecture, and although some com-
mentators trace the origins of Greek decoration
and architecture to primitive wooden structures,
such a view fails to take into account the
refinement of detail found in marble temples.
(See **Temple**). Greek architecture was rediscovered during the eighteenth century and
received a considerable promotion during the
early years of the nineteenth when the Elgin
Marbles became available for study and when
Greek independence was a cause espoused by
Byron. During the 1820s and 1830s many Greek
Revival buildings were erected in Britain, including the chapels at Kensal Green Cemetery by
John Griffith.

Greek Cross A cross with equal arms, foot and
head.

Greek Key A pattern found on bands, formed
of a labyrinthine fret.

Greenhouse A glasshouse for sheltering plants
which could not survive in the open air.

Grees Steps, or a staircase.

Grey Stocks Bricks of the third quality of malm
bricks.

Grisaille A style of decorative painting done in
grey tints to imitate bas-relief.

Groin The edge formed by an intersection of
vaults, usually covered by ribs (See Fig **Vault**)

Grotesque Light and fanciful ornament consisting of figures, foliage and the like. The name
derives from the fact that many antique grotesques were discovered buried and any subterranean apartment is called a grotto. Another
term for grotesque is arabesque.

Grotto An artificial cave decorated with fantastic shellwork, often incorporating fountains and
water cascades. Grottoes were sometimes built
in houses and were popular in the eighteenth
century.

Ground Floor The storey of a building at
ground level, or nearly so, usually containing the
best rooms.

Greek Key

Guilloche Two forms of guilloche

Ground Glass Obscured glass.

Groundings Battens or firrings, the same – basically – as grounds. (Scots)

Ground Plate The lowest timber on which exterior walls are built.

Grounds Timber fixed to a wall on which finishings are fixed.

Ground Tablestones The projecting course of stones above the surface of the ground, called a plinth.

Grouped Columns Several columns on one pedestal. When only two are used, they are termed coupled.

Grout A semi-liquid mortar poured into joints of masonry or rubble.

Guilloche An ornament in Classical architecture, formed by two or more intertwining bands. It is sometimes used in a band or on a convex moulding.

Gula Cymatium.

Gurgoyle Gargoyle.

Guttae Small ornaments resembling drops used in the Doric Order on the mutules of the cornice, and beneath the taenia of the architrave under the triglyphs. (See Fig e **Orders**)

Gutter Any small open watercourse. A channel between the parapet and lower part of a roof to collect water.

Gymnasium A place for athletic games.

Gynaeceum Part of a house reserved for women.

Gypsum Alabaster. Also sulphate of lime.

Habitacle A niche. An old word for a dwelling.

Hacking In walling, the interruption of a course of stone by introducing another course upon a different level in consequence of a want of stones to complete the thickness.

Haffet A spandrel. A triangular bracket. (Scots)

Haffit A frame or the sides of a box. (Scots)

Hagioscope A squint.

Half-checked Joint A double rebate joint, or a halved joint. (Scots)

Halflet A pew end. (Scots)

Half Round A semicircular moulding or torus.

Half-timbering A structure formed of timber, with sills, lintels, struts, ties, braces, etc, sometimes filled in with brickwork or lathing, and plastered.

Hall The principal room of a house in the Middle Ages. Also, the first room on entering a house; the public room of a corporate body; a court of justice, or any assembly room.

Hallan A biss, or division wall, boundary wall, or stall wall, constructed of a Caithness slab. (Scots)

Hall Church One where the naves and aisles are the same height.

Hallyngs The hangings of the hall.

Halpace, Halfpace, Hautepace The raised floor in a bay window, before a fireplace, or any raised step or dais.

Halving A method of jointing timbers by letting them into each other.

Ham A house, a street, or a village.

Hammer Beam A beam used in the principals of Gothic roofs, acting as a tie at the base of the principal rafter. Each principal has two hammer beams which occupy the situation of a tie beam, but they do not extend across the width of the roof. The ends of hammer beams are often carved with angels holding shields. (See Fig e **Roof**)

Hance The small arch which joins a lintel to a jamb.

Hand Hole An inspection chamber or an inspection hole. (Scots)

Handrail A rail upon slender posts, or balusters, to protect a stair well and to assist ascent and descent.

Hang Over The term used to denote the condition of a wall when the top projects beyond the bottom.

Hangings Linings of rooms, including tapestry, paper, etc.

Hanging Steps Steps built into a wall at one end and cantilevered out. (Scots)

Hanging Stile The stile of a door to which hinges are attached. (See Fig **Door**)

Hardware Ironmongery.

Harling A render on a wall, with a rough texture. (Scots)

Harmonic Proportion The relation of three quantities in harmonic progression. If any three adjoining terms are taken, the difference between the first and second is to the difference between the second and third, as the first is to the third. Elaborate systems of harmonic proportion related to musical harmonies were evolved by Alberti and by the Palladians.

Harmus A tile covering the joint between two common tiles.

Hasp The fastening to a common casement.

Hassack Kentish ragstone.

Haunches of an Arch The parts between the crown and the springing. (See Fig **Arch**)

Haunch of a Door, Hance This is an arched piece of timber placed under the lintel proper.

Header A brick or stone of which the longest dimension is the thickness of the wall.

Headstone Upright stone at the head of a grave.

Heart Bond In masonry, where one large stone the full breadth of the wall lies over two other stones.

90

Hearth The floor of a fireplace.

Hecatompedon A temple with a portico one hundred Attic feet wide, or one with a naos one hundred Attic feet in length. 101.341 English feet = 100 Attic feet. The Attic foot is based upon geometrical studies of the Parthenon, thought to be the ideal expression of great Doric architecture.

Heel of a Rafter The foot that rests on the wall plate.

Height of an Arch The distance from the line of the springing to the highest point of the intrados. (See Fig **Arch**)

Helices Spiral ornaments or volutes. The term is especially applied to the sixteen volutes under the abacus of the Corinthian capital, also called urillae. (See Fig g **Orders**). The helical line of a handrail is the spiral line, twisting, representing the form of the handrail.

Helioscene An exterior blind, louvred, which protects from the sun while permitting a clear view from the inside of the room.

Helm Roof One of four inclined faces meeting at an apex, with a gable at the foot of each face. (See Fig c **Roof**)

Hem The spiral projecting part of an Ionic capital.

Hemitriglyph A half triglyph.

Hence The narrow side of a chimneystack. (Scots)

Herm A pedestal terminating in a head or bust of Hermes or some other deity, found in Renaissance and post-Renaissance architecture.

Hermitage A small hut or dwelling in a secluded spot, usually built in a park, as a resting place, gazebo or visual stop.

Herringbone Work Masonry in which the stones are laid aslant instead of being bedded flat. Sometimes there is a band of coursed stones or bricks laid between each ashlar course. Herringbone work is frequently found in paving. (See Fig **Brickwork**)

Herse A portcullis, resembling a framework fashioned like a harrow, on which lighted candles were placed in church ceremonies and at funerals. It is the framework set over a coffin to carry the pall. Permanent metal frames over funerary effigies are also known as herses, so the term appears to mean any grid frame. A funeral herse was a canopy over the bier. Herses were capable of carrying an immense number of wax tapers.

Hewing Handworking of stone. (Scots)

Hexastyle With a portico of six columns.

Hick-joint Pointing After joints are raked out, superior mortar is inserted between courses, and made smooth.

Hieron The sacred enclosure of a Classical temple.

High Altar The principal altar of a church.

Hiling The covering or roof of a building.

Hinge The joints on which doors, gates, etc, turn. Gothic hinges are often very elaborate, and are ornamented with scrolls. (See also **Rising Hinge**)

Hip The external angle formed by the meeting of two sloping sides or skirts of a roof.

Hip Knob A finial at the end of the ridge piece of a roof, against which abut the bargeboards of a gable.

Hippodrome A place for equestrian exercises. The name was given to many Victorian music-halls and theatres.

Hoard, Hoarding Temporary wooden structures round a building which is in the course of erection.

Hogging A convex curve.

Hollow Newel An opening in the middle of a staircase.

Holy Water Stone, Stock The stoup or other receptacle for holy water.

Hood Mould A projecting moulding over the heads of arches, known also as a dripstone or label. (See Fig A **Mouldings**)

Horn The Ionic volute. (See Fig f **Orders**)

Hornwork An outwork of half-bastions joined to the main fortress by wings.

Horseshoe Arch An arch higher than a semi-circle, found usually in Moresque or Saracenic architecture. (See Fig **Arch**)

Hospital A building for the care of the sick, infirm, aged, and poor.

Hostrie, Hostel, Hotel An inn, a house for travellers.

Hothouse A glass building for raising plants. A conservatory, orangery, or greenhouse.

Houff A shelter or latrine. (Scots)

Hour-glass Stand A bracket or frame for the hour-glass found in post-Reformation times in churches near the pulpit.

Housing A tabernacle or niche. The term also means an excavation for the insertion of some part of the extremity of another element.

Hovel An open shed for cattle. The term is also used to denote a niche or tabernacle.

Hypaethral With no roof, open to the air.

Hyperthyrum The cornice over the architrave of a door or window. The term is also applied to a lintel.

Hypocaust A duct for heating by means of hot air.

Hypogaeum An underground room.

Hypostyle A covered colonnade or pillared hall.

Hypotrachelium The neck, groove, or frieze of the capital of a Tuscan, Doric, or Ionic column. The term is also applied to the upper part of the shaft below the cap. (See Fig e **Orders**)

Ice House A structure, partly underground, for the preservation of ice for use during warmer weather. The best examples were constructed during the eighteenth and early nineteenth centuries.

Iconostasis A screen separating the chancel from the nave, and pierced by three doors, found in Orthodox churches.

Image A painting or statue representative of saints, Our Lord, or the Blessed Virgin. Images were extensively destroyed during and after the Reformation.

Imbow To arch over or vault.

Imbrex A convex tile covering two adjacent concave tiles.

Imbricated Tracery A pattern formed like that of the tiles on a roof.

Impaled Two coats of arms on one shield separated down the middle.

Impluvium The cistern in the centre of a courtyard to catch water. The term is also applied to the courtyard itself.

Impost The capital, bracket, entablature, or pier from which an arch springs. The impost is generally said to be the point from which the arch springs. An impost block is a block placed between the capital and the springing of an arch. (See Figs **Arcade**, **Arch**)

Inband, Inban A quoin with its length built into the return of the wall or reveal. Any stone with its greatest length built into the depth of the wall. (Scots)

Inband Rybat A header stone in a jamb. (Scots)

Inbond A header on a reveal or a return. (Scots)

Inbond Jambstone A bondstone laid in the joint of an aperture.

Incertum Masonry of small rough stones and mortar, with irregular masonry on the face, not laid in horizontal courses, also called rubble.

Incised Slab A memorial sometimes carved with lettering, heraldry, etc, and sometimes inlaid with brass. The chiselled shape for the brass is called an indent. Incised slabs are often decorated with stylised effigies.

Income A jamb. (Scots)

Industrialised Building Mass-produced building parts were available to Georgian and Victorian house builders, while the iron-foundries produced a huge variety of artefacts which were used in a great number of all sorts of buildings of the Victorian era. While timber mouldings, etc, have been available in bulk for many years, the situation since 1945 has changed building technique considerably. Craftsmanship has declined and industrialised components have become more readily available. Many system-built schools were erected in Hertfordshire after World War II, and other industrialised systems have been widely used by many local authorities. The difficulties with industrialised-components systems include a lack of flexibility, a sameness, and, of course, the dependence on more and more production. Like all mass-production the system depends upon a very large demand. There is considerable evidence that a retreat from systems is due to failure of design and construction, and the intractable problems caused by certain systems have rendered them unattractive. As cheap solutions they have proved expensive.

Infirmary A public building for the reception of infirm persons. A hospital.

Inglenook A recess for a seat built in the chimneybreast or adjacent to a fireplace.

Ingoing A reveal. (Scots)

Inlaid Work Work in which the surface of the material is cut away to allow the substitution of metal, stone, cement, wood, ivory, or other substance with a flush surface. Buhl work, marquetry or mosaic are all examples. Inlaying of metal in metal is called damascening.

Inn, Hostel Any house used as a lodging house. A tavern. Formerly, inns were lodgings for scholars or law students, as at Oxford or Lincoln's Inn. Many old inns, in the sense that they are taverns, restaurants or hostels, still exist, for example, in Glastonbury or Ludlow.

Inserted Column An engaged column.

Intaglio Sculpture where the subject is hollowed out or incised.

Intake A plinth. (Scots)

Intarsia A wooden mosaic made up of different woods.

Inn The George and Pilgrims Inn, Glastonbury. A late-medieval inn

Intavolata A cymatium.

Intercolumniation The distance between columns measured from the lower parts of the shafts in multiples of the diameter of a column. The main types of intercolumniation as defined by Vitruvius are: pycnostyle, where columns are one and a half diameters apart; systyle, where they are two diameters apart; eustyle, where they are two and a quarter diameters apart; diastyle, where they are three diameters apart; and araeostyle, where they are greater than three diameters apart.

Interdentils The space between dentils.

Interlacing Arches Semicircular arches in an arcade, which overlap, commonly found in Norman work.

International Style The style of architecture that evolved from World War I onwards in Central Europe, and then became widely accep-

a

b

Interlacing Arches
a) Arcading of interlacing arches on the south wall of the chapterhouse of Much Wenlock Priory.
(Salop County Council Record Office SRO 770/ Small Box 1—No 6)
b) Arcading of interlacing arches on the north wall of the chapterhouse of Much Wenlock Priory.
(Salop County Council Record Office SRO 770/Small Box 1—No 8)

ted throughout Europe and America from the late 1920s. It is characterised by smooth surfaces, large areas of glass, usually in horizontal bands, asymmetry, cubic forms, no mouldings and a cleanly trimmed appearence. It was regarded as progressive, left-wing, and the only acceptable style by dogmatists. Buildings in this style were difficult to maintain, expensive to construct, wasteful of energy through heat loss and insulation difficulties, and ultimately just as eclectic as the architecture they attempted to replace. The style was also divorced from tradition and the decorative aspects of craftsmanship, being allegedly based upon a machine aesthetic.

Intersticium The space between the nave and choir under the central tower of a cruciform church, where the transepts cross the body.

Intertie A horizontal, connecting piece of timber placed between beams or posts to bind them together.

Intrados The interior and lower line or curve of an arch. The upper curve is called the extrados. (See Fig d **Arch**)

Inverted Arch An arch turned upside down, used in foundations.

Ionic Order The second of the Orders employed by the Greeks, and the third used by the Romans. The distinguishing feature is the capital, which is ornamented with four spiral projections or volutes. (See Fig f **Orders**)

Ironmongery Metal fixings such as bolts, locks, hinges and other fastenings, etc.

Ironwork Some very fine medieval ironwork remains, notably in the ornamental door hinges, scrolls, decorative nail-heads and handles of church doors. Monuments were frequently crowned with iron filigree work and some good examples survive in Westminster Abbey. Iron screens and railings survive in quantity from the seventeenth and eighteenth centuries, but by far the biggest heritage of ironwork is Victorian. Nineteenth-century manufacturers catered for a vast range of items, including pipes, crestings, balusters, railings, pissoirs, stalls, hothouses, lamp-posts, gravestones, manhole covers, notices, name-plates, etc.

Isodomum Masonry with courses of equal thickness.

Ironwork
a) Cast-iron tomb at Madeley, Shropshire
b) Iron bridge over the Severn at Ironbridge,
Shropshire. The earliest bridge of cast-iron, designed
by Abraham Darby in 1778
c) Ironwork above the fascia of the Black Friar,
London, built in 1905 by H. Fuller Clark
d) Cast-iron spandrels of Holborn Viaduct (1863) designed by William Haywood
e) Cast-iron shopfront at Witney, Oxfordshire,
c 1870
f) Cast-iron balustrade at Abbey Mills Pumping
Station

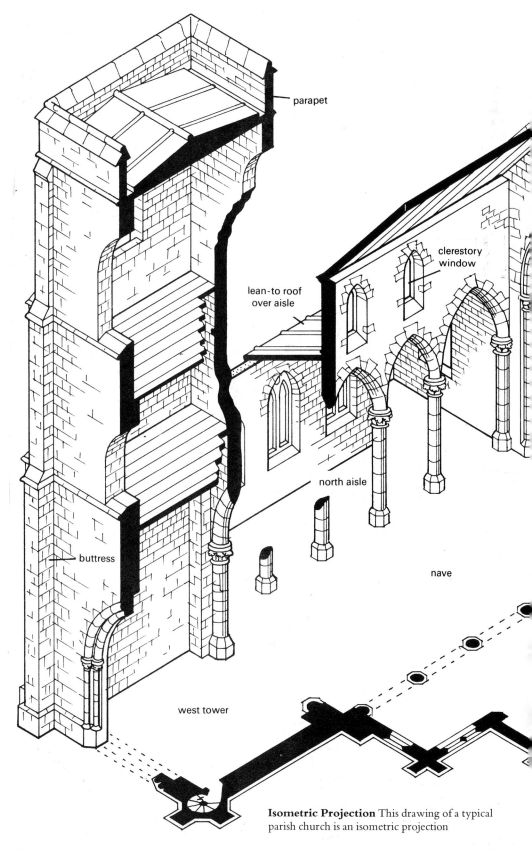

parapet

clerestory
window

lean-to roof
over aisle

north aisle

nave

buttress

west tower

Isometric Projection This drawing of a typical
parish church is an isometric projection

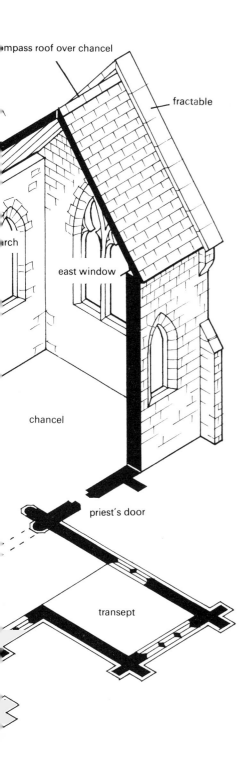

compass roof over chancel

fractable

arch

east window

chancel

priest's door

transept

Isometric Projection A system of drawing objects similar to Axonometric, but in which the plan is distorted to produce an illusion of perspective. (See also Fig C **Projections**)

Italian Architecture The style introduced by the architects of Italy at the end of the fifteenth century. Based on the art and architecture of

a

b

Italianate
a) The Finsbury Bank for Savings of 1840. This is a distinctly Italianate design based on the ideas imported by Barry
b) Italian Romanesque mausoleum at Brookwood Cemetery, near Woking

antiquity, the Renaissance came to England during the reign of Henry VII, and gradually, through the writings of Alberti, Serlio and others, superseded the medieval styles. Renaissance influences were all-powerful·in England until the Gothic Revival of the nineteenth century. The style known as Italianate was, however, a distinctly nineteenth-century phenomenon, and was made fashionable by Barry in his great London clubs which are interpretations of Italian Renaissance palaces. Ornaments, cornices and architraves of this style became *de rigueur* in most of the grander domestic buildings with stucco fronts built in Kensington and Bayswater in Victorian times.

Jack Arch An arch one brick thick.

Jack Rafter A short rafter, such as one fixed to a hip of a roof.

Jacobean Of the period of King James I and VI, at the beginning of the seventeenth century. Although Inigo Jones introduced Palladian Classicism in Jacobean times, the term applies to a coarser English Renaissance style, where French, Italian, and Flemish motifs were intermingled.

Jam Nuts Lock nuts. (Scots)

Jamb The side of a window, door, etc. A jamb lining is the vertical lining of a doorway. The term is applied to the inner part, as the portion outside a window or door is called a reveal.

Jawe Piece A strut or brace in a roof. Also called a jopy or jope.

Jerkin-head Roof A roof of which the end is somewhere between a gable and a hip, for the gable rises to a point where the collar beam is usually fixed, or about half way to the ridge. It is also called a shread-head.

Jesse, Tree of Jesse A representation of the genealogy of Christ in which the persons forming the descent are placed on scrolls of foliage branching out of each other. It was often represented in sculpture, painting, and embroidery. It

Jesse
Jesse reredos of 1470 in the south transept of the Church of St Cuthbert, Wells. The figure of Jesse is at the bottom while in the niches above were his descendants, including Our Lord. The whole was much mutilated by the 'reformers'

a

b

Jacobean Architecture
a) Gatehouse to Stanway House, Gloucestershire, of *c* 1630. Note the three shaped gables, and the bay windows. The archway is flanked by fluted columns on pedestals, and above the entablature is an open segmental pediment
b) Church of St John the Baptist, Stokesay, Shropshire. A canopied seventeenth-century pew of Jacobean style

c

is found in a spectacular form in the tracery of one of the windows at Dorchester Abbey in Oxfordshire, and in the reredos in the south aisle in St Cuthbert's Church in Wells. Jesses are also found in the form of branched candlesticks.

Jetty, Jettie, Jutty A part of a building that projects beyond the rest, and overhangs the wall below. The term is also applied to the projecting floor joists that carry the overhang of a timber-framed building or jettied storey. (See Fig **Timber Framing**)

Jib Door A door in a partition or wall set to have a continuity of surface with its surroundings. It is usually unobtrusive and sometimes even invisible.

Joggle The joint of two bodies so constructed to prevent them sliding past each other. The term is used in masonry to signify the indentation made in one stone to receive the projection in another. What a carpenter would call a rebate is a joggle in masonry. A joggle piece is a truss post in a roof formed to receive a brace or strut with a joggle. In Scotland it is called a joggle post.

Joinery Framing or joining of wood for finishings, including the making of doors and all better class woodwork.

Joist Horizontal timbers on which flooring is laid and to which a ceiling is fixed. Joists rest on walls or on girders and sometimes on both. (See **Bridging Joist**)

Jopy, Jope A strut or brace in a roof. The same as jawe piece.

Jube, Jubé The rood loft or gallery over the entrance to the choir.

Jump An abrupt rise in a level course of brickwork or masonry.

Jutting The same as overhang or jetty.

Jyméwe A hinge.

Kage, Cage The term is applied to chantry chapels enclosed with screens or lattices.

Kamptulicon An elastic covering for floors that had a brief vogue in Victorian times.

Keel The fillet, raised edge, or sharp arris, formed on roll mouldings, by which the heavi-

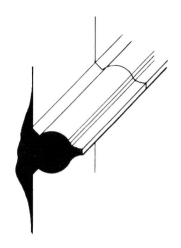

Keel Moulding

ness of the roll was relieved. The section is like the keel of a ship.

Keel Moulding A ridge or edge on a rounded moulding. (See Fig)

Keep The chief tower or donjon of a castle.

Keeper A striking-plate for a staple or a lock.

Kentish Rag Hard limestone much used as an external building material. Many Victorian churches were clad in ragstone.

Kep A doorstop. (Scots)

Kerb A stone at the edge of a footway in a street which divides it from the carriageway. Sometimes spelt kirb, kurb or curb.

Kernel (See **Crenelle**).

Key A pattern also called a fret or a Greek key pattern. (See Fig **Greek Key**). Anything that completes or holds together the parts of the fabric, eg strutting-pieces between joists. A key is also a piece of wood let into another against its grain to prevent warping. The term is also used to describe the instrument to drive back the bolt of a lock. The boss of a vault is called a key or a knot.

Keyed Dado That which has wood laid across its grain to prevent warping.

Keystone The highest and central stone or voussoir of an arch or a rib vault, sometimes called a sagitta. It is often carved, with consoles or other sculpture. (See Figs **Arch, Arcade**)

Killesse, Cullis, Coulisse A gutter, groove or channel. A dormer window is sometimes called a killesse window, while a hipped roof is sometimes called a killessed roof.

Kiln A building for the accumulation and retention of heat to dry or burn materials, eg timber or bricks.

Kilt Weathering to steps of stone. A kilt fillet is a tilting fillet. (Scots)

King Post The centre post of a roof standing on the tie beam and reaching up to the ridge. It is also called a crown post or prick post. Where two posts are used set at equal distances from the centre they are termed queen posts, but formerly all such posts were termed kings, crowns, or pricks. (See Fig d **Roof**)

Kiosk An open pavilion or summerhouse with a colonnade. A bandstand, or a small free-standing shop.

Kirb Same as kerb or curb.

Kirk A church. (Scots)

Kitchen An apartment where cooking takes place.

Knapped Flint Split flints laid to expose the black surfaces of the flints.

Knee The return of a dripstone at the springing of an arch. The projection of architrave mouldings at the ends of the lintel in the dressings of a Classical door or window. A part of the back of a handrail of convex form, the reverse of a ramp, which is the back of a handrail of concave form. Any piece of timber of a bent or angular form, usually fixed as a corbel under the ends of beams.

Knee Piece, Knee Rafter A crook rafter in the

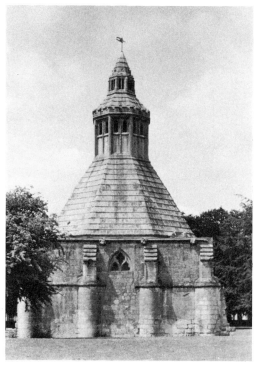

Kitchen
The abbot's kitchen at Glastonbury (second half of the fourteenth century). Probably the best-preserved medieval kitchen in Europe. It is a square building with fireplaces in the corners resulting in an octagonal interior, with an octagonal pyramidal roof surmounted by a tall lantern or femerell

principal truss of a roof. It is a rafter which is crooked downwards so that it may rest firmly on the walls.

Knee Timber A bent piece of timber formed out of a tree that grows crookedly, so that the fibres of the wood follow the curve.

Knocker A hinged hammer, usually ornamental, fixed to a door to attract the attention of those within. The knob which the hammer strikes is called a door nail.

Knot, Knob, Knoppe, Knotte A boss. A round bunch of leaves or flowers or similar ornament found on capitals, labels, or intersections of ribs. A knot is also a whorl in timber formed where there was a junction with a branch.

Knotting The preliminary process of painting to prevent knots from showing. Traditionally, knots were covered with red lead then white lead and oil, and lastly with a coat of gold size.

Knuckle The joint of a hinge.

Knulling A very flat bead-and-reel moulding.

Kurb Same as kerb or curb.

Kynges Table A table moulding, but the exact meaning is obscure.

Label A drip or hood mould over an aperture usually returned square. (See Fig A **Mouldings**)

Label Stop An ornamental boss at the ends of a hood mould or label. (See Fig B **Mouldings**)

Labyrinth A subterranean series of winding and interconnected passages. A maze. A mandala, symbolic of the grail or the pilgrimage, found in cathedral floors. A labyrinth fret is a fret with many maze-like turnings, similar to a key pattern or Greek key.

Laced Windows Window openings set above each other and flanked by strips of brick of a different colour to that of the wall.

Laconicum An apartment in an ancient bath.

Lacquer A solution of shellac in alcohol, sometimes coloured.

Lactarium A dairy-house.

Lacunar A ceiling or the under-surface of a cornice or entablature. A ceiling is only so described when it has sunken coffers without spaces or bands between them. When there are such bands, it is called laquear.

Lady A size of slate.

Lady Chapel A chapel dedicated to Our Blessed Lady, usually placed to the east of the High Altar, but sometimes in other positions.

Lagging The planks on the centring of an arch on which the arch voussoirs are laid in construction.

Laird's Loft A private gallery in a church for a Scots laird and family. (Scots)

Lady Chapel
The Lady Chapel of Hereford Cathedral. This is a remarkably pure example of the Early English style, and dates from *c* 1220–40. Note the dog-toothed mouldings round the windows. (*Hereford City Library Reference No 4621*)

Lancet Arch An arch with a sharply pointed head. (See Fig g **Arch**). A lancet window was a common feature of the Early English style.

Land Gutter A valley gutter. (Scots)

Landing The platform at the end of a flight of steps.

Lantern A small structure on top of a dome for the admission of light, for ventilation, or for ornament. In Gothic architecture the term is applied to louvres on the roofs of halls, etc, but it usually means a tower, open from below, commonly found over the crossings of churches, for example, at Ely Cathedral. A lantern also means the open structure at the tops of some towers, usually square, circular or polygonal.

Lantern Cross A cross with a lantern-shaped top, often enriched with sculpture.

Laordose The screen at the back of an altar, probably a corruption of reredos.

Lap Part of a body lying over another, eg slates.

Laquear (See **Lacunar**)

Lararium The apartment in a Roman house where the household gods were deposited.

Larder Properly, a store for undressed meat.

Larmier The corona.

Latch A catch by which a door is held shut.

Latchet A fixing welt. (Scots)

Lath Strips of timber used for fixing slates, tiles or plaster.

Lath Brick A large brick twenty-two inches long and six inches broad.

Lath Floated and Set Fair Three-coat plasterer's work: the first is called pricking up; the second is floating; and the third, or finishing, done with fine stuff, is the setting coat. Lath laid and set is two-coat work: the first coat is called laying, and the second is generally coloured.

Latin Cross A cross with the head and arms short and the lower arm or tail long.

Latten An alloy resembling brass, often used in tombs.

Lattice Window A reticulated window made of laths of wood, strips of iron or other materials, used where air rather than light is to be admitted. A lattice window is a term also applied to a window with lozenge-shaped leaded lights, or rather less accurately, to any hinged window.

Laundry A room or place where clothing, etc, is washed, mangled, dried, steamed and ironed.

Lavatory A cistern or trough for washing purposes. Lavatories are provided in cloisters of monastic establishments. The term is also given to the piscina in a church, but is very loosely nowadays given to any closet or small room fitted up with basins and other apparatus for washing, urinating, or defaecating.

Layer A course in brickwork or masonry.

Layer Boarding Gutter boarding.

Laying In plastering, the first coat on lath of two-coat work. If laid on brickwork or on stone, it is called rendering.

Lay Light A ceiling light.

Lazar-house, Lazaretto A hospital for the poor and for those with contagious diseases.

Leaded Lights Windows where the glass is held in cames of lead, usually in lozenge-shaped panes.

Leaf One side of a door, or a shutter.

Leaf and Dart A moulding similar to the egg and dart.

Leaning Place The sill wall under a window.

Lean-to A building whose rafters pitch against or lean on another building or wall. It is often termed a to-fall or too-fall, usually a shed with a single-slope roof falling away from the adjacent building.

Lear Board The plank on the feet of the rafters to carry the side piece of the lead of a gutter under the bottom rows of the slating or tiling.

Leaves Ornaments based on natural leaves. The leaves of a door.

Lectern The reading-desk in the choir of medieval churches. They were occasionally of stone or marble, but more usually of wood or brass.

Lectorium The place where the Epistle was read in a church.

Ledge The horizontal plank of a common door to which the battens or planks are nailed. A surface or shelf to support an object.

Ledgement A string course or horizontal band of mouldings. A ledgement table is the moulding on the plinth of a Gothic building.

Ledger A flat stone laid over a tomb. Horizontal timbers parallel to the walls are also termed ledgers.

Lesene A pilaster strip, ie a pilaster with no base or capital, found in Saxon churches.

Levecel A penthouse or projecting roof over a door or window. An open shed.

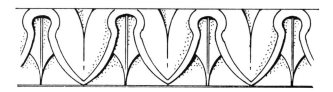

Leaf and Dart

Lever Boards Boards fastened in an aperture which can be turned to admit light or air, also called louvres.

Library A room or suite of rooms for the keeping of books.

Lich-gate A roof over the entrance to a church-yard beneath which bearers paused when bringing a corpse for interment.

Lierne A rib in a vault that does not arise from an impost and is not a ridge rib, but crosses from one intersection of the principal ribs to another.

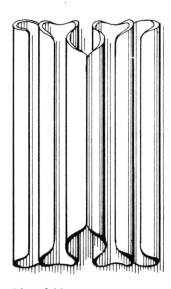

Linenfold

A vault with such ribs is called a lierne vault. (See Fig D **Vault**)

Lights The openings between the mullions of a window, also called days.

Linenfold Panelling of the Tudor period ornamented with a representation of folded linen.

Linings The coverings of the surface of any body with another substance.

Lintel, Lintol A beam placed over a doorway, window or other opening to support the wall over it.

List, Listel A fillet.

Listing The cutting of the sapwood from both edges of a board.

Lobby A small room communicating with one or more apartments.

Lobe of an Arch A foil of a Gothic arch.

Lock A piece of machinery for fastening a door, drawer, chest, etc. Those on outer doors are stock locks; those on chamber doors are spring locks or rim locks; and those hidden in the door are mortise locks. The lock rail of a door is the middle horizontal rail to which the lock is fixed.

Lockband A course of bonding stones.

Locker An aumbry.

Locutory A place in a monastery where talking was allowed.

Lodge A small house at the gate of an estate, or any small house in a park. The quarters of masons working on a medieval building, hence Freemasons' lodges.

Loft An upper platform, or the gallery in a church. In modern usage it is the space under the rafters of a building and above the ceiling of the upper floor.

Logan A rocking-stone, or upright stone capable of being rocked to and fro.

Loggia A lodge, but more usually applied to a gallery open to the air, where one or more sides are open, usually colonnaded.

Lombard Style Architecture of the Romanesque period found in northern Italy and revived in Victorian times.

Long and Short Work Saxon quoins, consisting of tall quoins and short horizontal ones, laid alternately. The method gave a very good bond as the short quoins often extended the full thickness of the wall.

Long-stone-swings Stone lintels. (Scots)

Lookum, Leucomb A projection on the upper floor of a warehouse or mill to cover a wheel and fall, or a crane, with a trap-door.

Loop, Loup, Loophole A small narrow slit in a wall, used in fortifications, through which missiles and arrows could be discharged. They often had circular enlargements in the middle or at the ends and were often in the form of a cross. (See Fig **Balistraria**). The term loophole is also applied to a vertical series of doors in a warehouse through which goods are delivered by crane.

Lorymer The corona.

Lotus A plant much used as the inspiration for architectural ornament in Egyptian work.

Louvre A turret or lantern over a hall to allow smoke and steam to escape, also called a femerell. They were sometimes closed with boards placed horizontally and aslope, at a distance apart, to allow ventilation to take place. These boards are known as louvre, luffer, or lever boards. A louvre is today a term applied to the board only, or to glass used in the same way.

Low-side Window A small opening in a church near the west end of the chancel, and on the south side, lower than other windows and possibly a means of communication between a priest and a person outside. It was always shut-

Loophole
Loophole or vertical series of doors in a warehouse in Southwark, London, through which goods are delivered

tered rather than glazed, and there was usually a seat on the inside. It was sometimes termed a lychnoscope on the assumption that here lepers could see the service from the churchyard and presumably confess to a priest within.

Lozenge A diamond shape found in decoration, eg lozenge mouldings.

Lucarne A small opening in a spire or a roof. A dormer or garret window.

Luffer (See **Louvre**)

Lunette A semicircular opening or surface, eg above a door in an arch.

Luthern A dormer.

Luting Caulking. (Scots)

Lych-gate (See **Lich-gate**)

Lychnoscope (See **Low-side Window**)

Machicolations
The central tower of the St Charles Hospital, London, by H. Saxon Snell (1879–81), containing the chimney flues and water tanks. The machicolations are not defensive in this instance, but are largely decorative. *(GLC Department of Architecture and Civic Design Reference No 70/14289)*

Lying Light A ceiling or lay light. (Scots)

Lysis A plinth or step above the cornice of the podium of a Roman temple or similar building.

M-roof A roof of two common roofs with a valley between.

Machicolations Openings at the top of fortified walls formed by setting the parapet proud of the wall on corbels. The intervals between the corbels were left open so that arrows, boiling oil and sundry unpleasant objects could be rained on any attackers below. (See Fig **Battlement**)

Maenhir (See **Menhir**)

Malm Bricks Bricks made from a calcareous loam, reckoned to be among the finest of all bricks.

Mandala A symbol of the totality of the psyche in all its aspects. It is represented by circles, polygons, labyrinths, squares and other figures which have a centre. Rose windows are mandalas, and so is the Vesica Piscis. The medieval churches abounded in mandala symbols. The labyrinth was represented in the leadwork of stained glass and in the patterns of the floor tiles of cathedrals. It was a symbol of the Holy Grail, not only the chalice, but the object of desire which led the pilgrim through life to Paradise.

Manger A trough in the stall of a stable.

Manhole An opening formed for access to a sewer, an underground passage or a boiler.

Mannerism Cold academic Classicism, or the use of Classical motifs outside their normal context or in a wilful manner. Mannerism is generally associated with Italian architecture from Michelangelo until the beginning of the seventeenth century.

Manor House An unfortified house of the late medieval period. A house in the centre of a manor.

Mansard or Curb Roof A roof with two inclined planes. (See Fig c **Roof**)

Manse A parsonage house, now usually applied to the dwelling of ministers in the north and in Scotland.

Mansion A large house.

Mantelpiece, Mantlepiece The decorative shelf in front of the manteltree, supported by the jambs of a chimneypiece. The frame surrounding a fireplace.

Manteltree, Mantletree The horizontal beam over a fireplace, or the arch.

Margin The part of a slate uncovered by the slate above.

Marigold Window A circular window with radiating mullions.

Market Cross A cross set up in a market-place. Originally it consisted of a shaft with a cross of stone set on a number of steps, but subsequently became an elaborate arcaded structure. In Scotland it was called a mercat cross.

Marmoratum Opus Fine stuff of calcinated gypsum and crushed stones or marble rubbed to a fine marble-like surface.

Marquetry Inlaid work of thin plates of ivory, or coloured veneers of wood glued to a ground. (See **Buhl Work**)

Martlet A swallow or martin; in heraldry, with no legs.

Masonry The craft of jointing, cutting, and laying stones for building. Some ancient masonry consisted of stones laid dry, some blocks being so

Masonry
a) Ashlar work co—coping s—string P—plinth R—regular-coursed ashlar DN—deep and narrow coursed ashlar C—channel-jointed rustication with reticulated quoins F—channel jointed rustication frosted CH—chamfer or vee-jointed rustication RF—chamfered rock-faced rustication V—chamfered vermiculated rustication D—diamond-pointed rustication
b) Rubble A—random rubble B—coursed random rubble C—squared coursed rubble with ashlar quoins

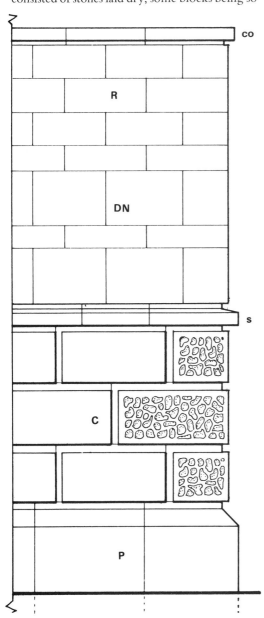

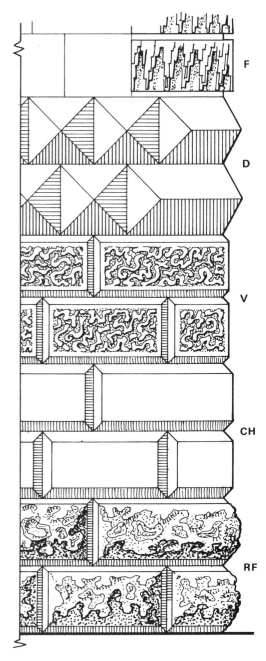

large they would not subsequently shift. Cyclopean masonry consists of large blocks of irregularly shaped stone with the interstices filled in with smaller stones. Stones laid in courses represent a degree of considerable sophistication. The opus incertum of the Romans consisted of random rubble made of stones of irregular shape. The reticulatum consisted of stones squared and set diagonally, often found in late-Norman work. (See **Ashlar**)

Mason's Mitre

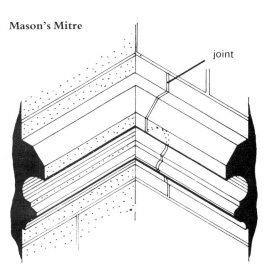

Mason's Mitre Where mouldings meet at right angles and the diagonal mitre does not coïncide with the joint, the moulding is carried through on the return face.

Mausoleum A monumental sepulchral building, so called after the tomb of King Mausolus, king of Caria, at Halicarnassus.

Medallion A square, elliptical, circular, or oval tablet on which are figures or busts in relief.

Medieval Architecture The architecture of Europe during the Middle Ages. It is generally called Gothic or Pointed architecture, but may embrace Romanesque or Norman work. (See **Gothic, Norman**)

Megalithic Consisting or constructed of large stones.

Menagerie A building for housing and preserving animals.

Menhir, Maenhir A tall upright stone of considerable antiquity.

b

A

B

C

a

b

Mausoleum
a) Mausoleum of Sir Titus Salt at Saltaire in Yorkshire attached to the Congregational Church. A Victorian industrialist's family tomb
b) Mausolea in Brookwood cemetery, near Woking

Mensa The slab on top of an altar.

Merlon The solid part of an embattled parapet, also called a cop. (See Fig **Battlement**)

Meros The plane face between the channels in a triglyph.

Mesaulae Small courts, or passages.

Mestling, Mastlin Yellow metal, brass, or latten.

Metalwork Objects made of metal.

Metatome (See **Metoche**).

Metoche, Metatome The space between the dentils of the Ionic Order, or the space between the triglyphs of the Doric Order.

Metopa, Metope, Metopse The space between the triglyphs of the Doric Order, either plain or decorated. (See Fig e **Orders**)

Mews A terrace of stables or coach-houses with living-quarters above, commonly associated with grander townhouses and situated at the backs of such houses, usually in London.

Mezzanine A storey of middle height between two higher ones; ie an entresol.

Mezzo-relievo (See **Relievo**).

Middle Post A king post.

Middle Rail The rail of a door to which the lock or bolt is usually fixed, also called the lock rail. (See Fig **Door**)

Mid-feather A cross-tongue or a parting slip. (Scots)

Minaret A tall slender circular turret with rings of balconies at intervals.

Minster The church of a monastery, or one to which a monastery was once attached. The name also distinguishes collegiate or conventual churches from secular or parish churches.

Minute A proportionate measure, and a subdivision of the module, ie one sixtieth part of the diameter of a column at the base of the shaft.

Misericord, Miserere The projecting bracket on the underside of seats in choir stalls in churches. When the hinged seats are raised, the brackets afford a modicum of rest to someone standing or leaning upon them. The brackets are often ornamented with grotesque or comic figures.

Mitchel A Purbeck marble stone twenty-four inches by fifteen.

Minster
Beverley Minster, Yorkshire, from the south. Note the two sets of transepts. The western towers are Perpendicular (*c* 1380–1420), the two transepts are Early English (*c* 1220–1260), and the nave is mostly Decorated (*c* 1308–1349)

a

b

c

Misericords
a) The fourteenth-century choir stalls at All Saints Church, Hereford, showing the misericords. *(Hereford City Library, Reference 10472)*
b) Detail of a misericord from All Saints Church, Hereford. *(Hereford City Library, Wilson and Phillips Collection, No 5821)*
c) Detail of misericord from All Saints Church, Hereford. *(Hereford City Library, Wilson and Phillips Collection, No 5827)*

Mitre The line formed by the meeting of two surfaces which intercept each other at an angle. A mitre arch consists of two flat slabs leaning together, joined in a mitre, thus forming a triangular head to the arch.

Moat A wide ditch surrounding a building and usually filled with water.

Modillion Projecting console brackets under the corona of the Corinthian and Composite Orders, and sometimes of the Roman Ionic Order. (See also Fig g **Orders**)

Modillions

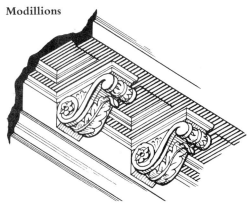

Modinature The general distribution, profiles and arrangement of the mouldings of an order, a building, or an architectural member.

Module A measure which regulates proportion. In Classical architecture it is the diameter of a column, or half its diameter, at the base of the shaft, and this module is divided into sixty minutes. (See Fig e **Orders**). The term also refers to any system of measurement to facilitate repetition of standard unit. The Modulor system of Le Corbusier is based upon the human figure.

Mole A pier to shelter ships.

Monastery An establishment for a monastic fraternity or sisterhood. Monasteries were established in England by both the Celtic church and the Benedictines. (See **Abbey**)

Monial A mullion.

Monkey The weight in a piling hammer, or the whole pile-driving instrument.

Monochrome A system of decoration in one colour.

Monolith A monument, obelisk, or a column of a single stone.

Monopteral A temple with no walls, supported on columns only, and circular in form.

Monostyle Columns in Gothic architecture consisting of a single shaft, as opposed to polystyle or compound shafts. The term is also applied to a building of one style throughout.

Monotriglyph Intercolumniation where only one triglyph and two metopes are introduced between column tops on the frieze.

Monstrance An open or transparent vessel in which the Host is exposed or relics are displayed.

Montant (See **Muntin**).

Monument An edifice to commemorate a person or event. The sepulchral monuments of the Middle Ages are very varied. Stone coffins tapering from head to foot are common, and these often have carved lids. Brasses let into slabs were also numerous. Altar tombs and canopied effigies are frequently found. After the Reformation, monuments of considerable coarseness and vulgarity invaded the churches, including many Elizabethan and Jacobean examples, where Renaissance motifs are used with eclectic extravagance. Many churches contain fine examples of Baroque and Classical monuments. By far the commonest are the mural slabs and cartouches of the eighteenth and nineteenth centuries. The Victorians reintroduced Gothic brasses and altar tombs. Tombstones were varied and interesting throughout history, and act not only as historical records but as repositories of the history of taste.

Monyal A mullion.

Moresque Art and architecture derived from that of the Arabs, Moors, or Saracens. (See **Arabesque, Arabian Architecture**)

Mortar Material to bind stones and bricks together. It is composed of burnt limestone and sand.

Mortise, Mortice In carpentry and joinery, a recessed cutting within a piece of timber which receives the projecting tenon of another piece, or a lock or other insertion. A mortise lock is one that fits into a mortise in a lock rail.

Mosaic Ornamental work formed by inlaying small pieces of glass, stone, pottery, marble, etc. It was much used in floors and on walls, where the tesserae, or small pieces, formed patterns either of a geometrical or naturalistic type.

Motte A steep mound on which the keep stood in an eleventh and twelfth-century castle. The motte and bailey was a system of defence consisting of a tower on an earth mound, enclosed by a bailey with palisade or wall and a ditch.

Moulded Capital A capital with mouldings, as opposed to a plain or block capital. (See Fig **Capital**)

Moulding An ornamental contour given to the
angles or features of a building, whether a projection or a cavity, such as a cornice, an architrave or an astragal. Regular mouldings in Classical architecture are the *fillet* or *list*; the *astragal* or
bead; the *cyma recta* and *cyma reversa*; the *cavetto*
or *hollow*; the *ovolo* or *quarter-round*; the *scotia* or
trochilus; and the *torus* or *round*. In Gothic architecture the diversities are great, but in
Norman work the mouldings consist almost
exclusively of rounds and hollows, with some
splays, often very shallowly worked. Norman
mouldings are frequently broken into *zigzags*,
and *billets* and *beaked heads* are common. The
Early English style has boldly cut mouldings,
with *keels* and fillets in abundance, and rounds
and hollows prevail. Decorated work is more

Mouldings

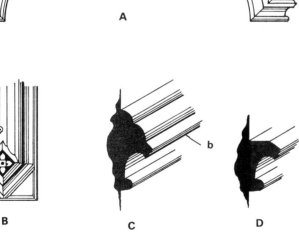

A

B

C

D

b

A hood mould, dripstone or label of brick from
 Ranworth Old Hall, Norfolk
B label stop of stone from Chippenham, Wilts
C moulding of B
D moulding of A
b beak

diversified with much enrichment. Perpendicular mouldings are flatter, with large elliptical hollows, and seem to owe something to
Classical forms. (See **Bolection, Boultine,
Cable, Cant, Chaplet, Dancette, Double-
cone, Dovetail, Echinus, Edge Roll, Fascia,
Gadroon, Half-round, Nebule, Ogee, Pellet, Ressault, Running Dog, Star, Wave** Figs
Anthemion, Ballflower, Bay-leaf Garland,

Bead and Reel, Beak Head, Billet, Bird's Beak, Chevron, Cyma Recta and Reversa, Dogtooth, Egg and Dart, Keel, Leaf and Dart, Nail-head, Panel Mouldings, Roll Mouldings)

Mould Stone A large stone to be carved with mouldings, usually at a jamb or as part of an architrave.

Mullet A five-pointed star with a central hole in heraldic devices.

Mullion A slender pier which forms the division between the lights of a window or a screen. Mullions are often moulded. Also known as a stanchion, monial, monyal, munnion, and in Scots usage, munion.

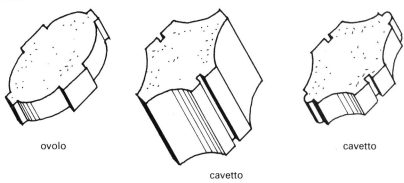

ovolo

cavetto

cavetto

Mullion A mullion and transom window dating from the sixteenth and seventeenth centuries. It is constructed of brick. Types of mullion brick are shown above with ovolo and cavetto sections

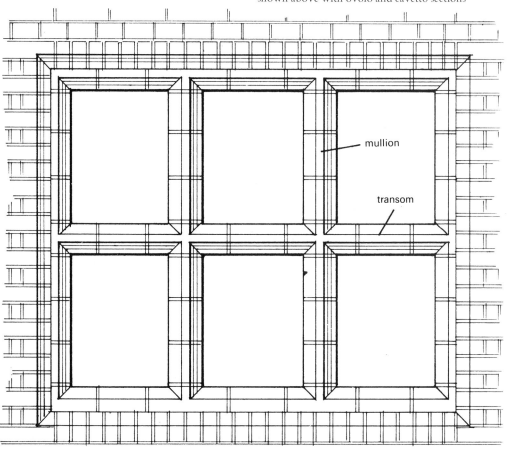

mullion

transom

Multifoil Arch A foil arch with numerous foils and cusps.

Muniment Room A fireproof room for the storage of papers.

Munnion A mullion.

Muntin, Montant An upright piece of timber in a frame. English joiners refer to the muntin as the intermediate upright bar of framing in a door, while the outside uprights are called stiles or styles. Muntins butt into the horizontal rails. (See Fig **Door**)

Mural Belonging to a wall. A mural monument is one fixed to a wall. A mural also means a painting on a wall.

Museum A place for the reception, display, and study of natural, literary, scientific, and artistic objects.

Music Hall A hall used for musical performances. Since Victorian times, however, the

Music Hall
Sectional view of the interior of the Strand Music Hall, London, by E. Bassett Keeling, 1864

term has come to mean a hall licensed for singing, dancing, and other entertainments exclusive of dramatic performance.

Mutilated Cornice and Pediment One that is broken or discontinued, also called a broken pediment. This device was much used during the Baroque period. (See **Pediment**)

Mutules The blocks under the corona of the Doric cornice, in the same situation as modillions in the Corinthian and Composite Orders. It may have a number of guttae or drops on the underside. The mutule is above the triglyph. (See Fig d **Orders**)

Mynchery A Saxon nunnery.

Nail A metal spike for fastening one piece of wood to another. Rose nails have square shanks; brads are headless nails; tacks are short, with heads; and cut nails are machine-made nails. In medieval times heads of nails were often ornamented and were features of doors.

Nail-head Moulding This is one used in Early English buildings, and consisted of a band resembling a series of pyramidal nail-heads.

Naked Floor (See **Single Frame**)

Naos The sanctuary of a Greek temple, or the sanctuary of a Byzantine church. (See Fig B **Temple**)

Narthex A division within an early church, sep-

Mural
Church of St James, Kinnersley, Herefordshire. The mural decorations above the nave arcade are by G. F. Bodley, and were executed by the Reverend Frederick Andrews

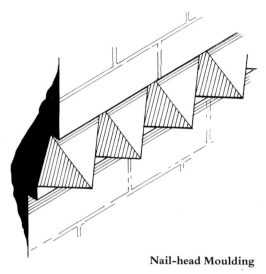

Nail-head Moulding

arated from the rest by a screen and situated near the door. It was also an ante-temple before a church, and was essentially a vestibule to the west of the church, acting as a porch. It was later called a Galilee. (See Fig **Basilica**)

Nave The part of a church west of the choir in which the congregation assembles. In most

Nave
The nave of Hereford Cathedral looking west. Note the Norman arcades with chevron mouldings. Above are the triforium and clerestory. *(Hereford City Library, Reference No 10339)*

churches it consists of a central division with two or more side aisles, but is often found without aisles. The nave was usually separated from the choir by a screen, and many such screens survive. The nave developed from Norman times into an elaborate structure illuminated from above by clear-storey or clerestory lights. (See also Figs **Basilica, Cathedral, Isometric Projection**)

Nebule Moulding An ornament in Norman architecture whose edge forms a wavy line. It is found in corbel tables and in archivolts.

Neck The plain part of a Roman Doric or other column between the astragal on the shaft and the annulet of the capital. Some Greek Ionic capitals have necks below them. Also known as the collarino or hypotrachelium. (See Fig a **Orders**) A neck moulding separates the capital from the shaft proper.

Needle A horizontal timber resting on shores or posts serving as a temporary support for a weight above, while the lower part of a wall is being underpinned.

Needle Spire A thin spire that rises from the centre of a tower roof, set back from the parapet.

Neo-Classicism A movement in architecture that had its beginnings in a rejection of Baroque and Rococo, but which was primarily concerned with a rediscovery of antiquity. The architecture of ancient Rome, celebrated in the etchings of Piranesi, was studied as the source of Classicism. Neo-Classicism, however, was rarely a mere copying of the works of antiquity, although accuracy was prized in archaeologically correct motifs: the movement was also concerned to return to first principles, basic forms, clear uncluttered geometry, and a rational approach to design. It was given additional impetus by the discoveries at Pompeii, by the publishing of measured drawings of Greek (and later Egyptian) architecture, and by the theories of those who demanded the noble clarity and simplicity of perfect shapes such as the sphere, the cone, the cube, the pyramid, and the obelisk. A stripped-down Neo-Classical architecture recurs in the twentieth century, and shows no sign of losing its appeal to designers.

Nerves, Nervures The ribs of a vault, or the mouldings on the ribs, bounding the sides of a groined apartment, distinguished from the ribs which cross diagonally.

Newel The central column round which the steps of a circular staircase wind. The principal post at the angles and foot of a stair.

Niche A recess in a wall for a statue, a vase or other ornament. Niches are often semicircular in plan and are arched. Gothic niches appear in profusion for the display of statuary.

Nidged, Nigged Ashlar Stone hewn with a pointed hammer.

Nimbus A circular halo round the head of a saint.

Nog A wooden brick.

Nogging Brickwork in a wooden frame. A nogging piece is a horizontal timber fixed to the uprights.

Nook Shaft A shaft or colonnette set in the angle of a pier, wall or corner.

Norman Architecture The style of architecture introduced by the Normans after 1066, and called Romanesque elsewhere, although there were buildings with Norman characteristics

Norman Architecture A typical bay of Peterborough Cathedral nave. Note the semicircular arches, the large triforium, small clerestory light, and general massiveness of the structure

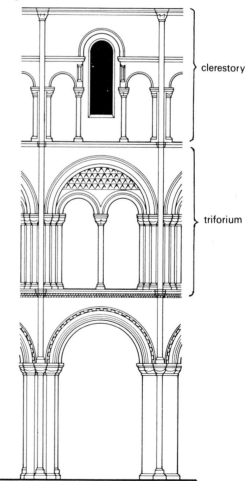

clerestory

triforium

Norman Architecture
a) The Church of St Michael and All Angels, Stewkley, Buckinghamshire. Dating from the twelfth century this is an aisleless Norman Church. Note the interlaced arcading on the tower.

b) The interior of the Church of St Michael and All Angels, Stewkley, Buckinghamshire in the late-Norman style of *c* 1150, showing the chancel and chancel arch, with chevron motifs and beak-head carvings

erected before the Conquest. It was, in its early stages, plain, massive and fortress-like, and ornaments were few. Doorways were deeply recessed and were usually arched with a semicircular arch. Windows were usually small and also had semicircular arches. Columns were massive and were sometimes channelled and moulded with spirals or zigzags. Buttresses were broad and of small projection. Vaults were simple barrels, or had simple groins without bosses. Apses were common and sometimes the arches had their springing well above the capitals, as at St Bartholomew's in London. About the middle of the twelfth century the Norman style started to give way to the Early English with the introduction of the pointed arch. (See **Romanesque**)

Nosing The prominent edge of a moulding or drip, or the projecting rounded moulding on the edge of a step.

Notching Hollows cut from one of the faces of a timber or piece of stone or brick.

Nuved Knotted.

Nymphaeum A picturesque grotto, or a structure containing pools, plants, fountains, and statues.

Obelisk A tapering shaft, column, or upright monument of stone, usually square in plan with a pyramidal top.

Observatory A building where the firmament is studied.

Octastyle A building having eight columns in front. (See Figs F,G **Temple**)

Oculus A round window.

Odeum A theatre.

Oecus A variety of hall.

Oeil-de-boeuf A window of circular or elliptical form.

Oeillet, Oillet, Oylett A small opening in a medieval wall through which arrows could be fired, also known as a loophole.

Offset The projection from the faces of the different parts of a wall where it increases in

Ogee
Ogee-arched niche with foils, flanked by crocketed pinnacles and surmounted by a finial. It is in St Swithun's Church, Merton, Oxfordshire

thickness. It is the part of a wall which is exposed upwards when the portion above is reduced in thickness. Offsets or set-offs are generally sloped in Gothic architecture and have projecting drips as in buttresses.

Ogee Arch A pointed arch the sides of which are each formed of a double curve, one convex and the other concave. It is common in both Decorated and Perpendicular work and is frequently found over tombs, shrines, and niches. (See also Fig g **Arch**)

Ogee Moulding A moulding the same as a cyma reversa (see Fig **Cyma Reversa**). The ogee moulding was also known as the ressaunt.

Ogival With a double curve, convex and concave, also known as ogee.

Ogive A pointed arch.

Oncome The corbel at the springing of an opening. The gathering of a flue. (Scots)

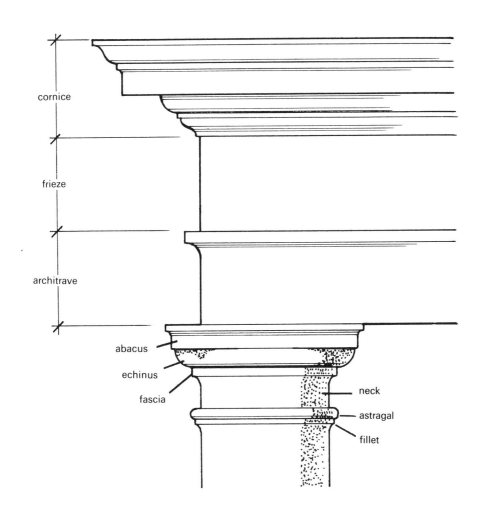

cornice

frieze

architrave

abacus

echinus

fascia

neck

astragal

fillet

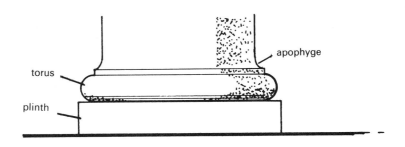

apophyge

torus

plinth

Orders
a) Tuscan Order, after Chambers

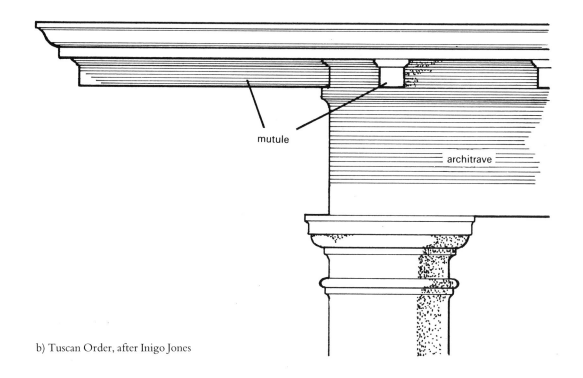

mutule

architrave

b) Tuscan Order, after Inigo Jones

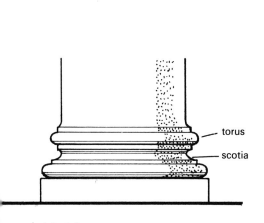

torus

scotia

c) Attic base

d) Composite capital. Note the mixture of Ionic and Corinthian motifs

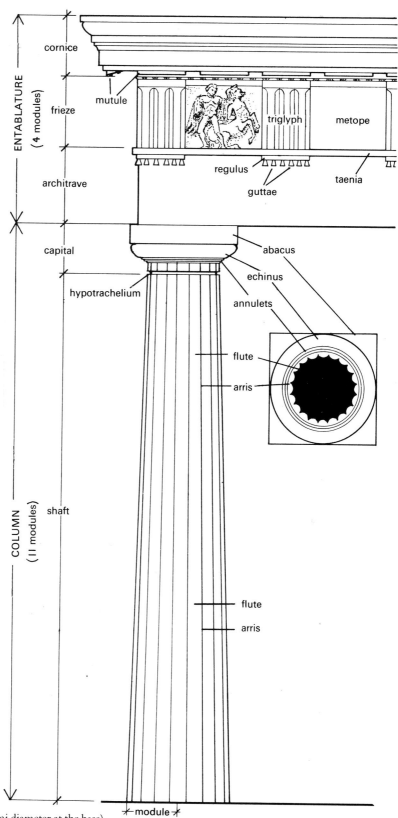

e) Greek Doric Order (semi diameter at the base)

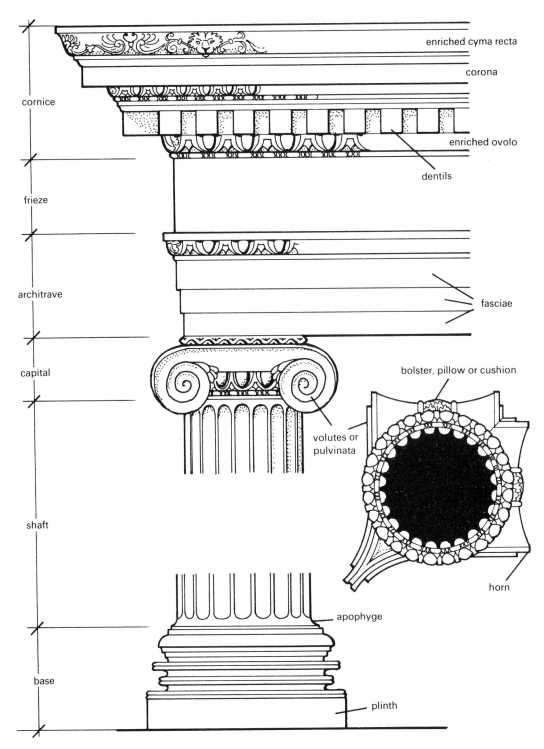

enriched cyma recta

corona

cornice

enriched ovolo

dentils

frieze

architrave

fasciae

capital

bolster, pillow or cushion

volutes or
pulvinata

horn

shaft

apophyge

base

plinth

f) Greek Ionic Order. The drawing also shows an
angle capital

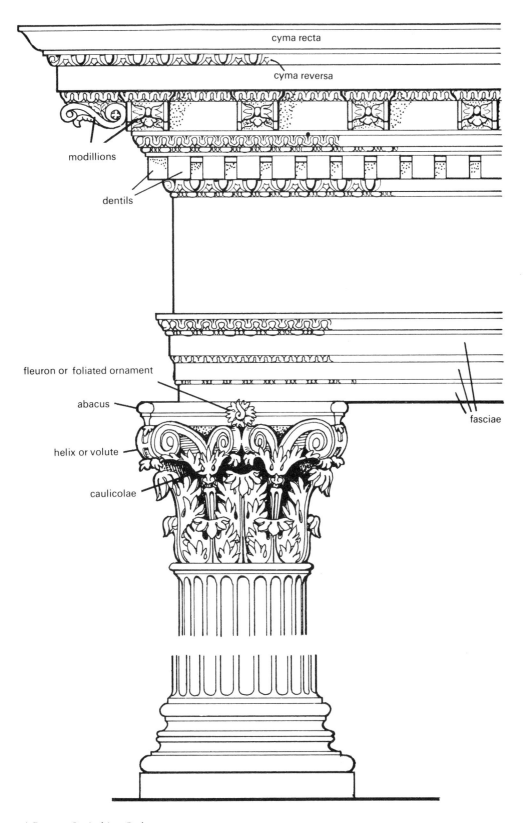

cyma recta

cyma reversa

modillions

dentils

fleuron or foliated ornament

abacus

helix or volute

caulicolae

fasciae

g) Roman Corinthian Order

One Pair of Stairs The first storey above the ground floor.

Onyx A type of quartz allied to agate, used for decorative work and cameos.

Opae The beds of the roof beams in a Greek building, the spaces between which are called metopes.

Open Well A stair which has a space or well between the outer strings, unlike the dog-leg which has no well between outer strings. (See Fig D **Stairs**)

Opisthodomus The enclosed space in the rear of the cell of a temple. (See Fig D **Temple**)

Opus Alexandrinum Paving of marble.

Opus Incertum A wall with rubble or concrete in the middle faced with rubble.

Opus Listatum Walling with alternate courses of brick and stone.

Opus Reticulatum Walling faced with squared blocks set diagonally.

Opus Sectile Ornamental geometrical paving of small pieces of marble.

Or Heraldic gold.

Orangery A gallery or building in a garden facing south for the growing of oranges.

Oratory A small private chapel or closet set apart for devotions. A faldstool at which a worshipper kneels. A place of prayer. A religious establishment of the Order of St Philip Neri, also known as the Oratorians.

Orb A knob of carved foliage at the intersection of the ribs of a Gothic ceiling or vault. A blank window or panel.

Orders In Greek, Roman, and Renaissance architecture, an assembly of parts consisting of columns with bases and capitals, and entablature, decorated and proportioned in consistency with the five Orders. These are Doric, Tuscan, Ionic, Corinthian, and Composite. There are Roman and Greek versions of Doric, Ionic, and Corinthian. The Greek Doric column has no base, whilst the Tuscan column is unfluted. In Vic-torian times curious mixtures of Orders were used by speculative builders in the stucco façades of terrace houses.

Organ Case The decorated case around the organ pipes, often in a prominent position in halls and churches. The positioning of the organ over the screen dividing the nave from the choir is a post-Reformation phenomenon.

Oriel, Oriole, Oryel A large bay or recessed window in a hall, chapel, or other apartment that projects from the wall. On plan it may be curved or polygonal, and is always on an upper floor, carried on a long corbel or bracket.

Orientation The placing of a building in relation to the points of the compass, especially the east in the case of churches. Correct orientation is with the altar and chancel at the east end and the main door at the west.

Orle A fillet under the ovolo or quarter-round of a capital. When it is at the top or bottom of the shaft of a column it is called a cincture. The term also means the plinth or the base of a column or pedestal. In heraldry it is a small bordure.

Ornament Small and detailed work for enrichment not essential to the structure.

Orthostyle Columns placed in a straight line.

Oubliette A secret prison cell reached only by a trap-door.

Oundy, Undy A wavy moulding.

Out-and-in-Bond Alternate headers and stretchers in quoins and jambs. Outban or outband refers to the long stone on the main face. Outbound is a masonry stretcher. (Scots)

Ova Egg-shaped ornaments.

Overhang, Oversail A jutting-out portion of a building, or a jetty or a projecting part. A projection over a base, ie the opposite of batter.

Overstorey A clear-storey or clerestory.

Ovolo A quarter-round or convex moulding much used in Classical architecture. Greek examples are flatter, more like part of the section of an egg, while Roman ovolos are more mechanical, usually quarter-rounds.

Oxter Piece Short timbers between ceiling joists and rafters near the eaves. A queen post is sometimes referred to as an oxter piece because it is approximately armpit height. An oxter is the space between the oxter piece and the eaves. (Scots)

Pace A dais. A step round a tomb.

Packing Small stones between larger ones in rubble walls.

Pad A padstone is the stone set on a wall to carry a truss. It is also called a template.

Paddle A sluice.

Pagoda A tall polygonal structure with orna-

Painted Glass
The east window of 1795 in the Church of St Alkmund, Shrewsbury, by Francis Eginton, set in cast-iron tracery

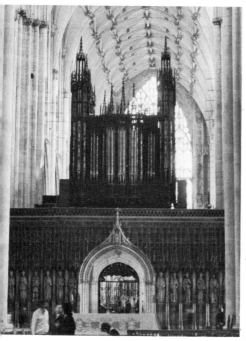

Organ Case
Organ Case in the Church of St Michael, Great Witley, Worcestershire, from the chapel at Canons, 1720. A Rococo example
The crossing and the chancel of York Minster. The chancel dates from the second half of the fourteenth century and the first half of the fifteenth. It is representative of the last phase of Decorated work as became Perpendicular in character. The screen is of 1475–1500, and the organ case is of 1902–3

mental roofs at each storey, originally a temple in Buddhist lands but adapted as an eyecatcher and pavilion in the eighteenth-century Chinoiserie manner in England.

Painted Glass Glass ornamented with painted decorations.

Palace A dwelling for royalty or the highest aristocracy, eg Blenheim Palace.

Palaestra A Greek gymnasium.

Pale A stake of wood placed vertically. Pale fencing is a fence of pales or palings. A palisade is an enclosure of stakes driven into the ground for defensive purposes. A vertical band in the middle of an heraldic shield.

a

b

Palladian
a) The Palladian bridge of 1737 by the ninth Earl of Pembroke and Roger Morris at Wilton
b) Chiswick Villa of 1725–29, modelled on the Villa Capra at Vicenza by Palladio. Note the octagonal dome with Diocletian windows, magnificent pedimented Corinthian portico at piano nobile level, and formal stairs
c) South front of Wilton House (1633–40) built by Isaac de Caux with Inigo Jones as consultant. An early example where Palladian influence may be seen

c

Palladian Architecture That which was derived from the ideas of Palladio (1508–80) and brought to England in publications and by the works of Inigo Jones. Palladianism was revived in England by Colen Campbell and Lord Burlington from the second decade of the eighteenth century, and remained a major influence until the advent of Neo-Classicism in the later part of the century. A Palladian Window is also termed a Serliana or Venetian Window.

Palmette An ornament like a palm leaf.

Pampre An ornament of vine leaves and grapes found in twisted or barley-sugar columns.

Pan A square in the framing of half-timbered houses.

Pancarpi Garlands and festoons of fruit, flowers and leaves for the ornament of doors, etc.

Pane A term applied to the side of any object. The light of a window. The space between timbers in a wooden partition.

Panel A sunken compartment in a wainscot, door, or ceiling, etc. Panels may be enriched with tracery, quatrefoils, heraldic devices, etc.

Panel Mouldings Panels are usually held in place within a framework by means of moulded beads. These mouldings may be bolection, or very simple. (See **Figs**). The panels themselves may be carved, raised and fielded, or have linenfold decorations.

Panier An upright corbel over a pilaster and under a truss.

Pantile A curved S-shaped tile used for roofing.

Pap A teat cast on a pipe to facilitate tapping for a branch. (Scots)

Paperhangings Paper covered with designs fixed to walls.

Papyrus Capital A species of capital seen in Egyptian architecture.

Paradise, Parvise A court or atrium in front of a church usually surrounded by a cloister. The term is also applied to a burial-ground or to the cloister garth. Many towns retain Paradise Streets which recall the Medieval usage, eg in Oxford. A parvise has sometimes been said to

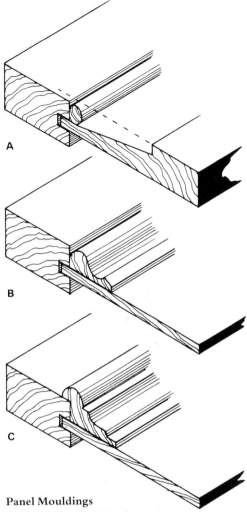

Panel Mouldings
A fielded panel and bead
B plain panel and flush moulding
C plain panel and bolection moulding

be a room over a church porch, but this is an erroneous use of the term.

Parament The furniture and hangings of an apartment.

Parapet A low wall to protect any place where there is a drop. It may be battlemented, plain, pierced, or ornamented.

Parclose A screen separating chapels or tombs from the body of the church.

Parge Work, Pargeting Plasterwork with ornamental patterns much used in Elizabethan times, especially on façades. Vines and figures were the commonest decorations.

Parget Plaster lining flues.

Parker's Cement Also called Roman cement, this was prepared from clay nodules powdered and burnt then mixed with sand and water. It set hard and fast and was much used during the nineteenth century for rendering purposes.

Parlour A room for conversation in a monastery. The term became used to denote the front room of a nineteenth-century middle- or working-class house.

Parpend A bond stone faced at both ends. Parpend ashlar is stonework faced on both sides. (Scots)

Parpent Wall A strong or substantial partition wall. (Scots)

Parquet Polished floors of hardwood blocks laid in patterns, usually of a herringbone type. Parquetry is inlaid work of thin veneers forming a floor, also called inlaid or plated parquet.

Parrell A chimneypiece.

a

b

Pavilion
a) Attingham Hall, built in 1783–5 to designs by George Steuart. Note the very thin Ionic columns carrying the pediment, and the Giant Order of Ionic pilasters on the side wall. The colonnades link the house to the side pavilions
b) Perspective view of St Thomas' Hospital, Lambeth, London. This fine Italianate group of buildings was designed by Henry Currey and was completed in 1870–1. The 'pavilion' principle of planning is demonstrated, where wards were separated by linking corridors
c) Triumphal arch at Wilton, by Sir William Chambers (c 1755). The lodges act as pavilions on either side of the central composition, and are by Wyatt

c

Parsonage A building which serves as the dwelling of a priest.

Parting Bead A beaded slip in the centre of the pulley stile of a sash window to separate the two sash cords.

Partition A wall that is non-loadbearing, dividing one room from another.

Party Wall The fireproof wall between buildings to separate them, eg terrace-houses.

Parvise (See **Paradise**)

Passage An avenue leading to the apartments of a building.

Patand The sleeper or bottom rail as the foundation for a wall.

Patera A circular ornament, resembling a dish, worked in relief. The term has also come to mean any flat ornament resembling the flowers on Gothic cornices, or a Classical rosette.

Paternoster Ornament in the form of a string of beads. A continuous band of elevators.

Patio An inner courtyard.

Pavement A path or road laid or beaten in with stones or other materials. Pavements can be cobbled; covered with Kentish ragstone; paved in square setts, bricks, or flags, or covered with tarmacadam or cement.

Pavilion A turret, a small building, or a wing of a building. A pavilion roof is one hipped equally on all sides. A pavilion usually suggests an ornamental or pleasure building, such as a gazebo or a summerhouse, or even a structure with a verandah attached to a sports ground.

Pebbledash Rendering of small pebbles thrown on to a second coat of cement before it is dry.

Pedestal A substructure placed under some columns in Classical architecture. It consists of a base or plinth, a dado or die and a cornice. It is also the support for a statue or vase.

Pediment In Classical architecture, a low-pitched gable crowning a portico and often containing sculpture. In Renaissance architecture, gables and openings are adorned with triangular

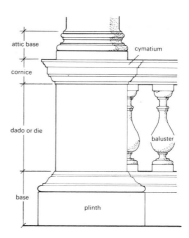

Pedestal The drawing shows a pedestal and balustrade

or segmental pediments. An *open* pediment has raking sides that stop short of the apex, and some authorities call this type a *broken* pediment. A true *broken* pediment also has an incomplete horizontal cornice, and occurs in eighteenth-century doorcases where the horizontal cornice is interrupted by a fanlight. A *scrolled* pediment is an *open* segmental pediment in which the segments terminate in scrolls. (See Figs **Aedicule**, **Temple**)

Peel-tower (See **Pele-tower**)

Pelasgic Building Walls of huge stones without mortar.

Pele-tower A tower, usually a fortified house, found in the north and in Scotland. Also spelt peel or pile.

Pelican A common sculpture in Gothic buildings showing the pelican vulning herself to feed her young, representing piety and the symbolism of the sacraments.

Pellet Moulding A flat band on which are circular discs forming an ornament common in Norman times, but also found in much nineteenth-century work.

Pen, Pen-check, Pend A bird's-mouth rebate in stone. (Scots)

Pend A covered passage through a terrace of houses. (Scots)

Pendant An elongated boss suspended from

Perpendicular and later vaulting. A pendant post is a short post placed against a wall, the lower end on a corbel or capital and the upper end fixed to a tie beam of a medieval principal roof truss.

Pendentive The portion of a domical vault which descends into the corner of an angular building where a dome is placed on a square base. It is essentially a concave spandrel that forms the junction between the corner of a square compartment and the base of a circular dome or drum. (See Fig b **Dome**) The term is also used in Gothic architecture to describe that part of a groined ceiling carried by one column or springing, and bounded by the ridges of the transverse and longitudinal vaults.

Penitentiary A place in a monastery where a penitent confined himself. That part of a church to which penitents were admitted. A prison.

Pentalpha A five-pointed star found in medieval tracery and decoration.

Pentastyle A portico of five columns.

Penthouse An open shed or projection over a door, window or stair. Any structure with a lean-to roof. A flat on the roof of a building, separately roofed.

Perch A bracket or a corbel.

Pergola A covered garden walk with flanking pillars and joists overhead, the whole covered with climbing plants.

Peribolus An enclosing walk or colonnade round a sacred enclosure.

Peridrome The space between columns and a wall of a cella.

Perpendicular
a) The central tower over the crossing at Wells, a magnificent essay in the Perpendicular style. The crowning pinnacles are beautiful examples of West Country Perpendicular
b) The Lane aisle at Cullompton Parish Church of the early sixteenth century showing the fan vaulting, a typical Perpendicular panelled motif
c) The Prior's House, Wenlock Priory. One of the finest surviving domestic buildings of the late-fifteenth century, this façade consists of a two-storey gallery with continuous windows between buttresses. Note the panelled effect. *(Salop County Council Record Office SRO 770/Large Box No 42)*

a

b

c

Peripteral A building surrounded by columns. (See Fig E **Temple**)

Periptery The range of columns around the cella of a temple.

Peristyle A range of columns surrounding a building or an open court. A peristylium is the court or cloister itself.

Perithyrides Ancones.

Perpend or Perpent Stone, Perpender A stone that reaches through a wall from one side to the other, alternatively known as a bonder or bond stone. A perpent wall or a perpeyn wall is a pier or buttress.

Perpendicular Style The last of the styles of Gothic architecture which flourished in England, also known as Third Pointed. It developed during the fourteenth century and continued to the sixteenth, almost unbroken for a quarter of a millennium. Perpendicular is peculiarly English and is characterised by straight verticals and horizontals, especially in window tracery where transoms are important, and there is little of the dashing verve of the Decorated style. Arches are very flat and vaulting is complex, usually of the lierne or fan type. A feature of Perpendicular work is the introduction of mouldings framing doorways, thus creating spandrels which are frequently ornamented. The rhythm of window tracery is usually continued in blind panels of stone, and some Perpendicular interiors are completely covered with masses of panelling, creating a rigid, tightly controlled architecture. Mouldings are generally mechanical and shallowly cut. Surviving glass is subdivided in relentless panels, and colours are generally much lighter than Decorated work, with a tendency for increased use of yellows. (See also **Gothic, Tracery**)

Perron External steps and a landing giving access to the principal floor of a building.

Persiennes Outer shutters with louvres.

Perspective A system of drawing objects that produces an image of the object as actually seen.

Pest House A lazar-house or lazaretto for contagious diseases.

Pew An enclosed seat in a church, or any fixed wooden seat in a church. The bench-ends of pews were usually finished with finials of the poppy-head type. Box pews were enclosed with panelled partitions and usually date from the eighteenth century.

Piano Nobile The main floor of a building containing the main reception rooms. It was higher than other storeys and usually sandwiched between a basement or ground floor and the upper floors.

Piazza A square open space surrounded by buildings. In the seventeenth and eighteenth centuries it came to mean any covered ways or arcaded arches with buildings over them, as in the Covent Garden piazza, but this was an ignorant use of the term.

Picked Masonry finished with a pointed tool. (Scots)

Picture Gallery A room or rooms for the display of paintings, drawings, etc.

Picturesque Largely an eighteenth-century concept, picturesque landscapes tended to be romantic compositions reminiscent of the works of Claude Gellée (Claude Lorrain) and Poussin. Asymmetry and natural features such as mountains, waterfalls, crags, etc, were necessary ingredients.

Piedroit A pilaster with no base or capital, known also as a lesene.

Piend An arris, hip, apex, or ridge. (Scots)

Pier Any isolated mass of construction, such as the solid between two windows or a support with no base or cap (as distinct from a column) for an arcade. An arch that springs from a pier is called a pier arch.

Pilaster
Massive Composite pilasters in Abingdon, Berkshire, of a Giant Order

Pilaster A shallow, pier-like, rectangular column that conforms with the Order used and is engaged with a wall. A pilaster strip is one with no base or cap, otherwise known as a piedroit or a lesene.

Pile A large timber or concrete pole driven into the ground in order to provide a foundation in marshy soil.

Pile-tower (See **Pele-tower**)

Pillar Any free-standing vertical pier, which need not be circular on plan, and which is distinct from a column. No column which conforms to an Order could be described as a pillar. Pillars may be clustered or compound.

Pilotis Pillars that help to carry a large building, leaving the ground-floor free.

Pin A cylindrical piece of wood used to connect two pieces of timber, also known as a dowel.

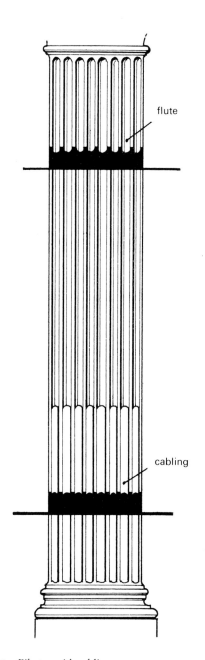

Pilaster Pilaster with cabling

Pinnacle A summit or apex, the crown of a buttress or a vertical abutment terminating in a spirelet, a cone, or a pyramid, often crocketed.

Pinnings Small stones in the interstices of masonry. (Scots)

Pinning Up Driving wedges under the upper work to bring it to bear on the work below.

Pipe A conveyance for water or soil from a

Pilotis
Roehampton Estate, London, by the former LCC
Architect's Department

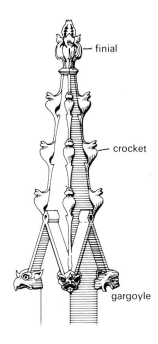

finial

crocket

gargoyle

Pinnacle

Piscina
Decorated piscina and sedilia with four cinquefoiled
ogee arches with crockets and finials flanked by
crocketed pinnacles in the chancel of the Church of
St Swithun, Merton, Oxfordshire

building, usually of metal or earthenware. A
pipe eye is a cleaning eye in a pipe.

Piscina A water drain connected to a stone bowl
within a niche in the south wall of the chancel. It
was used to receive the water in which the priest
washed his hands and that used to rinse the chalice. Within the niche there was frequently a stone
shelf or credence table for the sacred vessels.

Pit of a Theatre The part on the ground floor

between the lower range of boxes and the stage
of a theatre. The orchestra pit is that part occupied by the musicians.

Pitch The slope of the sides or skirts of a roof.

Plafond, Platfond A ceiling or soffit.

Plain Joint A butt joint. (Scots)

Plaisance A summerhouse or a pleasure pavilion.

Planceer The soffit or under-surface of the
corona.

Plane Tiles Flat tiles.

Plank Any flat timber less than four inches wide
or greater than one and a half inches wide. A
plank roof is formed of trusses made of planks
cut to a curve.

Planted When a moulding is wrought on a separate piece of stuff and is then fixed in place, it is said to be planted. Beads, etc, are usually planted.

Plaster A mixture of lime, sand, water and hair used for covering walls and ceilings, etc. Plaster of Paris is a calcined sulphate of lime which, when mixed with water, rapidly hardens and expands thus filling cracks, etc.

Platband A flat fascia, band or string, whose projection is less than its breadth. The lintel of a door. A plat or platt in Scots usage is a broad step below the threshold, or a landing.

Plate A general term given to all horizontal timbers laid upon walls to receive other timbers, eg a wall plate laid on walls to receive the roof structure above.

Plate Glass Glass cast in sheets and polished, of good quality, distinguished from crown glass and sheet. Although plate glass was known before the nineteenth century, only in the 1830s were manufacturing techniques perfected which made plate glass widely and cheaply available. Shops and gin palaces seem to have been the first places to use plate glass which was often etched with fantastic or arabesque designs. (See **Gin Palace**)

Plateresque An ornate style of architecture of Spanish origin, dating from the 1500s, incorporating Gothic, Moresque and Renaissance ornament in gross profusion.

Plate Tracery The earliest form of tracery, dating from the Early English period, consisting of openings cut in flat stonework with no projecting mouldings. It could be likened to fretwork rather than to the later more sophisticated tracery. (See Fig a **Tracery**)

Platform Timbers carrying a flat roof, or the roof itself. Any raised dais. Platform boarding is the boarding on a flat roof or on a dais.

Plinth A square member forming the lower division of the base of a column (see Figs a, f **Orders**) or the plain projecting face at the bottom of a wall immediately above the ground (see Fig **Pedestal**). In Classical buildings the plinth is generally divided into two or more gradations, usually moulded at the top. A plinth block is a plain block at the base of an architrave against

which a skirting or plinth is stopped. In Scots usage a plinth is an eaves course.

Plough and Tongue A continuous mortise and tenon along the edges of two boards, the one with a groove and the other with a projecting tongue.

Ploughshare Twist The winding surface of a vault where the wall ribs start at a higher level than the rest.

Plug A piece of timber driven into a wall and sawn off so that it is flush with the face. It is used for fixings. Plugging in Scots usage is dubbing out, or rough rendering behind the skirtings.

Plumbing The art of casting and working in lead and using it in building. The term is now used to cover all pipework within a building.

Pocket The space in the pulley stile of a sash window.

Podium A continuous pedestal or basement, or a dwarf wall.

Point Block A high building block, usually of flats.

Pointed Arch An arch formed by a radius equal to the span of the opening, and struck from both sides of it on the springing line, or any arch with a pointed head. It is a characteristic of Gothic architecture. The styles of Gothic architecture are also known as First, Middle or Second, and Third Pointed. (See Figs **Gothic, Tracery**)

Pointing Raking out of old mortar between joints in brickwork and masonry and replacing with new mortar. In Scots usage it is pecking stone faces with a pick or pointed tool.

Pole Plate A plate fixed to the lower ends of a truss to receive the ends or feet of the rafters.

Polychromy The decoration of exteriors and interiors of buildings with several colours or tints, usually with different materials.

Polystyle With many columns.

Pommel A knob, knot or boss. The ornament on top of a pinnacle, a finial, etc. Any ornament of globular form.

Poppy Head The terminating feature of the end of open pews.

Porch An exterior adjunct over a doorway, forming a covered approach. If it has columns and a pediment it becomes a portico. In medieval examples rooms are sometimes found over porches.

Porphyry A very hard stone composed of crystals of white or red plagioclase felspar set in a fine dark red ground. It is capable of taking a very high polish and varies in colour from claret to purple, although there are other colours known, including black.

Portal An arch over a door, or the frame of a gate. The small square corner in a room separated from the apartment by wainscoting.

Porte-cochère A porch big enough to admit vehicles.

Porte-cochère
Porte-cochère at Deptford Cemetery chapel

Portcullis A massive frame or grating of iron or wood reinforced with iron used to defend gateways. It slid up and down in a groove and was usually kept suspended over the entrance, but was let down when danger threatened. (See **Yett**)

Portico A range of columns forming a porch in front of a building, or a roofed space open or partially closed at the sides forming the entrance to a building. A portico often has a pediment or antae. If it projects and the columns are freestanding, it is called prostyle, but if the columns are between flanking walls, it is described as in antis. If it has four columns it is called tetrastyle; if six hexastyle; if eight octastyle; if ten decastyle. (See also **Colonnade**, Figs **Temple**)

Portico
This Corinthian portico to the Congregationalist Church at Saltaire, Yorkshire, was designed by Lockwood and Mawson and built in 1859

Portland Cement A cement made from limestone and clay, very light in colour.

Portland Stone A white stone from Portland off the South Coast, commonly used for public buildings in London after the Great Fire (1666).

Post An upright piece of timber. A post and paling is a fence of posts fixed into the ground with pales nailed between them. Half-timbered buildings with exposed posts and with the intervals filled in with plaster are called post-and-pane work.

Postern A private entrance to a castle, house, town, or monastery.

Posticum The epinaos.

Poyntell A pavement of small lozenge-shaped tiles or squares laid diagonally.

Preaching Cross A cross erected in the highway.

Precast Concrete Concrete cast in moulds in a factory or elsewhere before being built into an edifice.

Preceptory A manor or estate of the Knights Templars on which a church was erected together with a house.

Prefabrication The manufacture of building components in a factory or elsewhere before erection.

Presbytery The part of a church where the altar is placed. It is reserved for officiating priests. The term also means a priest's house or a parsonage.

Press A cupboard. (Scots)

Prestressed Concrete Reinforced concrete, where the reinforcement is by steel cables set in ducts, so that tension can be altered by tightening or loosening the cables. Prestressing induces compression in the tension area of a beam before loading, thus making more efficient use of both steel and concrete.

Prick Post Queen posts, or other intermediate posts in a frame. (See Figs **Roof**)

Pricking Up The first coat of plaster on lathing.

Priming The first ground for succeeding coats of paint.

Principal Brace A brace under the principal rafters.

Principal Rafter A large rafter framed, as in a truss, to bear the greater weight. (See Figs **Roof**)

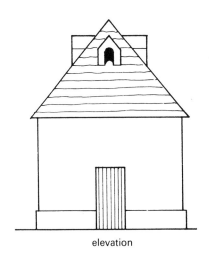

elevation

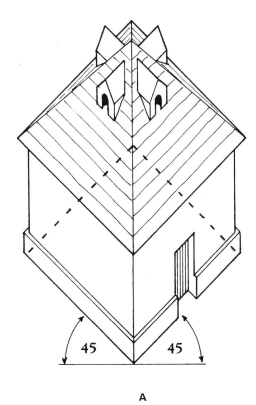

A

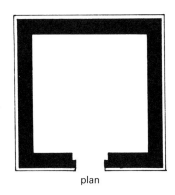

plan

Principals of a Hearse The turrets or pinnacles of waxwork and tapers crowning the posts and centre of a medieval hearse or herse.

Print A plaster cast of an ornament.

Priory A monastery governed by a prior or prioress.

Prismatory Sedilia.

Prison A building for the confinement of transgressors.

Procession Path The aisle or passage behind the high altar and reredos in cathedrals and conventual churches, also known as the ambulatory.

Prodomus A portico before the cell of a temple.

Profile The vertical section of a body, especially a moulding.

Projections Any parts of a structure that jetty out, are cantilevered, or project. Architectural projections are representations to explain the building.

Pronaos The portico in front of a temple and the vestibule flanked by walls behind the portico. (See Fig c **Temple**)

Prop A support.

Proper An heraldic term denoting natural colouring.

Proportion The just magnitude of each part, and of each part to an other; the relation existing between parts or elements rendering the whole harmonious in terms of balance and symmetry.

Propylaeum Any court or vestibule before a building or an entrance gate to such a court or vestibule.

Projections The drawings show axonometric projections A and B, and an isometric projection C, to explain the building. These are projections from the elevation and plan

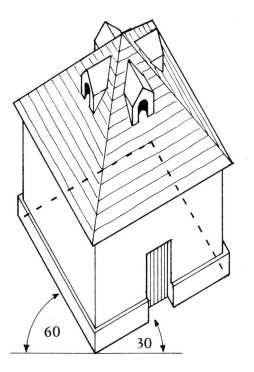

60

30

B

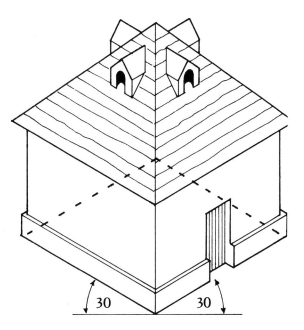

30   30

C

Propylon A gateway before the entrance of an Egyptian temple.

Proscenium In Classical times the stage of a theatre, but now the term means the space between the curtain and the orchestra pit, including the arch and frame facing the auditorium.

Prostyle A portico where the columns stand out freely in a row. (See Figs A, C, D **Temple**)

Prothesis A room or place for the preparation and storage of the sacraments.

Pseudodipteral A temple or building where the general arrangement is dipteral, but where the inner range of columns surrounding the cell is omitted, although the portico would suggest otherwise. (See Fig G **Temple**)

Pseudoperipteral A disposition of columns around a Classical building in which the columns at the sides are engaged with the wall. (See Fig H **Temple**)

Ptera The colonnade around the cell of a temple in Greek architecture.

Pteroma The space or ambulatory between the cell of a Greek temple and the columns of the peristyle.

Puddling Filling behind a wall, or filling of a cavity.

Pugging A coarse mortar on rough boarding placed between joists to aid sound insulation.

Pulley Stile One of the vertical side-pieces of a window sash-frame, in which the pulleys and counterweights are housed.

Pulpit An elevated stage or desk from which sermons are delivered in churches or other ecclesiastical buildings. Pulpits are of wood or stone with a few modern examples of concrete or metal. They are often elaborately carved and occasionally have sounding-boards or testers above to act as canopies.

Pulpitum A stone screen between the nave and choir.

Pulvinata A pillow or cushion, as in the volute of the Ionic order. It is also the dosseret above a

a

b

Pulpit
a) Carved Jacobean Pulpit in St Swithun's Church, Merton, Oxfordshire
b) Eighteenth-century three-decker pulpit in the Church of St Winifred, Branscombe, Devon
c) Pulpit of 1868–74 in All Saints Church, Babbacombe, Devon, by William Butterfield

c

Pyramid
A tomb in the churchyard of St Anne's, Limehouse. (Eighteenth century)

capital and below an arch in Byzantine work, also known as a pulvin.

Pulvinated A convex-profiled frieze. (See **Aedicule**)

Punched, Puncheoned A stone face brought flat with a blunt pick.

Puncheon A short upright piece in framing, or a stud.

Purbeck Marble A species of dark stone from the Isle of Purbeck in Dorset, very hard and capable of taking a high polish. It was widely used in Gothic architecture, especially in the thirteenth century for shafts or colonnettes. The dark, slim shafts against limestone walls gave a sharp effect, and compound piers were often surrounded with shafts of Purbeck marble. Effigies and tombs were frequently made of the material.

Purfled Ornamental work in stone or other material resembling embroidery or drapery.

Purlin A horizontal piece of timber lying on the principal rafters of a roof to give intermediate bearing to the common rafters. Purlins often span from party wall to party wall in terrace-houses. They are also called ribs or bridgings,

side wavers or side timbers. (See **Roof**)

Putlog Hole A small hole left in walls for the erection of scaffolding, also known as a staykfald hole. Cross-pieces of timber scaffolding are called putlogs. In Roman work putlog-holes resemble dove-holes, so Vitruvius called them columbaria.

Putty A paste of whiting and linseed oil, with either white lead or lamp black added, used for fixing glass in frames.

Pycnostyle One of the five species of intercolumniation defined by Vitruvius. In this case the columns are set at a distance from each other equal to one and a half diameters of a shaft. (See **Intercolumniation**)

Pylon The battered masses of building on either side of the entrance to an Egyptian temple. Any free-standing structure of this form.

Pynum-table The coping stones of a gable.

Pyramid A solid standing on a square or polygonal base, with sloping sides meeting at an apex. Structures of this form were built as sepulchral monuments by the ancient Egyptians, but sepulchral pyramids were erected in the eighteenth, nineteenth and twentieth centuries on a much smaller scale in European countries. Pyramids had symbolic significance, and such forms are found in religious buildings in several cultures.

Pyramidion The small flat pyramid on top of an obelisk.

Pyx The box or vessel in which the sacrament is reserved.

Quadra A square border or frame round a panel. The fillets of the Ionic base on either side of the scotia. The plinth or lowest member of the podium.

Quadrangle A figure with four angles and four sides. The term is given to a square or rectangular court surrounded by buildings, a usual feature of monastic establishments and therefore of colleges.

Quadrel A square artificial stone of white earth.

Quadretura Trompe l'oeil architectural designs painted on ceilings and walls in the seventeenth and eighteenth centuries.

Quadrifores Folding doors with the height divided in two.

Quadriga A sculptured group consisting of a chariot and driver pulled by four heroic horses, usually found on monuments, triumphal arches, etc.

Quarrel, Quarry A square of lozenge-shaped pieces of glass used in lead casement windows, a small square or diamond-shaped floor tile, or a similarly shaped opening in Gothic tracery.

Quarry A place where stones are procured by cutting them out of the earth.

Quarter Grain Timber grain achieved by the cutting of pieces in the direction of the annular rings. (See **Felt Grain**)

Quarter Round The same as ovolo and echinus. A moulding whose section is the quadrant of a circle.

Quarters The posts in partitions, also called uprights and studs. All quartering under five square inches in section is called scantling. An old term for quatrefoils.

Quatrefoil A form disposed in four arcs, with cusps, in the shape of a flower with four leaves. Bands of quatrefoils are much used as ornaments in the Perpendicular style. When placed diagonally they are called crossquarters. The old term for a quatrefoil was a quarter. (See Fig a **Tracery**)

Quay A bank with slightly battered or straight sides formed on the side of the sea or a river to enable boats to unload.

Queen A size of slate.

Queen Posts Prick posts or side posts, placed symmetrically on a tie beam and forming a truss with the principal rafters over. (See Fig b **Roof**)

Quicklime Lime ready for the addition of water, ie burned but not slaked. It is actually calcium oxide.

Quillons The cross-guard of a sword.

Quire Choir.

Quirk A piece taken out of the corner of a room; a re-entering angle. A quirk moulding has a sharp return from its extreme projection to the re-entrant angle in a V-shape; it is an acute-angled channel by which the convex parts of Greek mouldings are separated from the fillets. Quirks or V-shaped incisions are common in Gothic work.

Quoin, Coyn The external angle of a building. The dressed stones at the corners of buildings, which, if raised from the surface with channels between them, are called rustic quoins. (See Fig **Masonry**)

Rabbet A rebate or groove.

Race-bond A vertical joint in ashlar. (Scots)

Rack A case over a manger where hay is placed. Any similar high-level structure of bars.

Rad and Dab A substitute for brick nogging in partitions consisting of cob, or a mixture of clay and straw filled in between laths of split oak or hazel. It is also called wattle and daub, or dab.

Raffle Leaf A leaf in ornamental foliage with small indentations at its edges, eg an acanthus leaf.

Rafters Inclined timbers forming the sides of a roof, which meet at the ridge and to which the roof covering is fixed.

Ragged End A roughened end. (Scots)

Raggle, Raglet Chase or chasing for any purpose. (Scots)

Raggled Housed, or chased. (Scots)

Raglin A ceiling joist. (Scots)

Ragstone, Ragwork Flat-bedded stones, generally about the size of a brick, though not regular, usually laid horizontally. Kentish ragstone is a hard limestone much used for church building.

Rail A horizontal piece of timber between the panels of a door, or wainscoting, etc. Uprights are called stiles. (See Figs **Door**)

Rain Conductor A rainwater pipe. (Scots)

Rainwater Head A box-shaped structure of cast iron or lead into which rainwater is poured from a gutter in order to convey it to a pipe.

Raising Piece A timber, set under a beam and over the posts or puncheons in half-timbered work, carrying out the same function as a wall plate.

Rake The slope of a roof.

Ramp That part of a handrail that rises very steeply where there is a landing or a series of winders. It is a slope that connects two different levels instead of a step.

Rampant Arch An arch which has the springings on different levels.

Rampart A stone or earth wall round a fortress or a defended city.

Rance A shore or prop. Rancing is shoring. (Scots)

Random Tooling Called droving in Scotland, it consists of hewing the surface of the stone by advancing a wide chisel over the face at one eighth of an inch per stroke, leaving a series of regular indentations.

Ratchements of an Herse A kind of flying buttress which springs from a corner principal to meet another, thus forming a ridged top to a herse or hearse.

Ravelin An outwork of a salient constructed beyond a main ditch.

Rayonnant A type of Gothic tracery where mullions and window tracing appear as rays bursting forth.

Rear Arch An arch spanning an opening on the inside of a wall.

Rear Vault The small vault between the glass of a window and the inner face of a wall where the wall is thick and splayed in Gothic work. It usually springs from the jambs, or from corbels or shafts fixed against the inner edges of the jambs. The shafts are termed escoinson shafts.

Rebate, Rabbet A channel or recess cut along the edge of a body. Stones rebated to fit together are said to be joggled.

Redan A small ravelin or outwork.

Reed, Reeding A moulding consisting of three or more small beads side by side.

Refectory The dining-hall of a college, convent, etc.

Reglet A flat narrow moulding.

Regrating, Skinning Taking off the surface of old stone to make it look fresh.

Regula, Regulus The band below the taenia and above the guttae in a Doric entablature. (See Fig d **Orders**)

Reignier Work Ornamental inlaid patterns in the manner of Buhl work.

Reind, Rind A fillet. (Scots)

Reinforced Concrete Concrete is strong in compression and weak in tension. Steel is strong in tension. In order to strengthen concrete, steel rods are cast in where tensile strength is needed. Thus beams, columns, etc, may be constructed.

Reins of a Vault The sides or walls that carry the arch.

Relieving Arch An arch built over a lintel to take the weight off it, also known as a discharging arch. (See Fig b **Arch**)

Relievo, Relief The projection of any sculpture or ornament. Alto-relievo stands out well from the ground; mezzo-relievo projects half the figures; and basso-relievo projects the figures less than half their true proportions.

Reliquary A casket to contain relics. Reliquaries were of wood, iron, stone, or costly metals, and were embellished.

Renaissance Art and architecture based on Italian prototypes from the early fifteenth century until it gave way to Mannerism and the Baroque. In England, the first Renaissance work in architectural terms is found in the tomb of Henry VII by Torrigiani of Florence in Westminster Abbey. The Renaissance in England was influenced by Netherlandish and French motifs, as well as by Perpendicular Gothic forms in windows, etc. The result was a curiously English mixture, as at Longleat, Burghley, and Hardwick. Truly Italianate buildings only began with Inigo Jones, whose Palladian Classicism at the Banqueting House, Wilton, and other buildings set the standards of taste not only for the Jacobeans, but for the latter part of the eighteenth century as well.

Rendering The plastering of a surface with stucco, plaster, or some other finish.

Replum The panel of a framed door.

Reprises Seats on sills for jambs or mullions. (Scots)

Reredorter A privy at the back of a dormitory in a convent or monastery.

Reredos The wall or screen at the back of an altar, usually much ornamented with niches, statues, pinnacles and the like.

Reservoir Any artificial pond or cistern for the collection of water.

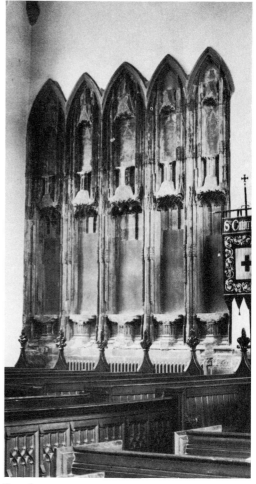

Reredos
Reredos in the Chapel of St Catherine (north transept) of the Church of St Cuthbert, Wells. A much mulilated, but very beautiful reredos of the thirteenth century

Respond A half-pier attached to a wall to support an arch, etc, usually at the end of an arcade. (See Fig **Arcade**)

Ressault The recess or projection of a member from or before another.

Ressaunt An ogee moulding.

Rest A padstone. (Scots)

Retable A shelf behind the altar, or a carved altar-piece behind the altar and below the reredos.

Retaining Wall, Revetment A wall built to retain a bank of earth.

Reticulated Constructed like the meshes of a net. Reticulated masonry is constructed with diamond-shaped stones, or with square stones placed diagonally. Reticulated tracery is Decorated work made up of interlocking ogees forming a net-like framework. (See Fig e **Tracery**)

Retrochoir The chapels and other parts behind and about the high altar.

Return The continuation of a moulding or projection in an opposite or different direction, eg the terminations of the dripstones or hood moulds of a window or door, or the seats and desks set against the screen at the west end of the choir.

Reveal The side of an opening in a wall between the framework and the outer face of the wall. If cut diagonally or at an angle it is called a splayed reveal or simply a splay. (See Fig a **Sash**)

Revestry A vestry.

Revetment (See **Retaining Wall**)

Rhone A half-round gutter.

Rib A projecting band on a ceiling or vault, often ornamental, but often structural. Gothic ribs are enriched with complex mouldings and have carved bosses at their intersections. (See Figs **Vault**)

Riddell A curtain around an altar.

Riddell Post A vertical post, usually capped by an angel, to support the riddells, or curtains, to the sides and back of an altar; there are therefore four riddell posts around the altar. These posts are peculiar to England. They were widely used in the fifteenth century, but were discarded during the Reformation. Their use was revived in the latter half of the nineteenth century, especially through the influence of Sir Ninian Comper, the architect.

Ridge The upper angle of a roof. The term is also given to the timber against which the upper ends of the rafters pitch, also called the ridge piece. The tiles over are called ridge tiles, and these are often ornamental. A ridge pole, in Scots usage, is a ridge roll or a wooden roll to take a lead ridge covering. (See Fig d **Roof**)

Riser The upright face of a step from tread to tread.

Rising Hinge A hinge that causes a door to rise as it is opened to clear a carpet and have an inclination to shut itself by gravity.

Risp A door rattle.

Rivet A small metal bolt with a head.

Rocaille Rock-work of pebbles and other stones used in the building of grottoes, follies, and other decorative conceits. (See **Rococo**)

Rocking Stone A logan.

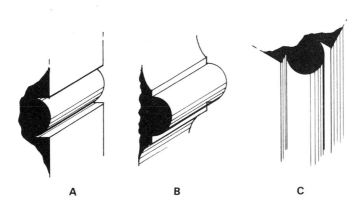

A   **B**   **C**

Roll Mouldings A—flush bead moulding B—torus or half-round C—angle bead or bowtell

Rococo A light, frothy, elegant and playful late phase of the Baroque, more than rocaille, but with much of the shell-like, coral, or marine forms associated with grottoes and the like. Naturalistic forms, Chinoiserie and Gothick elements fuse in this remarkable eighteenth-century art form.

Roll A piece of wood prepared with a rounded form for dressing lead over.

Roll Moulding A moulding used in Gothic work, especially in dripstones, usually with pronounced fillets and throating. A roll moulding is also a bowtell or a common round.

Roman Architecture The architecture of ancient Rome and its empire which was important not only in itself, but as an inspiration to the many Classical revivals that have occurred. Although the Romans used the Orders, and indeed developed peculiarly Roman versions of them, the arch was not ignored as it had been by the Greeks. Roman architecture is therefore much more plastic and adventurous, with structural possibilities exploited to the full. The Orders were often used to clothe walls and arcaded structures. Vaults and domes were constructed of stone, brick, and concrete, while surfaces were stuccoed or clothed in marble or mosaic. The structural use of the arch and the vault made great engineering works possible so that huge cities and an efficient government could exist. The Romans developed tenement blocks as well as villas, and solved problems of mass housing on a metropolitan scale. Public buildings and monuments tended to be grandiose, glorifying the divine Emperors or Roman arms as well as the deities in the Roman Pantheon. Greek monumental buildings, including temples, tended to be remote background edifices for ritual or ceremony. Roman architecture paid more attention to use and to interiors. The baths and basilicas were examples of public buildings for use, while the theatres, amphitheatres, and circuses catered for spectacle on a vast scale. The triumphalism of Roman architecture became absorbed into Early Christian basilican churches, while the plastic use of concrete to span vast areas catered for large-scale public activities. Roman heating, services, and hygiene were models for civilised living not to be attained again until modern times. Lessons of Roman construction were kept alive by the Eastern or Byzantine Empire, and to a certain extent by the religious orders. (See **Orders**, Fig H **Temple**)

Romanesque A style of architecture in Europe from the tenth century until the end of the twelfth, characterised by the use of the semicircular arch and by simple geometrical planning, massive walls and columns, and by the use of apses, often domed. Bays in churches are usually square to facilitate vaulting which was in use on a small scale throughout, but only on a large scale from about 1000 AD. Capitals are usually free adaptations of Roman or Byzantine forms, while mouldings are vigorous and barbaric. Romanesque work in England is known as Norman. Some authorities include work from the seventh century in the Romanesque period, but Early Christian and Byzantine influences are apparent before 900 AD. Very late Saxon work is undoubtedly influenced by Romanesque art. (See **Norman**)

Roman Cement Parker's or brown cement, a common early-nineteenth-century rendering.

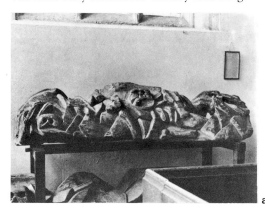

Rood
a) Fragment of the Golgotha scene from the base of a rood in the church at Cullompton, Devon
b) Rood and screen in the Church of St Dionysius, Bradninch, Devon. Note the fan-vaulting coving, and the cornice with three strips of foliage scrollwork

Roman Order The Composite Order. (See Fig d **Orders**)

Rood A cross or crucifix, often flanked by figures of St John and Our Blessed Lady. The rood was often wooden and set up on a beam across the chancel arch or above the rood loft over a screen separating the choir from the nave. The rood figures in such a position were often more than life size and incorporated representations of Golgotha. The rood loft was a gallery over the screen built to carry the heavy rood, with associated figures and tapers and with access from stairs in the adjacent masonry. The Reformation and subsequent iconoclasm destroyed many lofts and most roods, although an interesting fragment of a Golgotha survives at Cullompton in Devon. Rood lofts were sometimes situated above the chancel arch, as at Northleach in Gloucestershire. The term rood tower refers to the central tower over the crossing. (See **Golgotha**)

Roof The external covering on top of a building, sometimes of stone but more often of wood overlaid with slates, tiles, lead, etc. Medieval timber roofs are very varied, and only a few examples can be mentioned here. The simplest wooden structure is a *cruck*, composed of two curved timbers set on or in the ground meeting at a point, serving as the principal frame as well as the main truss. (See Fig **Cruck**). Roofs that are triangular in section can be composed of a series of main trusses at certain centres resting on the wall plates and carrying the purlins on which the common rafters rest. The commonest trusses are: the *king-post*, with a central vertical post, tie beam, braces or struts, and principal rafters; the *queen-post*, like the king-post, but with two vertical posts on either side of the centre line of the truss; and the *Hammer-beam*, springing from corbels carried on curved braces and supporting hammer-beams which in turn carry arched braces that carry the principal rafters and collar beams.

The various parts of such trusses are: *braces* which are diagonally placed to strengthen the frame; *collar beams* which tie the principal rafters together at high level; *common rafters* which are timbers rising from the wall plates to the ridge, and supported by the purlins; *hammer beams* which are horizontal brackets, or brackets carrying arched braces; *king posts* which rise from tie beams or collar beams to the ridge piece; *principal rafters* which carry the purlins; *purlins* which are horizontal timbers spanning from truss to truss

a

b

Roof
a) The Perpendicular nave roof of the Church of St Swithun, Merton, Oxfordshire. Note the carved corbels, carrying the wall posts from which the braces spring to support the main beams. These beams in turn carry posts that support the ridge and purlins
b) Boarded Wagon-roof with angel brackets and cross-ribs to the panels, and bosses showing the carved rood beam surmounted by the royal arms in place of the rood. From the Church of St Andrew, Cullompton, Devon

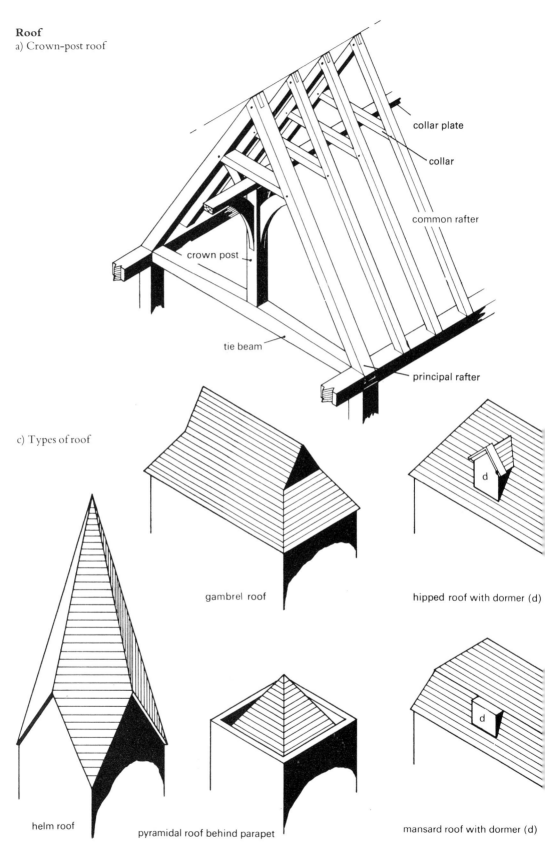

Roof
a) Crown-post roof

collar plate

collar

common rafter

crown post

tie beam

principal rafter

c) Types of roof

gambrel roof

hipped roof with dormer (d)

helm roof

pyramidal roof behind parapet

mansard roof with dormer (d)

b) Queen-post roof

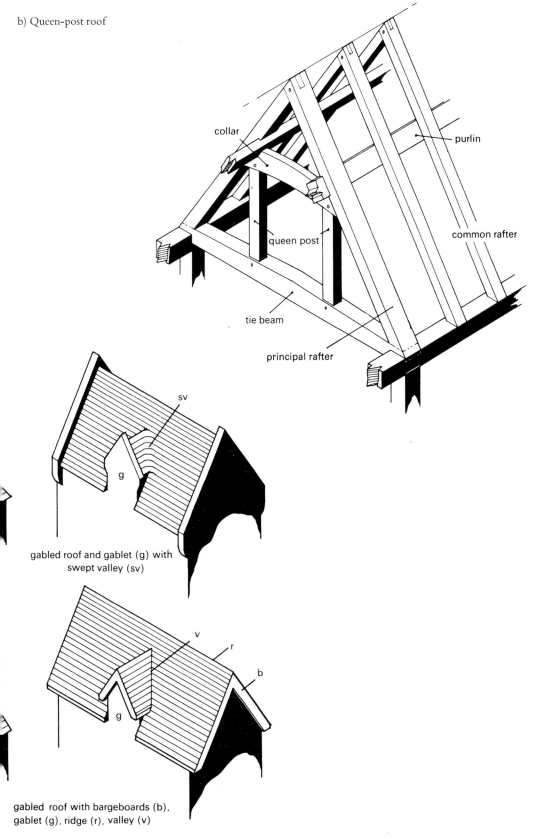

collar

purlin

queen post

common rafter

tie beam

principal rafter

sv

g

gabled roof and gablet (g) with
swept valley (sv)

v

r

b

g

gabled roof with bargeboards (b),
gablet (g), ridge (r), valley (v)

145

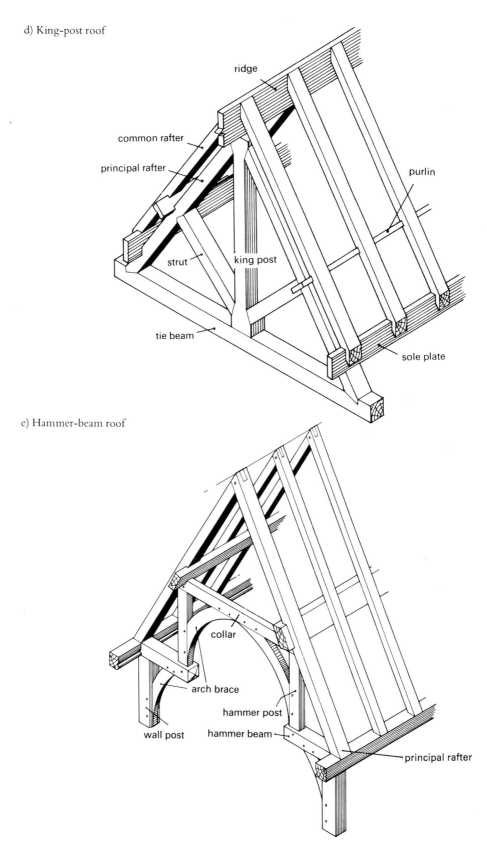

d) King-post roof

ridge

common rafter

principal rafter

purlin

strut

king post

tie beam

sole plate

e) Hammer-beam roof

collar

arch brace

hammer post

wall post

hammer beam

principal rafter

f) Scissor-truss roof with arch bracing

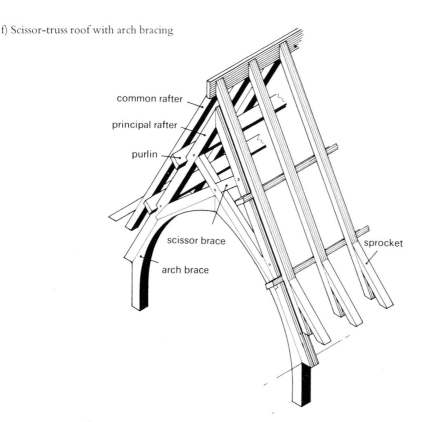

common rafter

principal rafter

purlin

scissor brace

arch brace

sprocket

and which carry the common rafters; *queen posts* which rise from tie beams or collar beams to carry the principal rafters; *struts* which are straight braces; *tie beams*, which are the main ties of trusses, preventing them from spreading and which carry the king and queen posts; and *wall plates* which lie on the walls to give fixings for the trusses and rafters.

Coupled roofs have no ties or collars, whereas *close couple* roofs have ties. A *collar* roof has the tie above wall-plate level. A *double* or *purlin* roof has purlins as intermediate supports for the common rafters. *Gambrel* roofs are hipped, with small gables below the ridge. *Helm* roofs rise to a point, with gables at the foot of each face. *Hipped* roofs have no gables, the ends being inclined like the sides. *Lean-to* roofs have one slope built against a higher wall. *Mansard* or *curb* roofs have two inclined planes. (See also **Belfast, Common, Compass, Cut, Double-framed, Jerkin-head, M-Roof, Saddleback, Span**)

Rose, Rosette An ornament like a rose used to decorate strings, etc.

Rosette A patera, or rose.

Rose Window A circular window with com-partments of tracery. A wheel window has definite spokes and is less floral in design.

Rostrum A beak like the prow of a ship. An elevated dais or platform.

Rotunda A building that is circular, often with a colonnade. A circular domed room.

Roughcast Rendering of mortar, with coarse aggregate thrown on to a wall, known in its coarse form as pebbledash.

Roundel A bead or astragal. A circle. A circular panel.

Rubbed Jointing Masonry joints rubbed to ensure a close fit. (Scots)

Rubble-work Masonry of rough undressed stones. Random rubble is uncoursed. Coursed rubble is laid in layers. Squared rubble is roughly dressed. (See Fig b **Masonry**)

Rudenture Cabling.

Ruderation Walls of rough pebbles and mortar. Also a method of laying pavements.

Run Fall. (Scots)

Running Dog A Classical ornament in a frieze, also called a Vitruvian scroll, with wave-like repetitive motifs. (See Fig **Vitruvian Scroll**)

Rural Architecture Picturesque cottage architecture.

Rustic-work, Rustication Ashlar masonry, the joints of which are worked with grooves or channels to emphasise the work. Grooves may be moulded or plain. *Banded* rustication has only the horizontal joints grooved. *Chamfered* rustication has V-joints. *Cyclopean* rustication consists of big rough-faced blocks. *Pyramidal* or *diamond* rustication has the blocks to resemble pyramids or hipped roofs. *Frosted* rustication has carving simulating stalactites or icicles, to give a grotto-like effect. *Vermiculated* masonry has irregular grooves and holes over the face. A rusticated column has blocks of square ashlar at intervals along the shaft. Rustic quoins are stones at the corners of a building or at reveals which project beyond the face of the wall. (See Figs **Masonry**)

Rybat A reveal. (Scots)

Sabaton A broad-toed mail shoe in heraldic devices or sepulchral effigies.

Sacellum A small roofless enclosure. In church architecture the term means a chapel within a church, usually a memorial chapel.

Sacrarium A sacred apartment in a Roman house. The cell, or the adytum of a temple. The name is now given to the part of the chancel enclosed by the altar rails.

Sacristy, Sacristry A vestry attached to a church where vestments, sacred vessels, and other furniture used in worship are kept.

Saddle A board, of wood on the floor in a doorway between the jambs. A saddle in Scots usage is the apex stone to a gable or a splayed coping.

Saddle-back Roof A common pitched roof with gable ends on a tower.

Saddle-bars Iron bars set into stone to which lead panels are tied.

Sagitta An uncommon name for a keystone.

Sail-over A projection.

Salient A projection of any part of a building.

Sally A projection. The end of a timber cut with an interior angle, or bird's mouth.

Sally-port A postern gate. An underground way from one part of a fortified structure to another.

Salon, Saloon A lofty or spacious apartment situated in the centre of a building, often vaulted or domed, the equivalent of two storeys high, and frequently illuminated from high level. A public apartment for a specified purpose. A bar, usually of the better class.

Sanctuary The presbytery or eastern part of the choir of a church where the high altar is placed.

Sanctus Bell, Sancte-bell A small bell sounded at important moments of the Mass. The bell was placed in a small turret or sanctecote situated over the chancel arch above the roof of the church. (See Fig **Bellcote**)

Sandstone A stone composed of grains or particles of sand, either mixed with other mineral substances or adhering together without any visible cementing matter.

Saracenic (See **Arabian, Moresque**)

Sarcophagus A stone coffin, but very grand, usually ornamented and heroic in scale.

Sarcophagus
The tomb of Princess Sophia (d 1848), daughter of King George III. The design was by Ludwig Grüner of Dresden, and the quattrocento-style sarcophagus was carved by the Signori Bardi. The podium is by Edward Pearce. In the background is the Greek Doric prostyle tetrastyle portico of the Anglican Chapel at the General Cemetery of All Souls, Kensal Green, London

Sash

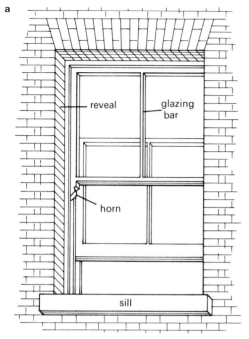

sash with hidden sash boxes

Horns became fashionable during the nineteenth century, but are not Georgian.

sash with exposed sash boxes

Sarking Thin boards for lining. Boards over the rafters before battening and tiling. Boarding for slating is called sarkin in Scotland.

Sash A frame for holding the glass in a window and capable of being raised and lowered in vertical grooves. Sashes are single- or double-hung, and are counterbalanced by weights in the lining. The frame in which sashes are fitted is called a sash frame, and the ropes on which sashes are suspended are called sash lines or cords.

Saves, Savers, Saving-stones Stones built over a lintel to distribute the load of the jambs, usually in the form of a relieving arch. (Scots)

Saxon Architecture Many Saxon buildings were of wood, but from the ninth century the more important buildings such as churches or monasteries were of stone, or were timber-framed structures. The Germanic tribes who settled in England from the fifth century onwards had a tradition of building with timber, but with the reintroduction of Christianity from Iona and Lindisfarne, and from Europe via St Augustine of Canterbury, stone-building techniques were reintroduced. The typical Saxon church is a hall rather than a basilica, usually with a chancel approached through an arch. Walls are of rag or rubble and quoins are placed alternately flat and on end, a form known as long and short work. Walls are ornamented externally with flat vertical pilaster strips, and on towers these strips are broken by plain horizontal strings. Walls are sometimes decorated with simple blind arcades of arches on vertical pilaster strips, either of semicircular or triangular arches formed of two straight stones resting against each other at the apex. Jambs are often composed of long and short work. Where there are imposts they are massive. Windows are small and are often found in pairs divided by small shafts or colonnettes shaped like balusters, which are encircled by bands of plain mouldings. Capitals are formed of long stones and may have rude carvings. Saxon details and methods of construction undoubtedly continued to be employed after the Conquest in 1066, and it is clear that a Norman style of architecture rapidly became peculiarly English as the two cultures mixed.

Scabellum A high pedestal to support busts or statues.

Scaffold A temporary erection of poles and planks to facilitate building. A gallery is also known as a scaffold. In the temporary structure sense, the upright poles are called *standards*; the horizontal timbers parallel to the walls are called *ledgers*; while the timbers at right angles to the walls, and fixed to them, are called *putlogs*. Putlogs provide the supports for the planks on which operatives can stand while working on the wall.

Scagliola A species of plaster or stucco with colouring matter introduced so that the finished, polished material resembles marble. Scagliola was known in Classical times, but reached a new perfection in the eighteenth century.

Scale Steps Steps with parallel nosings and equal goings. A scale and platt is a stair with straight flights and landings. (Scots).

Scallage, Scallenge A lich-gate.

Scallop An ornament resembling a scallop shell. (See Fig e **Capital**)

Scalpturatum Inlaid work, the pattern being chiselled out and filled with coloured marble.

Scamilli According to several nineteenth-century sources, these are plain blocks under columns or statues. Unlike pedestals they have no mouldings and are smaller in size. This meaning, however, has now been disputed. Gwilt says that the term *scamilli impares* means the horizontal lines of a classical building which incline almost imperceptibly from the ends to the centre to correct the optical illusion of bending.

Scandulae Shingles.

Scantling The dimensions of a piece of timber in breadth and thickness. The term also denotes a piece of timber under five square inches in area, such as partition quartering, or parts of a roof. In masonry, scantling is the length, breadth, and thickness of a stone.

Scape, Scapus The shaft of a column. The apophyge of the shaft.

Scappling, Scapling, Scabbling A method of tooling the face of a stone with a pick. The face is worked to a flat but not smooth surface.

Scarcement A plain flat set-off in a wall or foundation used as a shelf to carry the ends of joists.

Scarfing The joining of two pieces of timber so that the two pieces appear as one continuous piece.

Scarp The bank below the ramparts of a fortress.

Scene An alley or rural portico where theatrical performances could be given.

Scheme, Skene Arch A segmental arch.

Scissor-truss Roof A cross-shaped frame at intervals to support the purlins of a roof. (See Fig f **Roof**)

Sconce An earthwork or fortress. A screen. An arch formed across the angles of towers, ie a squinch.

Sconcheon The portion of the side of an aperture from the back of the jamb or reveal to the interior of the wall.

Scontion, Scuntion, Scuncheon A sconcheon, or the return of a pilaster. (Scots)

Scotia A concave moulding at the base of a column between the fillets of the torus mouldings, or under the nosing on a stair.

Scouchon, Skouchin (See **Squinch**)

Scratch Work A form of decoration consisting of a coat of coloured plaster covered with a white coat which is then scratched to reveal the colour. Also known as sgraffito.

Screed A large area of cement, usually forming the base for a tiled floor, or as a finish.

Screen A partition, enclosure or parclose, separating a portion of a room or a church from the rest. Screens are found in churches shutting off aisles from choirs, chapels from aisles, chancels from naves, and to protect tombs, etc. Many fine chancel screens survive, usually of wood but sometimes of stone. (See **Rood, Golgotha**)

Screens Passage A space at one end of a medieval hall, usually under the gallery and situated between the kitchen and a screen.

Scribbled Hammer-dressed joints in masonry with margins chiselled. (Scots)

Scroll A convoluted or spiral ornament. A

a

b

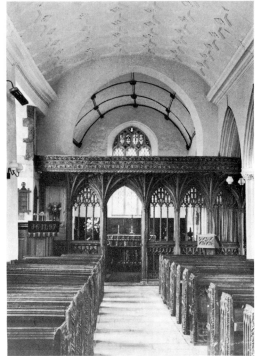

c

d

Screen

a) *above left* Church of St Dionysius, Bradninch, Devon. The fifteenth-century screen

b) *left* Detail of the Bradninch screen

c) *above right* Church of St John, Plymtree, Devon. An exceptionally fine chancel screen. Note the fifteenth-century bench ends, and the eighteenth-century vaulted ceiling

d) *above* Hereford Cathedral choir screen. Designed by Sir George Gilbert Scott, but sadly removed in 1967. It was manufactured by Skidmore of Coventry in 1862 and was shown at the International Exhibition of that year. It was made of iron, brass, and copper, and was set with about three hundred cut and polished stones. It was a masterpiece of High Victorian craftsmanship. Note the Vesica Piscis over the trumeau. *(Hereford City Library Reference 6387)*

volute of an Ionic, Corinthian, or Composite capital, or a moulding in the form of a scroll.

Scullery, Squillery The place where dishes, etc, are washed.

Sculpture Properly speaking, carved work. The terms modelling, casting and carving are also used to denote sculptured work.

Scutcheon The angle of a building or a part of a building, also called a sconcheon. A shield charged with armorial bearings in Gothic work. The term is also applied to the plate on a door from the centre of which the handle is suspended, or to the plate over the keyhole. (See Fig **Escutcheon**). In Scots usage, an escutcheon is known as a shield.

Section The representation of a building or part of a building cut asunder vertically to show the interior; or any moulding cut asunder transversely and represented to show its profile.

Sedilia Seats recessed in the south wall of the sanctuary of a church for the officiating clergy. Sedilia usually comprise three seats, and may be associated with the piscina. They are usually canopied and are often of stone. Also known as the prismatory.

See A seat, or a dais.

Segment A part cut off. A segmental arch is an arch which is only part of a semicircle.

Sell, Cell A habitation for an anchorite. For other meanings see **Cell.**

Semicircular Arch An arch in the form of a half-circle.

Sepulchre A grave, a tomb or a place of interment. A cenotaph is an empty memorial. (See **Easter Sepulchre**)

Serliana A Venetian window, ie an arched opening flanked by two rectangular openings. The openings have a cornice, pilasters or en-

Sedilia
a) Decorated canopies of the early-fourteenth century in Exeter Cathedral. Note the very elaborate superstructure and very fine detail
b) Early English sedilia in Exeter Lady Chapel. Note the detached shafts

gaged columns, and are generally found in Classical motifs. The term is named after the architect Serlio (1475–1554).

Setback Buttress This is like an angle buttress, but is set back from the corner on the face of the wall so that it does not join its counterpart at 90°, but leaves the corner of the building freely expressed. (See **Buttress**)

Set-off, Offset The part of a wall which is exposed upwards when the portion above it is reduced in thickness. In Gothic work, the set-offs are sloped, and have a projecting drip or throating on their lower edges.

Sett A squared stone used for paving.

Settlements Those parts in which failures by sinking in a building have occurred. The distortions produced by the unequal compression of the foundation.

Severans Probably a string or a cornice.

Severey, Severy A compartment or bay of a building or scaffold. The term is more usually given to a bay of a vault.

Sewer A large drain or conduit for carrying wastes.

Sexpartite A quadripartite vault is a bay divided into four cells. A sexpartite vault indicates that there is a rib dividing the bay in two, usually at the ridge or apex, so six compartments are formed in the bay. (See Fig B **Vault**)

Sgraffito (See **Scratch Work**)

Shaft The body of a column or pillar. The part between the capital and the base. In Gothic work the term is given to the small columns which are clustered round pillars, or used in the jambs of doors or windows. Gothic shafts are frequently of Purbeck marble and are polished. The part of a chimney-stack between the base and the cornice is called the shaft.

Shaft Ring A shaft ring or annulet is a Gothic detail of the twelfth and thirteenth centuries and consists of a ring around a shaft, at various heights, tying it back to the wall or pillar. (See Fig **Band of a Shaft**)

Shake A fissure in timber caused by its being dried too quickly.

Shakefork An heraldic Y.

Shamble, Shambles A name surviving in many streets meaning an abattoir or place where animals are slaughtered.

Shanks Spaces between the two channels of the Doric triglyph.

Sheet Glass Glass blown, opened out after slitting, and flattened.

Sheet Lead Cast lead as opposed to rolled lead.

Shelf A board fixed to a wall to carry objects.

Shell A very thin structure based on the eggshell principle, made of concrete and self-supporting.

Shilf Broken slates.

Shingles Wooden tiles used for roofing, also known as scandulae. Shingles are also loose stones used for gravel or concrete aggregate, known in Scotland as shivers.

Shivers Chips of broken stone. Shiver bottoming is hard-core filling. (Scots)

Shoar A shore.

Shoe The inclined piece at the bottom of a rainwater pipe to discharge the water into a gulley.

Shore A prop to support the side of a building.

Shouldered A shouldered arch consists of a lintel carried on quarter-arches supporting a short vertical. Shouldering is a fillet of haired lime laid on the upper edge of slates to prevent water penetrating.

Shreddings The same as firrings or furrings.

Shrine A fereter or repository for relics, sometimes a most substantial erection.

Shroud The crypt of a church.

Shuttering The temporary mould into which concrete is poured. It is made of timber or metal.

Shutters The doors or frames which cover a window from the outside or inside.

Side Posts Posts placed in pairs at an equal distance from the middle of a truss.

Side Timbers Purlins.

Sill, Cill, Sole, Sule The horizontal piece of timber or stone forming the bottom of a window, doorway, or other opening, usually and properly designed to throw water off.

Sima Cyma or Cymatium.

Single Frame, Single Joist, Naked Floor One with only one tier of joists.

Single Hung A sash window where only one sash moves.

Sinister The heraldic left (ie right when viewed from front).

Skeleton Frame A framed building with an outer watertight skin or curtain wall, or cladding.

Skew The sloping top of a buttress where it slants off into a wall, or the coping of a gable, also called a skew-table. A skew and crest is a cope with a roll moulding as a crest. Skews in Scots usage are slates in swept valleys.

Skew-back Part of an abutment carrying an arch.

Skew Corbel The stone built into the bottom of a gable to support the coping above, also known as a summer stone or a springer.

Skew-put The lowest stone of a gable.

Skirting The narrow board placed round the margin of a floor at the base of an internal wall. The skirts of a roof are the eaves.

Skylight A frame containing glass set in a roof.

Skyscraper A very tall building based on a steel or concrete frame.

Slab Any thin rectangular piece of stone. The hearth of a fireplace.

Slaistering A wet rendering. The term is derogatory and suggests slovenly work. (Scots)

Slate A kind of stone capable of being split or cut in very thin regular slabs and used for cladding or roofing. Slatehanging is a slate-covered wall.

Sleeper Timbers or plates laid under the ground floor of a building on which joists rest. The walls which support these timbers are called sleeper walls. They are found giving intermediate support to floor joists. A sleeper wall may also be placed between two structural elements, such as piers, in order to strengthen them and stop them shifting. The term sleepers may also be applied to any beams carrying joists or other structural pieces.

Slip-bolt A barrel-bolt. (Scots)

Slips Glazing beads or fillets. (Scots)

Sluice A dam which can be raised or lowered to regulate the flow of water.

Slype A covered corridor in a monastic building.

Snacket The hasp of a casement.

Sneck The lifting lever to lift a latch. Small stones in squared rubble. A sneck-head is a latch catch. Snecked harling leaves certain stones in the wall unharled. (Scots)

Socle, Zocle A plain block or low pedestal without mouldings.

Soffit, Soffite, Soffita A ceiling. The lower surface of an arch or vault. The under-surface of the corona of a cornice. The underside of any part of a building including arches. (See Fig **Arch**)

Solar A loft, garret, or upper chamber. A rood loft.

Solarium An upper chamber or sun terrace. A loggia.

Sole The foundation of a building, or the hearth of an oven. A sill, or the base of an embrasure.

Sole Plate (See Fig d **Roof**)

Solomonic Column A twisted, barley-sugar column.

Solum The area within the walls of a building after removal of the topsoil. (Scots)

Sopraporta A design or painting over a doorway of a room.

Sound-boarding Short boards between joists, carried on fillets and supporting pugging, to dampen sound.

Sounding-board, Sound-board A canopy or tester over a pulpit.

Souse A corbel.

Sowdels Saddle-bars.

Space Frame A framed roof structure of geometrical forms, usually made of light-weight tubing, and capable of covering large areas without intermediate support.

Spandrel, Splandrel The approximately triangular space between an arched doorway and a rectangle formed by the outer mouldings over it, drawn from the apex in a horizontal line, and from the springing in a vertical line. The surface between two arches is an arcade. Spandrels are sometimes called the hanses or haunches.

Span of an Arch The distance between the imposts.

Span Piece A collar beam.

Span Roof A roof of two inclined sides. The naves of churches are usually span-roofed, while aisles are shed-roofed, or lean-to roofed.

Spar, Sper, Spur Quarters, wooden bars, etc, but more commonly rafters. A spur is the term given to an ornamental bracket supporting the breastsummer and placed flanking doorways. A spar piece is the collar beam.

Sparred Shelving Slated shelving. (Scots)

Spawled A block of stone after the chips or spawls have been knocked off. To spall or spawl stone is to chip or chip off portions of its face.

Speak-house A parlour.

Specus The canal in which water flowed in aqueducts.

Spere, Spure A screen across the lower end of a medieval hall in a domestic building, marking off the screens passage between the hall and the kitchen.

Speroni Anterides.

Sperver, Sparver, Esperver The timber frame at the top of a bed or canopy, including a tester.

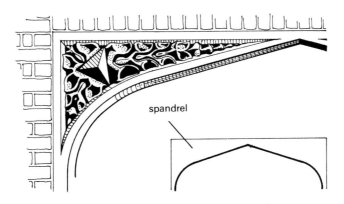

spandrel

Spandrel The example of a Tudor spandrel comes from Honingham Hall, Norfolk. See also **Arcade**

Sphaeristerium A building for ball-games.

Spire An acutely pointed termination of turrets and towers forming the roof and often carried up to a great height. Spires are of stone, or of timber covered with slates, tiles, shingles, or lead. The earliest spires rose directly from the bases on which they sat, so they corresponded with the towers in terms of plan, with no gutters or parapets. Early English spires were very elevated and many were octagonal and set on square towers so that the angles not covered by the tower were occupied by pinnacles or by masses of masonry that sloped back towards the spire. A *broach* spire is one that is octagonal but rises from a square tower without a parapet or gutter, with these masses of masonry, or sometimes slate-covered broaches, built into the sides of the spire and carried to points. Broach spires are also found during the Decorated period. A *needle* spire is a very thin, tall spire rising from within a parapet on a tower. The term spire is sometimes given to the base of a column, or sometimes to the torus or astragal.

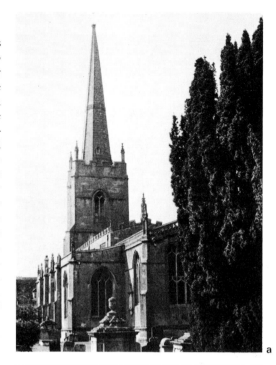

a

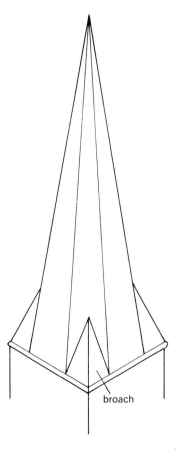

broach

Spire A broach spire

b

c

Spire
a) Church of St Lawrence, Lechlade, Gloucestershire. Note the needle spire set behind the parapet
b) The remarkable three spires of Lichfield Cathedral. Note the lucarnes in the spires
c) Christ Church, Spitalfields, by Nicholas Hawksmoor, built 1714–29. Note the giant Tuscan Order of the portico. The face of the tower appears very wide by virtue of its flanking buttresses, and the whole tower is crowned by a broach spire. This extraordinary composition, with its eclectic use of many motifs, has Mannerist and Baroque aspects. The giant portico is partly a triumphal arch and partly a gigantic Venetian window

Spirelet A small spire or flèche.

Spital A hospital.

Splandrel A spandrel.

Splay, Embrasure The expansion given to openings by slanting the sides to admit more light. Anything that is bevelled or sloped.

Springing, Springer The impost or point which an arch unites with its support. The bottom stone of the arch on the impost is called the springer. The term springer is sometimes given to the bottom stone of a gable. Springed, or sprung, indicates roof boarding or sarking with bevel joints to prevent water penetration. The springing course is the horizontal course of

stones from which an arch springs. In Scots usage a spring-board is a string, while a spring snib is a sash fastener.

Sprocket A wedge-shaped piece of timber, especially one fixed to the foot of a rafter on its upper side to raise the level of the eaves, and tilt the roof slightly at the eaves. (See Fig f **Roof**)

Spudds and Rings Rings of iron into which doorposts are placed, with a projection or spudd for insertion into a corresponding hole in the step or sill.

Spur, Spure Carved timberwork at a doorway supporting the bressumer. A short strut or stay set diagonally to support something. A shore, a prop, a sustaining pillar, a sloping buttress. An angular outwork or projection from the general face of a curtain or wall to assist in defence. The angular edge of the pier of a bridge. A spur-stone is a stone that projects from the corner of a building to prevent its being damaged by carts, etc.

Square
Part of Myddelton Square, Clerkenwell, by William Chadwell Mylne, of 1829–30. A typical late-Georgian square

Square A figure of four equal sides and right-angled corners. An area of such form surrounded by houses, and usually paved or planted in the centre.

Squared Rubble Rubble-work where the stones are roughly squared.

Squillery A scullery.

Squinch A small arch formed across an angle, eg to support the alternate sides of octagonal spires. Squinches may be corbelled pieces built out

Squint
St Mary's Church, Charminster, Dorset. Norman chancel arch (c 1100) with nail-head ornament. Note the hagioscope or squint, and the door to the missing rood loft. The pointed arches of the nave are Transitional Norman, and the scallop shell capitals should be noted

course by course across a corner to support something above. (See Fig c **Dome**)

Squint An opening through the wall of a church in an oblique direction to enable people in the transepts or aisles to see the high altar. Squints are usually placed on either side of the chancel arch. They are also called hagioscopes.

Stable A building for the accommodation of horses.

Stack (See **Chimney**)

Staddle Stones The stones forming mushroom shapes to give a secure base to timber-built barns. They not only protect the timber from the wet ground, but prevent rats and mice from climbing up.

Stadium A place for athletics.

Staff Bead A corner or angle bead.

Stage A floor or storey. In a theatre it is where the action takes place. The stage of a buttress or tower is the part between one splayed projection or string and the next.

Stained Glass Glass stained through its thickness during its manufacture is called pot-metal glass, while white glass coloured on the surface is called flashed glass. Stained glass is secured in lead cames and is arranged in patterns.

Stair, Staircase That part of a building where there are steps to enable persons to get from one storey or level of a building to another. The *apron* is a board that covers the trimmer joist of a landing. *Balusters* are vertical bars that support the handrail and protect the open sides. The *balustrade* consists of a handrail, a string, balusters and newels. *Bearers* are members that support the steps. *Blocks* are fixed to the upper edges of bearers and give additional support to the treads: the term is also given to the small pieces of wood of triangular section that are glued to the angles between the treads and risers on the underside. *Brackets* serve the same purpose as blocks. *Cappings* are the cover mouldings planted on the upper edges of strings. *Easing* is a curved portion connecting two strings. A *flight* is a continuous set of steps from one landing to another. The *going* or *run of a step* is the distance measured

Stair
a) The extraordinary stair to the chapterhouse at Wells Cathedral
b) Part of the staircase of 14 Fournier Street, Spitalfields, built in 1726. Note the tread brackets carved with flowers and foliage scrolls. The balusters are turned and twisted, and the newels are fluted Ionic columns

horizontally between two risers. The *going of a flight* is the horizontal distance between the face of the bottom riser and that of the top riser. *Headroom* is the height measured vertically from the line of the nosings to the lower outer edge of the apron or to the soffit of a flight above. A *landing* is a platform between the flights, or the floor at the top of a stair. A quarter-space landing is one on which a quarter-turn has to be made between the end of one flight and the beginning of the next. If the landing extends for the combined width of both flights and a complete half-turn has to be made, it is known as a half-space landing. The *line of the nosings* is a line drawn to touch the projecting edges or nosings of the treads. *Newels* are vertical members placed at the ends of flights to support the strings, handrails, trimmers, and bearers. The top of a newel is called a cap and its lower end is the drop. *Nosing* is the front edge of a tread which projects beyond the face of the riser. The *pitch* or *slope* is the angle between the line of nosings and the floor or landing. The *riser* is the vertical part or front member of the step. The *rise of a step* is the vertical distance between the tops of two consecutive treads. The *rise of a flight* is the total height from floor to floor, or landing to landing, or floor to landing. The *scotia* is a concave moulding under the nosing. The *soffit* is the under-surface of the stair. The *spandrel* is a triangular surface between an outer string and the floor. *Strings* or *stringers* are the inclined timbers that support the steps. The *tread* is the horizontal member which forms the upper surface of a step. The *well* is the space between the outer strings of the several flights of a stair. A *closed-string* stair has strings of continuous raking members supporting identical balusters. An *open*, or *cut-string*

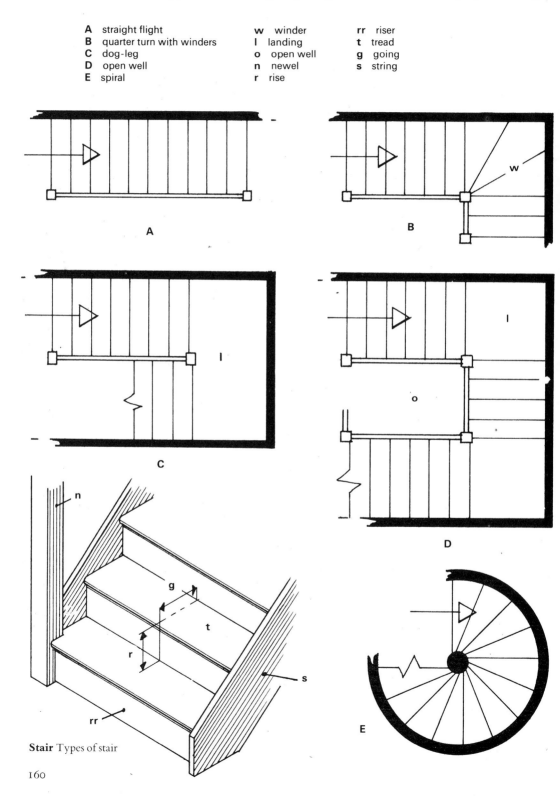

A	straight flight	**w**	winder	**rr**	riser
B	quarter turn with winders	**l**	landing	**t**	tread
C	dog-leg	**o**	open well	**g**	going
D	open well	**n**	newel	**s**	string
E	spiral	**r**	rise		

Stair Types of stair

stair, has strings cut to the profiles of the treads that support balusters of unequal length. In the latter case, two balusters per tread are usual in early eighteenth-century work, increasing to three by the mid-century, and accompanied, in the better class of work, by elaborately carved tread-ends. Different types of stair include the *dog-leg*, where two flights are parallel to each other with a landing joining them and no well between the outer strings; *geometrical* stairs which have no newels, are usually circular or elliptical on plan, and consist of stone steps with one end built into the wall and resting on the step below; *newel* or *spiral* stairs where the steps wind round a central column; the *open-well* stair which has a space or well between the outer strings, and thus differs from a dog-leg; *straight-flight* stairs; and *turning* stairs, including quarter-turn, half-turn, three-quarter turn and bifurcated where stairs divide into two branches. (See also **Close String, Cockle, Cut-string, Dancing Steps, Turngrece, Turnpike, Vice**)

Stalactites Corbelled squinches carved to resemble stalactites. Stucco or stone carved or shaped to resemble stalactites, especially in grottoes.

Stalk An ornament in the Corinthian capital from which spring volutes and helices.

Stall An elevated seat in the chancel of a church. It is a fixed seat enclosed either wholly or partially at the back and sides. In cathedrals or large churches it was enclosed at the back with panelling and surmounted by overhanging canopies of openwork, and formed part of serried rows of stalls. The open canopies were richly ornamented, enriched with pinnacles, crockets, tracery, and the like. The stall seats, if hinged, frequently had carved grotesques on the underside. (See **Misericord**). Stalls are also the divisions in stables or other places.

Stanchion A prop or other vertical support. The term was also given to the upright iron bars between mullions in Gothic work. Mullions are also known as stanchions, as are the quarters or studs of a partition.

Standard Massive items, not easily moved, such as chests or candlesticks, or the vertical poles of a scaffold. The supports for shelves are also called standards. In Scots usage, standards are door posts, quartering, or uprights in stud partitions.

Starlings Piles round the piers of a bridge. The term starling is also given to the cutwater of a pier of a bridge.

Star Moulding A decoration like a band of stars.

Staves Small upright cylinders to form a rack to contain the hay in a stable. A stave-church is a timber-framed and timber-walled church found in Scandinavia. A stave in Scots usage is a caulk.

Stay A brace. A stay-bar is a horizontal iron bar which extends along the top of the mullions of a traceried window.

Staykfald Hole A putlog hole.

Steening Brickwork laid dry with no mortar to form the shaft of a well.

Steeple The tower and the spire of a church, housing bells.

Stell An enclosure for sheep, usually circular.

Step A block of any material of a height within the lift of a person's foot.

Stereobata, Stereobate The stylobate.

Stiff-leaf Gothic foliage of the thirteenth century on capitals and bosses consisting of stylised foliage. (See Fig b **Capital**)

Stile The vertical part of a frame into which the ends of rails are fixed with mortises and tenons, as in a panelled door. (See **Door**)

Stile Liberty A type of Art Nouveau.

Stiles In joinery, the upright pieces of a frame, as of a door, or panelling. The horizontals are called rails. (See Fig **Door**)

Stillicidium Dripping eaves on Doric buildings.

Still-room A room where preserves, biscuits, etc, are made.

Stilted Arch An arch where the springing begins above the impost, giving the arch an elongated appearance.

Stoa A colonnade or portico, or a covered hall in the Byzantine style.

Stop Chamfer A seventeenth-century example of a stop-chamfered beam

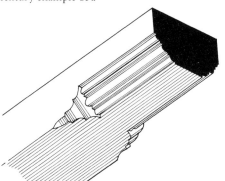

Stoep A verandah.

Stoneware Clay burnt and glazed used for drainpipes, etc.

Stoothing Battening of walls.

Stop Anything against which a moulding stops, such as a projecting stone or piece of wood.

Stop Chamfer The decorative treatment of the transition between a chamfer and a normal square arris.

Stopping Making good of cracks or defects in plastering, wood, etc.

Storey, Story One of the vertical divisions of a building. The space between two floors, or between two entablatures or any other horizontal division. Storeys are divided into basement, ground, first or piano nobile if the principal floor, second, third, etc, then attic, meaning above the main cornice. (See Fig **Georgian**). Entresols and mezzanines are intermediate storeys. Vertical divisions of towers are called stages. Storey posts are the main upright posts carrying the wall of a timber-framed building.

Stoup A vessel for holding consecrated water placed near the entrance to a church, usually in a simple niche, or cantilevered out. It is also called a holy-water stone.

Stove An enclosed fire-gate.

Straight Arch A lintel of voussoirs based on the principle of an arch but with a flat intrados, and common in Georgian architecture.

Straightening Plaster rendering for dubbing-out rubble or stone walls with irregular surfaces. (Scots)

Strainer Arch An arch across an aisle or a nave to prevent movement of the walls.

Straining Piece A brace or strut.

Strap An iron plate for the connection of two or more timbers to which it is bolted. Strapping or straps in Scots usage are battening, firrings, or plugged and nailed grounds.

Strapwork A form of decoration, usually of wood or plaster, consisting of interlaced bands like leather straps, much used in Elizabethan and Jacobean times. (See Fig **Altar Tomb**)

Stretcher A brick or stone laid with its longer face in the surface of the wall. A stretching course is a course composed of stretchers.

Striae Lists or fillets between the flutes of columns or pilasters.

Striated Chamfered or channelled.

Striges The flutes of a column.

String The sloping members of timber carrying the ends of the treads and risers of a stair. A string or stringcourse is a horizontal band or line of mouldings on a building. (See **Stairs**)

Strix A flute in a column.

Strut A brace. Any piece that keeps two other members apart. It is in a state of compression, unlike a tie which keeps two members together and is therefore in tension. (See Fig d **Roof**)

Stucco Calcareous cement, or plasterwork. Strictly speaking, stucco is calcium carbonate mixed with marble dust, glue, and hair.

Studio An apartment, usually with a north light, for artwork.

Studs The quarters or posts in wooden partitions.

Stuff Timber for joinery.

Stugged Pecked stone faced with a pointed tool. (Scots)

Stump Tracery Tracery where ribs pass through each other and are then abruptly cut off.

Stupa A domed sepulchre of Far Eastern origin.

Stylobate, Stereobata, Stereobate A continuous base or substructure in Classical architecture on which a colonnade is placed. (See Fig A **Temple**)

Subway Any underground passage for pedestrians, sewers and services, etc.

Sule A sill.

Summer A lintel, or a breastsummer.

Summer-, Sommer-beam A main beam or girder in a floor. The term breastsummer or bressumer is given to the main beam in the front of a timber-framed building, or over a shop-front.

Summer Stone The lowest stone of a gable stopping at the eaves. The first stone of the tabling is set into the summer stone. It is also called a skew corbel.

Sun Light Gas jets placed under a reflector.

Superaltar A shelf over the altar, or to the east of it, on which are placed vases, etc, not permitted to be placed on the altar itself.

Supercilium A lintel of a door.

Superstructure Work built on the foundations of a building.

Surbase The upper mouldings or cornice of a pedestal or dado.

Surbased An arch, vault or dome of less height than half its span.

Surmounted An arch, vault or dome rising higher than half its span.

Swag A festoon like a cloth or string of flowers or fruit held on two supports.

Swallow-tail A swallow-tail or dove-tail moulding is an ornament formed of running bands, sometimes called a triangular fret.

Swan-neck A double-curved member.

Symbol An attribute or sign accompanying a statue or picture to denote the identity. As a guide to the identity of some saints, the following motifs may prove useful.

almond tree in a flowerpot Our Blessed Lady at the Annunciation.
alms St Elisabeth.
altar prayer by altars: SS Clement and Canute; murder before an altar: St Thomas of Canterbury and St Winifred.
anchor SS Clement, Nicholas and Felix.
angel SS Matthew and others.
angel trampling a dragon or weighing souls St Michael.
anvil SS Giles and Adrian.
apples SS Dorothy and Nicholas.
armour SS George (especially), Michael (the War in Heaven), Maurice, Pancras, Victor, Eustace, Armil.
arms and legs removed St Adrian.
arrow SS Sebastian, Cosmas and Damian, Ursula, Giles, Christina, and Thomas.
arrow, crowned figure pierced by St Edmund the King.
asperge SS Benedict, Peter, Robert, Martha, and many others.
axe SS Boniface and Mathias.
bag or purse SS Matthew and Sitha, and Judas Iscariot.
ball of fire St Benedict.
balls St Nicholas.
barn St Bridget of Kildare.
basket SS Elisabeth, Dorothy, Philip, Sitha.
battleaxe SS Olaf or Olave, Alphege, Thomas of Canterbury.
beard, especially on women SS Mary, Barbara, Galla, Wilgefortis.
bed St Faith.
beehive SS Ambrose, Bernard, John Chrysostom.
beggar SS Elisabeth, Martin, Alexis, Giles, Medard.
beggar, with feet being washed St Edith.
bell SS Anthony and Benedict.
bellows St Genevieve.
blind, restored to seeing SS Magnus, Birinus, Vedast, Wulstan, and, exceptionally, Paul.

birds   SS Macentius, Paul the Hermit, Blaise, Remigius, and Francis.

boar   SS Anthony and Blaise.

boat   SS Jude, Mary Magdalene, and Julian.

boathook   St Jude.

bodkin   SS Leger and Simon of Trent.

books, three   St Hilary.

bottle and shears   SS Cosmas and Damian.

bow   SS Sebastian or Edmund.

bowels   SS Erasmus and Vincent.

box of money   St Matthew.

box of ointments   SS Mary Magdalene, Joseph of Arimathea, Cosmas and Damian.

boys in cauldron   St Nicholas.

branch   SS Brendan, Bridget, Kentigern or Mungo.

bread   SS Olave, Philip, Nicholas, Sitha, Cuthbert, Roche, Gertrude, Paul the Hermit.

breast   used as an altar it represents St Lucian; breasts cut off suggest SS Agatha, Sophia and her daughters.

briars   St Benedict.

broom   SS Petronella and Sitha.

bull   SS Eustace, Luke, and Polycarp.

calves   St Wulstan.

candles   SS Genevieve, Beatrix and Blaise.

cardinal's hat   SS Jerome and Mark.

carpenter's tools   SS Thomas, Joseph, Jude, Matthew.

cart   St Bavo.

casket   SS Cosmas and Damian, and Mary Magdalene.

cauldron   SS Lucy, Cecilia, Erasmus, John the Evangelist, Felicitas, Boniface, Cyprian, and others.

cave   SS Benedict, Blaise, Giles and Leonard.

chafing dish   St Agatha.

chain   SS Leonard, Ninian, German, Ignatius, Peter and Bridget of Sweden.

chalice   SS John the Evangelist, Benedict, Barbara, Giles, Richard, Thomas Aquinas, and Bruno.

chalice and winged serpent   St John the Evangelist.

chasuble   SS Alphege and Thomas of Canterbury.

chest   SS Ethelreda, Rumold.

children   St Nicholas.

church   SS Botolph, Helen, Osmund, Peter, Martin, and others.

cloak   SS Martin and Alban.

club   SS James the Less and Simon. Also SS Vitalis, Lambert, Magnus, Valentine and Jude.

coals   SS Lambert and Brice.

cock   St Peter.

coffin   St Ouen.

comb   St Blaise.

coronation   St Edward the Confessor.

corpse   St Silvester.

cow   SS Perpetua, Bridget, and others.

cripple   SS Elizabeth and Martin.

cross   All popes.

crown of thorns   SS Francis of Assisi, Catherine and King Louis.

crucified figures, upside down   SS Peter and Philip.

crucifix   especially SS Columba, Francis and Thomas Aquinas.

cup   SS John the Evangelist, Benedict, Edward and Mary Magdalene.

dagger   SS Olave, Canute, Edward, and Agnes.

dart   SS Lambert, Cosmas and Damian.

diagonal cross or saltire   St Andrew.

dish   St Oswald.

dog   St Roche.

dove   SS Bridget of Sweden, Catherine, Lo, Hilary, Gregory, and many others.

dragon   SS George, Michael, Margaret, Julian, German and others.

dragon and crozier   St Margaret.

eagle   SS John the Evangelist, Gregory, and Augustine of Hippo.

eyes   SS Lucy, Leger and Alban.

falcon   SS Bavo, Edward and Mary.

female figure with several small virgins   St Ursula.

fetters   SS Leonard, Ninian and German.

figure carrying the Gospel of St John   St Edmund.

figure holding a head in its hands   St Denis, or if female, St Winifred.

fire   SS Patrick, Barnabas, Aidan, Boniface, Lo, Martin, Bridget of Kildare and Januarius.

fish   especially associated with SS Raphael, Andrew, Simon, Jude, Boniface, Peter and Zeno.

flames, walked on   SS Anthony, Polycarp, Vincent, Bridget of Kildare and Agnes.

flaying knife   St Bartholomew.

flowers   SS Mary, Dorothy, Cecilia, and Sitha.

font   SS Patrick, Silvester and others.

fountain   SS Clement, Boniface, Augustine of Canterbury, Leonard, Humbert, Paul and especially Mary.

fruit   SS Dorothy and Anne.

furnace   St Victor.

geese   SS Martin and Vedast.

girdle   SS Thomas, Margaret and Thomas Aquinas.

goat   St Anthony.

grail   St Joseph of Arimathea.

gridiron   SS Lawrence, Vincent, Faith and Cyprian.

hair   SS Mary Magdalene and Agnes.

hammer   SS Adrian and William.

handkerchief   St Veronica.

hands   SS Adrian, Martin and others.

harp   SS Cecilia and Dunstan.

hawk   SS Julian, Edward and others.

head   SS John the Baptist, Clare, Denis, Alban, Firmin, Winifred, Osyth, and many others.

heart   SS Augustine of Hippo, Benedict, Clare, Francis, Catherine of Siena and others. With the IHS monogram, this symbol is especially that of St Ignatius.

hermit   very common, but usually SS Christopher and Jerome.

hind   St Giles.

holy water   St Martha.

hook   SS Vincent, Agatha, and Hippolytus.

horn   SS Cornelius, Oswald and Hubert.

horse and cart   St Bavo.

horses, three   St Hippolytus.

hunters   SS Eustace, German and Herbert.

jug   St Vincent.

keys   especially St Peter, but also Hubert, Sitha, Hippolytus, Genevieve, Mary, Martha, James, and others.

knife   SS Bartholomew, Matthew and Peter the Martyr.

ladder   SS Olave, Perpetua and Leonard.

ladle   St Martha.

lamb   SS Agnes, Genevieve, John the Baptist or Catherine.

lamb and flag   (agnus dei) St John the Baptist.

lamp   SS Lucy or Francis.

lance   SS Hippolytus, German, Oswin, Thomas, Michael, Barbara, Philip and others.

lantern   SS Gudula or Hugh.

lily   SS Joseph, Gabriel, Kenelm, Sebastian, Clare, Dominic, Mary and Catherine of Siena.

lion   SS Jerome, Adrian, Dorothy and Ignatius.

lion, winged   St Mark.

loaf   SS Olave, Philip, Nicholas, Sitha, Cuthbert, Roche, Gertrude and Paul the Hermit.

lute   St Cecilia.

mallets   St Denis.

manacles   St Leonard.

millstone   SS Vincent, Christina, Crispin.

money   SS Matthew, Philip, and Martin; and Judas Iscariot.

monstrance   St Clare.

nails   SS Giles, King Louis, and others.

neck   SS Agnes and Cecilia.

oak, being cut   St Boniface.

oar   SS Jude, Julian, and others.

oil   St Vitus.

ointment box   SS Mary Magdalene, Joseph of Arimathea, Cosmas and Damian, and Joanna.

organ   St Cecilia.

our Lord being carried across a river   St Christopher.

ox   SS Luke, Silvester, Leonard, Frideswide (especially round Oxford), Polycarp and Lucy.

painting   St Luke.

palm   SS John the Evangelist and Catherine: a symbol of martyrdom.

palm branch and saracen   St Pancras.

physicians   SS Cosmas and Damian, and Luke.

pig   St Anthony.

pincers   SS Dunstan, Agatha and Lucy.

pitcher   St Bede.

plough   St Kentigern or Mungo.

rack   St Vincent.

rain   St Swithin.

raven   SS Benedict, Oswald, Vincent, and others.

ring   SS Edward, Barbara, and Peter.

rock   SS Peter, Martin and Gregory.

rods   SS Benedict and Faith.

roses   an especial symbol of the Blessed Virgin, but also of SS Dorothy, Barbara, and others.

salmon and ring   St Kentigern or Mungo.

saw   SS Simon, James the Less, and George.

scales   St Michael and others.

scallop shell   SS James and Roche.

sceptre   royal saints such as Olave, Oswald, Edmund, Edward, Louis, and Margaret.

scourge   SS Ambrose, Boniface and others.

serpent   SS John the Evangelist, Benedict, Francis, Patrick, Magnus and others.

shears   SS Agatha, and Cosmas and Damian.

sheep   SS Margaret, Genevieve, and others.

ship   SS Jude and Ursula.

shoes   SS Crispin and Theobald.

sick people   SS Luke, Cosmas and Damian.

skin, flayed   SS Bartholomew, Crispin, and many others.

skull   SS Jerome, Mary Magdalene and others.

staff   SS Joseph of Arimathea, Etheldreda, Ninian, Christopher.

staff and banner   St James the Less.

staff, hat and scallop   St James.

staff (pastoral) being struck on tomb   St Wulfstan.

staff and two doves   St Joachim.

stag   SS Aidan, Julian and Kentigern or Mungo.

stag with crucifix   SS Eustace and Herbert.

star   SS Dominic, Bruno, Thomas Aquinas and especially the Virgin.

stigmata   SS Francis and Catherine of Siena.

stones   SS Pancras, Matthew, Timothy, Stephen, Barnabas, Jerome and Olave.

stones in a chasuble   St Alphege.

swan   SS Hugh, Cuthbert and Leger.

sword   St Paul.

sword piercing woman's heart   Our Blessed Lady.

sword through neck   SS Agatha, Agnes, Lucy and others.

T-shaped cross   St Philip.

thorn   SS Joseph of Arimathea, Mark, Jerome, Benedict, and Dominic.

tiara   any pope, or the Virgin.

tongue   St Leger.

tooth   St Apollonia.

torch   SS Blaise, Aidan, Barbara and Dorothy.

tower   SS Barbara, Ambrose, and others.

tree over head of sleeping girl   St Etheldreda.

turtle doves (a pair)   Our Blessed Lady at Her Purification.

vase   SS Mary Magdalene, Cosmas and Damian, and others.

veil   SS Veronica, Agnes, and others.

violin   St Cecilia.

well   SS Sebastian, Sitha, Cyr, and others.

wheel   SS Catherine and Quentin.

wine   St Elizabeth.

wolf   SS Vedast, Blaise, Columba, Edmund, and Kentigern.

woman teaching Our Lady to read   St Anne.

writing, by scribes   St John the Divine and the Evangelists.

The following general symbols may also be found accompanying representations of some saints:

arrow   signifies martyrdom accomplished with arrows, but is also a symbol of torture. SS Sebastian, Edmund and Christina.

asperge   used for sprinkling holy water. A symbol of purity.

book   emblem of an Evangelist or Doctor of the Church, a symbol of learning: St Catherine and St Sitha.

chalice   saint represented was a priest, or it symbolises SS John the Evangelist, Benedict, Richard of Chichester, or Barbara.

church   symbolic of high rank in the Church, or of the founding of a religious establishment.

cross   signifies a missionary: SS Alban and John the Baptist.

crown or sceptre   signifies royal rank or sainthood.

dove   signifies the presence of the Holy Spirit, or purity, or represents Chistianity itself.

fountain   represents the Virgin, or St Peter or preaching.

head   symbolises death by decapitation: SS John the Baptist or Denis.

lamp   virgins.

lily   essentially a Marian motif, but also a symbol of purity or virginity.

lilies among thorns   confessors.

palm   suggests victory or martyrdom.

scourge   represents mortification or self-punishment: SS Boniface, Ambrose, or Guthlac.

skull   suggests St Jerome and preparation for death.

sword   celebrates saints who died by decapitation.

wheel   patriarchs.

Symmetry Uniformity or balance of one part of a building and another. Equal disposition of parts and masses on either side of a centre line.

Synthronon The benches for the clergy in the apse of an early church.

Systyle One of the five species of intercolumniation defined by Vitruvius, in which the columns are two diameters apart. (See **Intercolumniation**)

Tabern A tavern.

Tabernacle The receptacle for the sacraments placed over the altar, or any niche or canopy. Sepulchral monuments, choir stalls and sedilia are all surmounted by rich canopy work known as tabernacle work.

Table Horizontal mouldings dividing storeys.

Table Tomb A flat stone supported by two or more upright stones over a grave. The finished object looks like a table. The term is also applied to a dolmen or cromlech.

Symmetry
A symmetrical composition at Greenwich Royal Hospital. In the centre is the Queen's House by Inigo Jones (1618–35), and on either side are late additions including the cupolas and colonnades by Wren

Tablet A wall slab or monumental tablet.

Tabling Coping of walls. (Scots)

Tablinum A room in a Roman villa with one side open to the atrium.

Taenia, Tenia The fillet or band at the top of a

Tabernacle
Tabernacle work on a canopy over Bishop Drokersford's tomb of the fourteenth century in Wells Cathedral

Doric frieze separating it from the architrave. (See Fig e **Order**)

Tambour The ground on which the leaves of a Corinthian capital are placed. The wall or drum carrying a cupola.

Tarras Strong cement.

Tas-de-charge The lowest course of an arch or vault.

Tassel, Tassel, Torsel, Tossel The plate of timber for the end of a beam or joist to rest on.

Tavern A public house for the sale of alcoholic beverages.

Tavern
The Old Bell Tavern, Holborn, before demolition. Basically an eighteenth-century façade

Tebam A rostrum.

Tectorium Opus A form of ancient plastering.

Telamones Atlantes.

Temenos The sacred precinct of a Classical temple.

Template, Templet A short timber or block of stone laid under a girder, sometimes called a padstone. A pattern for setting out.

Temple A building dedicated to pagan deities. Classical temples were usually rectangular, with a body or cell, a portico, and a sanctuary. A temple has a portico in antis when the antae

partially close the portico at the sides. The various arrangements of columns are described elsewhere. (See **Colonnade, Intercolumniation**)

Tenia (See **Taenia**)

Tenon, Tenant A projecting rectangular piece on the end of a timber to be inserted into a mortise.

Tepidarium An apartment in a Roman bath.

Teram A scroll at the end of a step.

Term A pedestal like an inverted obelisk supporting a bust, or merging with a bust. It is also

Temple A—G are Greek examples, H is Roman

A elevation of Doric prostyle tetrastyle temple	**E** plan of peripteral hexastyle temple
B plan of distyle in antis temple	**F** half-plan of dipteral octastyle temple
C plan of prostyle tetrastyle temple	**G** half-plan of pseudodipteral octastyle temple
D plan of amphi-prostyle tetrastyle temple	**H** plan of pseudoperipteral tetrastyle temple

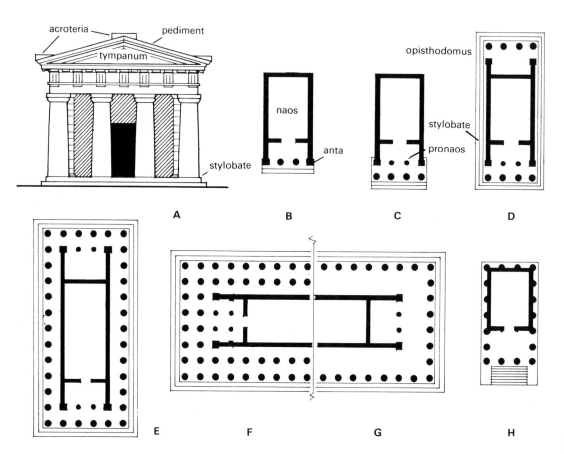

Terrace
a) Cumberland Terrace, Regent's Park. John Nash's great unified terraces of blocks linked by arches behind which are smaller houses. *(Photograph by E. R. Jarrett, kindly lent by Mr Terence Davis)*
b) Chester Terrace, Regent's Park, London. The longest unbroken terrace of houses in the Regent's Park development. It was designed by John Nash and built in 1825. *(Photograph by E. J. Jarrett, kindly provided by Mr Terence Davis)*
c) *overleaf:* Sir John Soane's design for part of Regent Street. *(Kindly lent by Mr Terence Davis)*

a

b

called a terminal. A terminus is the popular word for the end of a railway line, or its main station.

Terrace A raised space or platform adjoining a building, or a row of houses joined together as a unified design.

Terracotta Baked earth, unglazed, used for ornamentation.

Terrazzo A floor or dado finish of marble chips set in cement and then ground down and polished.

Tessellated Pavement A pavement of mosaic made of squares of marble, brick, tile, etc, called tesserae or tessellae.

Tester A canopy over a pulpit, tomb, bed, etc.

Testudo A vault over a hall, or any grand arched roof.

Tetrastyle A portico with four columns. (See Figs A, C, D, H **Temple**)

Thatch A roof covering of straw, rushes, or reeds, much favoured for the cottage orné.

c

Theatre A place for the performing of plays.

Thermae Public baths in Roman times that contained many amenities apart from baths.

Thermal Window A semicircular window subdivided with two mullions, also known as a Diocletian window. It is a feature of Palladian architecture.

Tholos The dome of a circular building or the building in toto.

Through A stone in a wall that reaches through it. A throughstane in Scots usage is a table tomb, ie a horizontal tombstone on pillars.

Tie An iron rod or a timber beam tying two bodies together. A tie beam is the beam that connects a pair of principal rafters. (See Fig a **Roof**)

Tierceron A secondary rib from the springing to the ridge rib in a Gothic vault. (See Figs c, d **Vaulting**)

Tile A decorative floor tile from Winchester Cathedral

Tigna A tie beam.

Tile A thick plate of baked clay or other material used to cover a roof. Thicker tiles are used for paving. Flat tiles are plain tiles, and curved ones are called pantiles. When walls are clad in tiles it is called tilehanging. Some very beautiful glazed or encaustic tiles with designs in colour exist in

Timber Framing
a) Broad Street, Ludlow, Shropshire. Timber-framed buildings. That on the left has jettied storeys and a dragon beam on the corner. That on the right has gables with nineteenth-century bargeboards and finials
b) The Feathers Hotel, Ludlow, Shropshire. This magnificent Elizabethan timber-framed building was put up in 1603. Note the balcony with flat, openwork balusters and the lozenge pattern on the first floor. The three gables, bays, and carved bargeboards are excellent examples of their type

medieval churches. The design was frequently inset with a differently coloured clay. Tiles were used to represent Christian symbols, the signs of the zodiac, or the labyrinth. Glazed wall tiles were much employed in Victorian times.

Timber Framing Half-timbering where walls are made of a timber frame and the spaces are filled in with brick or plaster. (See also **Breastsummer**)

Timbre, Tymbre The crest on top of a helm, or on top of a femerell or lantern.

Tinning of Ironwork Medieval decorative

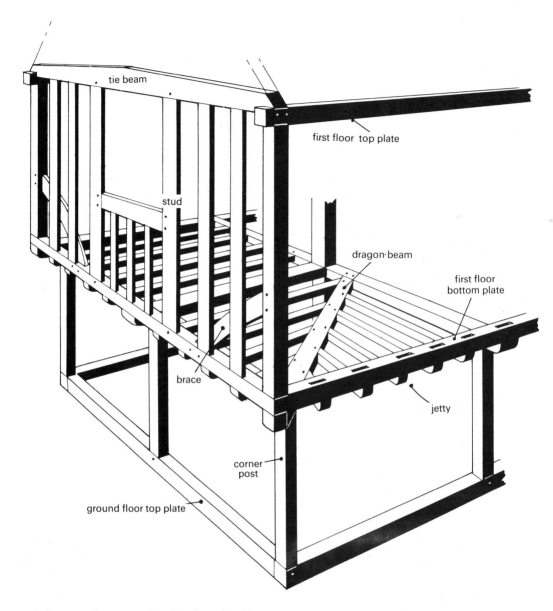

Timber Framing A typical timber-framed building

ironwork was sometimes tinned to protect it from rust.

To-fall, Too-fall A lean-to.

Tomb A sepulchre or grave, including a monument. A tomb chest is a stone coffin shaped like a chest, also known as an altar tomb. A table tomb is a horizontal tombstone supported on pillars.

Tongue A projecting feather to fit within a groove, as in tongue-and-groove work.

Toothing Stones (See **Tusses**)

Tomb

a) Church of St Laurence, Ludlow, Shropshire.
Tomb of Sir Robert Townsend (d 1581) and his wife.
It consists of a tomb chest with fluted Ionic engaged
columns carrying two recumbent effigies
b) Church of St Endellienta, St Endellion, Cornwall.
Tomb chest in the south aisle of *c* 1400
c) Altar tomb of the last decade of the eighteenth
century in the churchyard of St Dunstan, Stepney,
London
d) Tomb of Bishop Beckington, Wells Cathedral
(1451). Note the very fine fifteenth-century
ironwork and the two-tiered tomb, with cadaver
under the effigy of the bishop

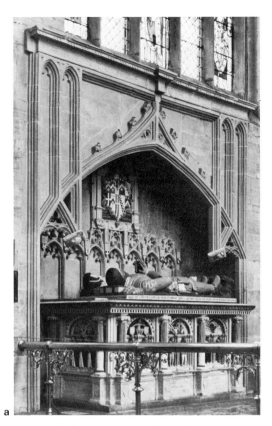

a

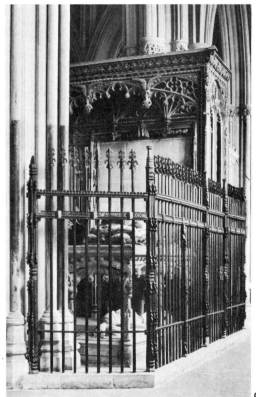

c

b

d

Tooth Ornament A Gothic ornament consisting of a square, four-leaved flower the centre of which projects in a point, rather like a pierced pyramid.

Top Beam A collar beam.

Top Rail The top rail of wainscoting.

Torus A large convex moulding at the base of a column. (See **Orders**)

Touchstone A smooth black stone used for tombs, eg Purbeck marble.

Tourelle A corbelled turret.

Tower A tall building, round, square, or polygonal in plan, used for defence, as a landmark, or for the hanging of bells.

Tower
a) *below* Church of St James, Kinnersley, Herefordshire. The west front with its blocked Norman door and Perpendicular window. The tower is early fourteenth-century, and has a saddleback roof.
b) *above right* The tower of the Church of St George-in-the-East by Nicholas Hawksmoor, 1717—22, cutting into almost Mannerist split pediments with scrolls. The bizarre octagonal lantern is a curiously original invention
c) *right* The Gothic Revival façade of St Mark's Church, Clerkenwell, designed by W. C. Mylne and erected 1826–8

a

b

Trab A wall plate.

Trabeation An entablature or beam. To say a building is trabeated means it is constructed on the post-and-lintel principle.

Tracery The intersection of the mullions and transoms of windows, screens, panels, or vaults. Early tracery, dating from the Early English period is usually plate tracery or flat masonry panels pierced with lights. From the thirteenth century moulded mullions and separate windows are continued at the head to form circular or other forms. Simple *bar tracery* formed patterns of a geometrical nature, but later, in the Decorated period, formed flowing tracery. Bar tracery is also Early English, and consists of moulded shafts

Tracery
a) Exeter Cathedral. The bishop's throne of 1316 (right), and the Decorated east window of the fourteenth century
b) York Minster. The west window, a sumptuous design of eight lights, in pairs, with a great heart-shaped mass of flowing tracery above (1338). This is a beautiful example of Decorated work
c) Fifteenth-century cloisters with tracery at Wells Cathedral

c

intersecting at the window head. *Geometrical tracery* features circles and foils. *Flowing tracery* features ogee curves in plenty, and is also called *curvilinear tracery*. It is a characteristic of the Decorated period. *Intersecting tracery* has mullions continuing in curves until they hit the frame of the window opening. *Panel tracery* introduces transoms, and is characteristic of Perpendicular work. *Reticulated tracery* is Decorated, suggestive of a net of ogee shapes. (See also **Imbricated, Rayonnant, Stump**)

Trachelium, Trachelion The neck of a column between the shaft ring and hypotrachelium.

Trail A running enrichment of mouldings in Gothic work.

Transe A through-passage.

Transenna A lattice screen.

Transept The transverse portion of a cruciform church; the arms on either side of the crossing. Large churches may have several transepts, or cross aisles. (See Fig **Cathedral, Isometric Projection**)

Transition A term used to denote the passing of one style to another, especially Norman to Gothic.

Transom A horizontal bar to divide a window into two or more lights in height.

Transverse Arch An arch dividing a compartment of a vault from another.

Traverse A screen with curtains to give privacy, or a gallery or loft of communication.

Tread The horizontal part of a step of a stair.

Trefoil A Gothic ornament of three foils in a circle or some other figure.

Trellis A reticulated frame of thin bars of wood used as a screen.

Trenail An oak pin.

Tresawnte, Tresawns, Transyte A narrow passage near the chapterhouse.

Tressel A trestle.

Tressure A border within an heraldic shield

a

b

narrower than the orle, generally doubled.

Trestle, Tressel A prop for a horizontal plank.

Tribune An apse, a raised platform, or a church gallery.

Triclinium A room where Romans feasted and received guests.

Triforium The gallery or arcade in the wall over the pier arches which separate the body from the aisles of a church, often associated with a wall-passage that runs behind the arcade and under the clerestory. (See Figs **Gothic**)

Triglyph The vertical tablets in a Doric frieze, comprising two glyphs and two half-glyphs. (See Fig e **Orders**)

Trilithon Two vertical stones supporting one horizontal stone like a lintel.

Tracery
a) Plate tracery. This example is from the Church of St Andrew, Peckham. Enoch Bassett Keeling (1837–86), architect. Note the quatrefoils and cusps
b) Geometrical tracery from the chapterhouse of Salisbury Cathedral
c) Intersecting tracery from North Stoke in Sussex
d) Curvilinear tracery from Selby Abbey, Yorkshire. Note the flowing lines and cusps, and the dagger form
over page
e) Decorated tracery of reticulated pattern from Worstead in Norfolk
f) Perpendicular tracery from Bath Abbey. Note the transoms, cusps, and curiously flat arches

c

d

Trim A frame or edging.

Trimmer A timber that supports the ends of joists, etc. A partition wall would be trimmed up between floor and ceiling, while the cutting of a trapdoor would involve the insertion of trimmers.

Tripod A table with three legs.

Triptych A picture with folding doors which close over it. When opened three pictures are revealed. A triptych usually forms a reredos.

Triumphal Arch An arch erected to celebrate a person or event, usually a military victory, and often surmounted by a quadriga.

Trochilus A scotia, or concave moulding.

Trophy A sculptured group of armour and arms.

Trumeau In Gothic work, the stone pier in the middle of a church door supporting the tympanum above.

Truss A combination of timbers to form a frame, placed at intervals, and carrying the purlins. As well as a frame, of timber or metal, the term also means a projection from the face of a wall, or a large corbel or modillion.

Tuck Pointing Lines to mark the joints of brickwork, made with ridges of lime putty after joints have been raked out and replaced with mortar coloured to match the brickwork.

Tudor Arch A four-centred arch. The point is

e

f

a

b

Tudor Style
a) The Victorian vestry hall of 1852 in Kensington, by J. Broadbridge. *(Public Libraries of the Royal Borough of Kensington and Chelsea, reference 352/NCS [1852] C91. Negative Reference B/101)*
b) Tudor-style lodges at Highgate

Tuscan Order
Portico of the Church of St Paul, Covent Garden, commenced in 1631, and designed by Inigo Jones

not very much raised above the springing and a typical Tudor arch has a very flattened appearance.

Tudor Style Late Perpendicular Gothic. A Tudor flower is an ornament of a flat flower or leaf placed upright on its stalk and used in cresting.

Tufa A porous stone much used by the Romans.

Tun A chimney-shaft.

Tunnel An underground channel supported by a vaulted roof.

Turngrece A winding stair.

Turnpike Stair A spiral staircase.

Turret A small tower or a large pinnacle.

Tuscan Order The simplest of the five Orders of Classical architecture. The shaft of the column is never fluted. The entablature is simple, and the capital has a square abacus. The base consists of a square plinth and large torus. (See Figs **Orders**)

Tusses Projecting stones left in a wall to which another building is to be joined. They are also called toothing stones. In Scots usage they are called tusks.

Tympanum The face of a pediment between the level and raked mouldings. The space between the lintel of a door and the arch over it.

Type A tester or sound-board over a pulpit. The capping of a cupola roof or turret.

Undercroft A vault or crypt under a church or chapel.

Underpinning Bringing a wall up to the ground sill. The term denotes the temporary support for a wall where new foundations are being built.

Uphers Fir poles used for very crude roofing.

Upstart A reveal stone higher than it is long. (Scots)

Urillae (See Helices)

Urn A vase for ashes or cremated remains. It is often used as a decorative motif on top of the dies of balustrades or on walls or in niches.

Vagina The lower part of a term or terminal in which a statuette or other motif is inserted.

Vair Heraldic fur, represented as ranged bell-shaped pieces.

Valance Hung drapery round a tester, etc. The wooden vertical boards resembling such hangings at the edges of railway-station canopies.

Valley The internal meeting of two slopes of a roof. (See Fig c **Roof**)

Vamure The walk on top of a wall behind the parapet.

Vane A metal banner fixed to the top of a tower to show the direction of the wind. Also called a weathercock.

Vase An ornamental vessel. The bell of a Corinthian capital.

Vault An arched roof over an apartment. The simplest vault is the *cylindrical*, barrel, or wagon vault that springs from opposite parallel walls, and presents a uniform concave surface throughout its length. It is also known as a tunnel vault. A *domical* vault sits on a square, circular, or polygonal base, the curved vaults rising directly from the walls. The junctions between curved surfaces are called groins. A sail vault also sits on a square, the diagonal of the square being the diameter of the dome, which starts to rise as on pendentives, but the curve continues smoothly. A *groin* vault is produced by the junctions of two barrel vaults at right angles. A *fan* vault is formed of curved cones fanning out from the imposts to intersect and meet or nearly join at the apex. It is characteristic of Perpendicular work. A *quadri-*

partite vault is divided into four pieces by diagonal ribs. A *rib vault* is a vault with ribs across the bay or compartment. The ribs form the structure which carries the stones or panels in between. A *sexpartite* vault is like a quadripartite vault, but with a ridge rib creating six compartments or cells. A *stellar vault* has ribs but also lierne ribs and tiercerons which form a star-shaped pattern on plan. A *lierne* is a rib that springs from rib to rib. The *ridge-rib* is the rib along the ridge of a vault. A *tierceron* is a rib that springs from out of the main springing points to a boss on the ridge-rib. A *transverse arch* separates one vaulted compartment from an other. A *vaulting-shaft* is a shaft, small column, pillar, or cluster of shafts supporting the ribs of a vault at their springing. Such shafts sometimes rise from the floor (in buildings influenced by the French style) and from corbels if essentially English in origin. (See also **Diaphragm**, **Rear**, **Welch Groin**). A vault is another term for a burial chamber.

Velarium The awning over an amphitheatre.

Vellar Cupola A dome over large staircases and salons.

Veneer A thin leaf of wood of superior quality to cover a wood of commoner variety.

Venetian Arch A form of arched opening, either a void or blind, consisting of a pointed or semi-circular large arch within which are two openings separated by a colonnette. Above the colonnette is a roundel or foiled opening. (See Fig **Arch**)

Venetian Door An arched central doorway flanked by tall flat-topped windows.

Venetian Style Italian architecture indigenous to Venice.

Venetian Window A Serliana, or arched central window flanked by narrower flat-topped windows. The whole is framed within a Classical form with columns or pilasters, entablature, archivolt, and key. It is a feature of Palladianism.

Vent A flue or funnel of a chimney. Any conduit for carrying off fumes.

Verandah An open gallery with a roof or canopy supported on light pillars or other supports and also called a stoep. It is usually placed before the windows of the principal rooms to

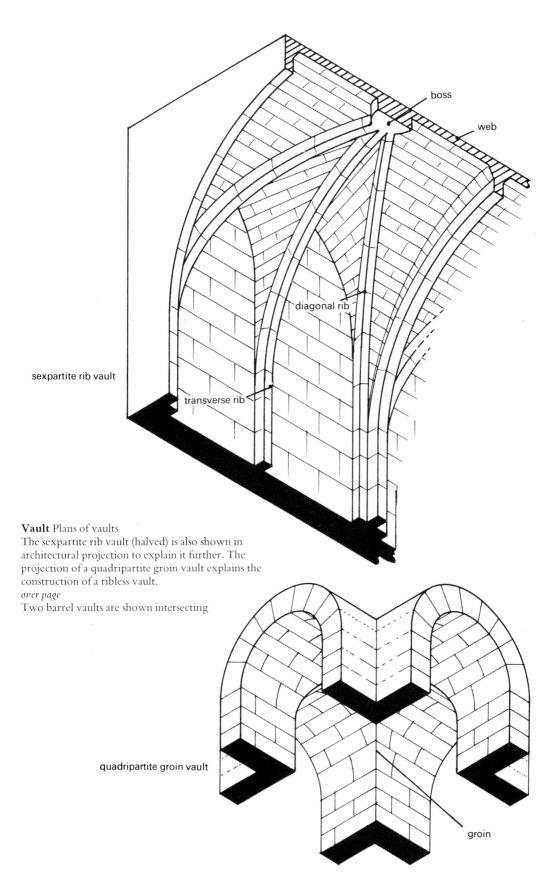

boss

web

diagonal rib

sexpartite rib vault

transverse rib

Vault Plans of vaults
The sexpartite rib vault (halved) is also shown in
architectural projection to explain it further. The
projection of a quadripartite groin vault explains the
construction of a ribless vault.
over page
Two barrel vaults are shown intersecting

quadripartite groin vault

groin

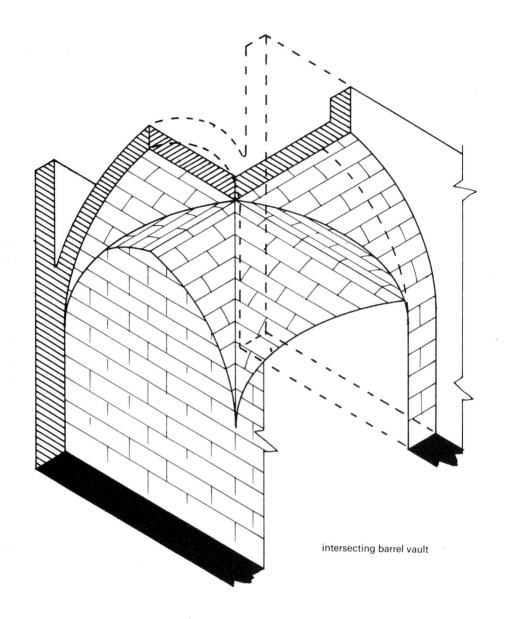

intersecting barrel vault

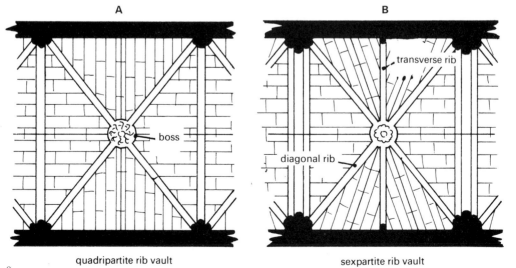

A

B

transverse rib

boss

diagonal rib

quadripartite rib vault

sexpartite rib vault

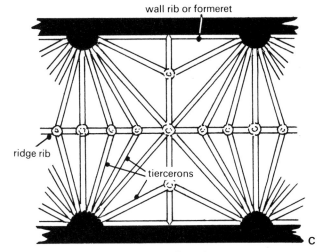

wall rib or formeret

ridge rib

tiercerons

C

tierceron rib vault

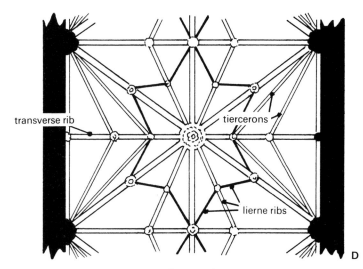

transverse rib

tiercerons

lierne ribs

D

lierne vault

E

fan vault

shelter them from the sun. It may be closed to form a conservatory.

Verge The shaft of a column, or a very small shaft in Gothic architecture. A verge-board is synonymous with a bargeboard.

Vermiculated Work Rustic work having the appearance of being eaten by worms, ie with irregular shallow channels over the surface. (See also Fig **Masonry**)

Vert Heraldic green.

Vesica Piscis An elliptical shape but pointed at the ends instead of curved: in reality a figure formed by the interpenetration of two equal circles. It is a common form of the aureole or glory surrounding representations of the Trinity and Our Blessed Lady. The figure is a symbol representing the fish, which contains the Greek letters of the name and title of Our Lord. It is the eye of the needle through which it is difficult to

Vermiculated Work
Vermiculated masonry in Wells. Note the stalactites on either side

pass. It is a common form in Gothic panels, tracery and other architectural features, especially in the tympanum above a doorway where it usually encloses a figure of Christ in Majesty. It will be noted that the Vesica Piscis

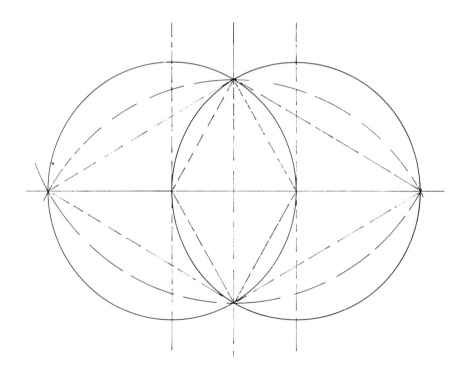

Vesica Piscis Note the equilateral triangles and the Gothic arches formed by the relationships between the two *mandala* forms. The all-embracing significance of such a figure, not only in terms of metaphysics, but of geometry, made it ideal as a basis

for construction, and got over the problems of vaulting spaces not square on plan. The functional versatility of the pointed arch was ideal for the complexities of a great medieval cathedral as well as those of a Victorian office block

Viaduct
a) The 'Proposed High Level Road and Viaduct from St Sepulchre's Church to Hatton Garden', designed by F. Marrable, and published by Cundall, Downes and Co. *(RIBA Library)*
b) The 'Birds Eye View of the London Grand Junction Railway from Skinner Street to Camden Town' lithographed by Bouvier, drawn by George Remington, Junior, and published by G. S. Tregear. *(RIBA Library)*

contains the basic forms of the pointed arch. (See **Mandala**)

Vestibule An apartment which serves as a communication between rooms. An entrance lobby or hall.

Vestry, Revestry A room adjacent to the chancel of a church, sometimes called a sacristy, in which sacred vessels and vestments are kept.

Vethym Six feet, or a fathom.

Viaduct A long bridge carrying a road, usually on a series of arches.

Vice, Vis, Vyse A spiral staircase wound round a pillar.

Vignette A running ornament of leaves and tendrils in cavetto mouldings of Gothic work.

Villa A country house. In the nineteenth century the term came to mean a detached house on the outskirts of a town.

Vitruvian Scroll A continuous band of ornament like a series of waves, found in Classical architecture. It is also called running dog.

Vivo The shaft of a column.

Volute A spiral scroll forming the principal part of the Ionic capital, and also found in the Corinthian and Composite Orders. Also called a helix. (See Figs d, f, g **Orders**)

Vomitorium A principal exit from an amphitheatre.

Voussoir A wedge-like stone or brick forming part of an arch. (See Fig d **Arch**)

Voussure A vault.

Voutain A term apparently connected with the jointing of the webs of a stone vault.

Wagon Ceiling, Wagon Vault A ceiling or vault over a rectangular space consisting of a simple half-cylinder. (See **Vault**)

Wainscot Timber lining to walls, or timber panelling.

Waling Shoring.

Wall Plate A timber laid horizontally on a wall to which joists, rafters and roof trusses are fixed.

Wall Press A built-in cupboard. (Scots)

Ward A court in a castle, surrounding the keep, also called a bailey.

Water-leaf A carved leaf found in Gothic work of the twelfth century, consisting of a very wide leaf with no modelling, bowing out and returning at the corners of a capital, slightly reminiscent of a Corinthian capital. (See Fig a **Capital**)

Water-table A horizontal offset in a wall, sloped on the top. In Scots usage it is a barge, or projecting ledge at the base of a chimney.

Villa

a) Sandridge Park, Devón, of 1805, by Nash. On the right is the conservatory. *(Kindly lent by Mr Terence Davis)*

b) Park Village East, Regent's Park. Note the valancing on the eaves of the villa on the left. Drawn by T. H. Shepherd and engraved by W. Radcliff, published in 1829. *(Kindly lent by Mr Terence Davis)*

c) Cronkhill, Shropshire, *c* 1802. An Italianate villa by John Nash *(National Buildings Record HSP 1794)*

c

Wattle and Daub Mud or clay on thin lathing to fill the framework of timber-framed buildings. Also called rad and dab.

Wave Moulding A Decorated moulding of a convex section flanked by hollows.

Weathercock A vane.

Weather Boarding Boards nailed with a lap on each other to prevent the penetration of water and laid horizontally to clad a building.

Weathering An inclination given to horizontal surfaces to throw off water.

Weather Moulding A hood mould, or projecting moulding with a weathered top.

Weather Tiling, or Slating Walls clad in tiles or slates.

Web Infilling between the ribs of a Gothic vault ie one of the compartments of a groin or rib vault also known as a cell.

Weepers Statues in attitudes of mourning round a tomb.

Weights of a Sash Two weights on either side of a sash by which it is suspended by cords over pulleys.

Welch Groin A groin formed by the intersection of two cylindrical vaults, one of which is of less height than the other.

Well A deep shaft to contain water. In a flight of stairs it is the space left beyond the ends of the steps.

Wheel Window A Catherine-wheel window, or circular window with radiating spokes, loosely called a rose window.

Wheelers Winders. (Scots)

Wheelers and Kneelers Battlements.

Wicket A small door in a larger one.

Wind Beam A collar beam.

Winders Steps radiating from a centre.

Window An aperture in a wall to admit light. If divided, each part is known as a light. Classical windows are usually rectangular openings without splays, but sometimes they are arched, or are circular or semicircular in form. Venetian windows are of large size and divided by columns or piers resembling pilasters into three lights, the middle one of which is wider than the two flanking it and sometimes arched. Saxon windows are small, often with large splays, and are often arched. In towers they are usually of two lights divided by small pillars resembling balusters with arched or triangular heads. Norman windows are often small, but in larger buildings are of considerable size. They are usually arched with semicircular heads, and may be occasionally paired, divided by shafts, and placed within a larger semicircular opening. Circular windows were common. In the Early English style, windows are pointed, long, and narrow (lancets), and are found singly or in groups. Plate tracery is found in this period, as are circles, quatrefoils, etc. Decorated windows are very much enlarged and subdivided by mullions into separate lights with ornate tracery above. Clerestory windows are often trefoils or quatrefoils. Perpendicular

Vitruvian Scroll

windows have transoms and are usually very large in area, the structure being reduced to the minimum. Heads are usually four-centred arches. The noblest windows are usually found at the east and west ends, and in transepts. (See also **Bay, Catherine Wheel, Clerestory, Compass, Cross, Diocletian, Dormer, Fanlight, French, Laced, Lattice, Low-side, Oculus, Oeil-de-boeuf, Oriel, Rose, Sash, Serliana, Tracery, Wheel, Wyatt, Yorkshire Light**)

Window-bossing A recess under a window. (Scots)

Wine Cellar An apartment in a basement for the storage of wines, fitted with bins.

Wings The side portions of a façade, subordinate to the principal and central front, or small buildings flanking a main block. The wing of a moulding is a fillet.

Withe The partition between two flues in a chimney stack.

Wood Brick A piece of timber the same size as a brick.

Wreathed Column A barley-sugar or contorted, twisted column. A column festooned with vines or other leaves or tendrils, including ivy.

Wreathed String The circular portion of a stair string where there is a hollow newel.

Wrought-iron Malleable iron as opposed to cast, or brittle iron.

Wyatt Window A Venetian window with a square head instead of an arched central opening.

Xenodochium A room or building for the reception of strangers.

Xystus A spacious portico, attached to a gymnasium, where athletes exercised in inclement weather. In Roman architecture it was a long covered or open colonnade around a garden or court. An hypaethral walk.

Yard A paved area, generally at the back of a house. A long piece of timber.

Yett A grated door or portcullis made of wrought iron, and distinguished by the horizontals passing alternately through the thickness of the verticals and vice versa. (Scots)

Ymage An image.

Yorkshire Light A mullioned window containing two lights, one fixed and the other a sliding sash moving horizontally.

Ziggurat A stepped pyramidal temple with ramps and steps, found in ancient Mesopotamia.

Zigzag A Norman decoration consisting of mouldings running in zigzag lines, known as a chevron or dancette. (See Fig **Chevron**)

Zocle, Zocco, Zoccolo (See **Socle**)

Zophorus, Zoophorus A frieze with reliefs featuring animals.

Zotheca A small room or alcove.

Bibliography

Adam, W. *Vitruvius Scotius: A Collection of Public and Private Buildings in Scotland* (Edinburgh, 1720–40)

Adams, M. B. *Artists' Homes* (1883)

Ballantine, J. *A Treatise on Painted Glass* (1845)

Barr, J. *Anglican Church Architecture* (Oxford, 1843)

Barry, A. *The Life and Works of Sir Charles Barry* (1867)

Belcher, J. *Essentials in Architecture* (1920)

Benham and Froud *Illustrations of Mediaeval Metal Work* (1877)

Bentham, J. *The History and Antiquities of Ely* (1771)

Billings, R. W. *Baronial and Ecclesiastical Antiquities of Scotland* (Edinburgh, 1845–52)

Blore, Edward *The Monumental Remains of Noble and Eminent Persons, comprising the Sepulchral Antiquities of Great Britain* (1826)

Bloxham, M. H. *Principles of Gothic Ecclesiastical Antiquities* (1882)

Boase, T. S. R. *The Oxford History of English Art*, Vol 3 (Oxford, 1953)

Bond, Francis *Fonts and Font Covers* (1908)

—— *Dedications and Patron Saints of English Churches* (1914)

—— *An Introduction to English Church Architecture from the Eleventh to the Sixteenth Century* (1913)

—— *Screens and Galleries in English Churches* (1908)

Boutell, Rev Charles *Christian Monuments in England and Wales: An Historical and Descriptive Sketch of the Classes of Sepulchral Monuments which have been in use in this country from about the era of the Norman Conquest to the time of Edward the Fourth* (1854)

—— *The Monumental Brasses of England: A Series of Engravings upon Wood, from every variety of these interesting and Valuable Memorials, accompanied with Brief Descriptive Notices* (1849)

Bowman, H. and Crowther, J. S. *The Churches of the Middle Ages* (1845–53)

Brace, H. G. *Middle-class House Architecture* (1881)

Brandon, R. and J. A. *An Analysis of Gothic Architecture* (1847–49)

Brieger, P. *The Oxford History of English Art*. Vol 4 (Oxford, 1957)

Briggs, Asa *Victorian Cities* (Harmondsworth, 1968)

Brindley, William (with Weatherley, W. Samuel) *Ancient Sepulchral Monuments* (1887)

Britton, J. *Cathedrals, comprising Canterbury, York, Salisbury, Norwich, Oxford, Winchester, Lichfield, Hereford, Wells, Exeter, Worcester, Peterborough, Gloucester, and Bristol* (1821–35)

—— *Architectural Antiquities of Great Britain* (1807–35)

Burges, E. *Art Applied to Industry* (1865)

—— *Architectural Drawings* (1870)

—— *A History of Christian Altars* (1847)

Burn, R. S. *Architecture and Building; a Series of Working Drawings and Designs, with Essays by eminent Architects* (Edinburgh, 1863–65)

Campbell, C. *Vitruvius Britannicus* (1715, 1725, 1731, 1767, 1771)

Carter, J. (ed Britton, J.) *Ancient Architecture of England* (1837)

Chadwick, G. F. *The Works of Sir Joseph Paxton* (1961)

Chance Brothers and Company *Designs for Coloured Ornamental Windows* (Birmingham, 1853)

Clapham, A. W. *English Romanesque Architecture before the Conquest* (Oxford, 1930)

—— *English Romanesque Architecture after the Conquest* (Oxford, 1934)

Clark, Kenneth *The Gothic Revival. An Essay in the History of Taste* (Harmondsworth, 1964)

Clarke, Basil F. L. *Church Builders of the Nineteenth Century* (Newton Abbot, 1969)

Clayton, J. *Ancient Half-timbered Edifices of England* (1846)

Cobb, Gerald *The Old Churches of London* (1941–2)

Cockerell, C. R. *Iconography of the West Front of Wells Cathedral* (1851)

Colling, J. K. *Details of Gothic Architecture* (1851–56)

Colvin, Howard M. *A Biographical Dictionary of British Architects 1660–1840* (1978)

Cook, G. H. *The English Cathedral through the Centuries* (1957)

Cotman, J. S. *Architectural Antiquities of Norfolk* (1818)

Crook, J. Mordaunt (ed) *A History of the Gothic Revival, by Charles L. Eastlake* (Leicester and New York, 1970)

Curl, James Stevens. *A Celebration of Death. An introduction to some of the buildings, monuments, and settings of funerary architecture in the Western European tradition* (London and New York, 1980)

—— *The Egyptian Revival. An Introductory Study of a Recurring Theme in the History of Taste* (London, Boston and Sydney, 1982)

—— *The Life and Work of Henry Roberts (1803–76), Architect* (London and Chichester, 1983)

Cutts, E. L. *Church Furniture and Decoration* (1854)

Davis, Terence *John Nash: The Prince Regent's Architect* (1966)

—— *The Gothick Taste* (Newton Abbot, 1975)

Dollman, F. T.   *Examples of Ancient Pulpits in England* (1849)

Downes, Kerry.   *Hawksmoor* (1959)

Dresser, Christopher.   *The Art of Decorative Design* (1862)

—— *Modern Ornamentation* (1886)

—— *Principles of Decorative Design* (1880)

—— *Studies in Design* (1876)

Esdaile, Katherine A.   *English Monumental Sculpture since the Renaissance* (1927)

Evans, Joan.   *The Oxford History of English Art* Vol 5 (Oxford, 1949)

Fairbairn, William.   *On the Application of Cast and Wrought Iron to Building Purposes* (1857)

Fergusson, J.   *History of Architecture* (1869)

Fletcher, Sir Banister.   *A History of Architecture on the Comparative Method* (many editions)

Fletcher, B.   *Model Houses for the Industrial Classes* (1877)

Fox-Davies, Arthur Charles.   *A Complete Guide to Heraldry* (N.D.)

Fullarton, A.   *Grammar of House Planning* (Edinburgh, 1864)

Gibbs, J.   *Book of Architecture, containing St. Martin's Church, etc* (1728)

Gloag, John.   *Victorian Comfort: A Social History of Design from 1830–1900* (Newton Abbot, 1973)

—— *Mr. Loudon's England: The Life and Work of John Claudius Loudon, and his influence on architecture and furniture design* (Newcastle upon Tyne, 1970)

Gomme, Andor and Walker, David.   *Architecture of Glasgow* (1968)

Goodhart-Rendel, H. S.   *English Architecture since the Regency* (1953)

Gough, R.   *Sepulchral Monuments in Great Britain* (1796)

Gunnis, Rupert.   *Dictionary of British Sculptors 1660–1851* (revised edition n.d.)

Gwilt, Joseph.   *An Encyclopaedia of Architecture, Historical, Theoretical, and Practical* (revised by Wyatt Papworth, 1903)

Halfpenny, J. and W.   *Chinese and Gothic Architecture Properly Ornamented* (1752)

Hall, Sir J.   *Essay on the Origin, History, and Principles of Gothic Architecture* (1813)

Hamlin, A. D. F.   *A Text Book of History of Architecture* (New York, 1896)

Harvey, John.   *Gothic England* (1948)

Hay, George.   *The Architecture of Scottish Post-Reformation Churches, 1560–1843* (Oxford, 1957)

Hewett, C. A.   *The Development of Carpentry, 1200–1700. An Essex Study* (Newton Abbot, 1969)

Hitchcock, H. R.   *Early Victorian Architecture in Britain* (1954)

Hole, J.   *Homes of the Working Classes: 20 plates of the Model Village of Akroydon, etc* (1866)

Honour, Hugh.   *Chinoiserie. The Vision of Cathay* (1961)

Hope, A. J. Beresford.   *The English Cathedral of the Nineteenth Century* (1861)

de L'Hôpital, Winefride.   *Westminster Cathedral and its Architect* (n.d.)

Howard, F. E.   *The Mediaeval Styles of the English Parish Church* (1936)

Howarth, Thomas.   *Charles Rennie Mackintosh and the Modern Movement* (1952)

Hussey, Christopher.   *English Country Houses* (1955–8)

—— *The Life of Sir Edwin Lutyens* (1953)

Jackson, Sir T. G.   *Modern Gothic Architecture* (1873)

Jones, Owen.   *Grammar of Ornament* (1856)

—— *The True and the False in the Decorative Arts* (1863)

Jordan, Robert Furneaux.   *Victorian Architecture* (Harmondsworth, 1966)

Kerr, R.   *The Gentleman's House* (1869)

Kidson, Peter; Murray, Peter; and Thompson, Paul.   *A History of English Architecture* (Harmondsworth, 1965)

de Lasaulx, V. and Elliott, J.   *Street Architecture: a series of Shop Fronts* (1855)

Lethaby, W. R.   *Architecture* (1911)

—— *Form in Civilization* (1922)

—— *Philip Webb and his Work* (Oxford, 1935)

Lewis, J.   *Original Designs in Architecture, consisting of Plans, etc, of Public and Private Buildings in England and Ireland* (1780–97)

Loudon, John Claudius (ed).   *The Gardener's Magazine* (several issues in the early 1840s.)

—— *Encyclopaedia of Cottage, Farm, and Villa Architecture* (edition of 1846, enlarged by Mrs Jane Loudon)

Macaulay, James.   *The Gothic Revival 1745–1845* (Glasgow and London, 1975)

Macfarlane's 'Saracen' Works Catalogues (Glasgow, various dates)

Macgibbon, David, and Ross, Thomas.   *The Castellated and Domestic Architecture of Scotland from the Twelfth to the Eighteenth Century* (Edinburgh, 1887)

Macklin, Rev Herbert W.   *Monumental Brasses* (1905)

Madsen, S. Tschudi.   *Art Nouveau* (Madrid, 1967)

Mason, R. T.   *Framed Buildings of England* (Horsham, n.d.)

Meeks, C. L. V.   *The Railroad Station* (Yale and London, 1956)

Mickelthwaithe, J. T.   *Modern Parish Churches* (1874)

Milner, J.   *Treatise on the Ecclesiastical Architecture of England* (1835)

—— *History and Antiquities of Winchester* (1798)

Morris, F. O.   *The Country Seats, etc of Great Britain and Ireland* (1866–80)

Morris, W.   *Collected Works* (1910–15)

Nash, J.   *Mansions of England in the Olden Times* (1839–49)

Paley, F. A.   *Illustrations of Baptismal Fonts* (1844)

—— *Gothic Mouldings* (1877)

Parker, John Henry.   *A Glossary of Terms used in Grecian, Roman, Italian, and Gothic Architecture* (Oxford, 1850)

Petit, Rev J. L. *Remarks on the Principles of Gothic Architecture as applied to ordinary Parish Churches* (Oxford, 1846)

Pevsner, Sir Nikolaus. *The Buildings of England* A monumental county-by-county inventory of buildings. (Harmondsworth, various years)

—— *Pioneers of Modern Design* (Harmondsworth, 1960)

—— *An Outline of European Architecture* (Harmondsworth, 1963)

Powell, Nicholas. *From Baroque to Rococo. An Introduction to Austrian and German Architecture from 1580 to 1790* (1959)

Pride, Glen L. *Glossary of Scottish Building* (Glasgow, 1975)

Pugin, A. *Specimens of Gothic Architecture: Selected from various Ancient Edifices in England, etc* (1823)

Pugin, A. W. N. *Contrasts, or a Parallel between the Noble Edifices of the Fourteenth and Fifteenth Centuries and Similar Buildings of the Present Day* (1836)

Pullan, R. P. *The Architectural Designs of W. Burges* (1883 and 1887)

—— *Studies in Cathedral Design* (1888)

Richardson, A. E. *Robert Mylne, Architect and Engineer* (1955)

Rickman, Thomas. *An Attempt to Discriminate the Styles of Architecture in England, from the Conquest to the Reformation, etc.* (1848)

Roberts, H. *Dwellings for the labouring Classes* (1850)

Rolt, L. T. C. *Isambard Kingdom Brunel* (1957)

—— *George and Robert Stephenson* (1960)

Ruskin, John. *The Seven Lamps of Architecture* (various editions)

—— *The Stones of Venice* (various editions)

Salzman, L. F. *A Documentary History of Mediaeval Buildings* (Oxford, 1952)

Scott, Sir G. G. *Lectures on Mediaeval Architecture* (1879)

Sharpe, E. *A Treatise on the Rise and Progress of Decorative Window Tracery in England* (1849)

Shaw, H. *Specimens of the Details of Elizabethan Architecture* (1839)

Society of Antiquaries of London. *Archaeologia* (1773–1874)

Starforth, J. *Designs for Villa Residences* (Edinburgh, 1865)

—— *Designs for Villa Residences and Farm Architecture* (Edinburgh, 1866)

Stevenson, J. J. *House Architecture* (1880)

Stoll, Robert. *Architecture and Sculpture in Early Britain Celtic, Saxon, Norman* Photographs by Jean Roubier. (1967)

Stothard, C. A. and Kempe, J. A. *Monumental Effigies of Great Britain* (1817)

Street, G. E. (ed King, G. G.). *Unpublished Note Books and Reprinted Papers* (1916)

Styan, K. E. *A Short History of Sepulchral Cross-Slabs, with Reference to Other Emblems found thereon* (1902)

Summerson, Sir John. *John Nash. Architect to King George IV* (1949)

—— *Georgian London* (Harmondsworth, 1969)

—— *Inigo Jones* (Harmondsworth, 1966)

—— *Architecture in Britain, 1530–1830* (Harmondsworth, 1969)

Thompson, A. Hamilton. *Military Architecture in England* (Oxford, 1912)

Thompson, Paul. *William Butterfield* (1971)

Turner, T. H. and Parker, J. H. *Some Account of Domestic Architecture of England, 12th to 15th Centuries* (Oxford, 1851–59)

Waterhouse, P. *Pediments and Gables* (Oxford, 1886)

Weaver, Lawrence. *Memorials and Monuments Old and New; two hundred subjects chosen from seven centuries* (1915)

Webb, G. F. *Architecture in Britain: The Middle Ages* (Harmondsworth, 1956)

Whittock, N. *Shop fronts of London; their construction, decoration, etc.* (1840)

Wickes, C. *Illustrations of the Spires and Towers of the Mediaeval Churches of England* (1853–59)

Willis, Rev Robert. *Architectural History of some English Cathedrals* (Reprinted Chicheley 1972)

—— *Remarks on the Architecture of the Middle Ages* (Cambridge, 1835)

Winkles, B. *Cathedral Churches of England and Wales* (1836–42)

Woolnoth, W. *Ancient Castles of England and Wales* (1825)

Wornum, Ralph N. *Analysis of Ornament. The Characteristics of Styles: an Introduction to the Study of the History of Ornamental Art* (1869)

Wyatt, M. D. *Metal Work and its Artistic Design* (1852)

Acknowledgements

All photographs are my own unless otherwise stated. I am very grateful to Mr Terence Davis and to Mr A. W. Pullan for providing several plates. I am indebted to Salop County Council Record Office, Hereford City Library, the Library of the Royal Borough of Kensington and Chelsea, the RIBA Library and especially Mr David Dean, the GLC Department of Architecture and Civic Design, and the Guildhall Library, for the supply of the plates indicated. I am also grateful to all the vicars and other clergy, and the various cathedral authorities for permission to photograph, for which I was always happy to make a contribution towards the fabric fund.

My wife and daughters accompanied me in search of examples for this book, and I am very grateful to them for their patience, understanding and enthusiasm; they often spent hours in cathedrals and churches while I made my notes and took photographs.

My very old friend Mr Rodney Roach, who has collaborated with me for many years, enlarged the pictures and often processed my film in his usual expert fashion. I acknowledge a large debt to his kindness and enthusiasm.

Mr Archibald Hector Buck, most helpful of dear friends, once more subjected his sensibilities to the tiresome task of reading my text. His help has always been invaluable, while his expertise as a proof-reader has once more been given, even when the delights of a Test Match have offered their blandishments. The long sessions of going over scripts together have been both educational and hugely entertaining.

Many other friends have accompanied me in search of the architecture of the past; Mr John Sambrook has very kindly contributed his beautiful drawings to help with the explanation of architectural plans and terms and Mr Terence Davis kindly provided some pictures from his own collection for which help I am most grateful. Mrs Penelope Jessel aided my last labours on this book, and I warmly thank her for her kindness.

Miss Helen I. Logan typed the manuscript, and has my gratitude and sympathy.